Visit us at

www.syngress.com

Syngress is committed to publishing high-quality books for IT Professionals and delivering those books in media and formats that fit the demands of our customers. We are also committed to extending the utility of the book you purchase via additional materials available from our Web site.

SOLUTIONS WEB SITE

To register your book, please visit **www.syngress.com**. Once registered, you can access your e-book with print, copy, and comment features enabled.

ULTIMATE CDs

Our Ultimate CD product line offers our readers budget-conscious compilations of some of our best-selling backlist titles in Adobe PDF form. These CDs are the perfect way to extend your reference library on key topics pertaining to your area of expertise, including Cisco Engineering, Microsoft Windows System Administration, CyberCrime Investigation, Open Source Security, and Firewall Configuration, to name a few.

DOWNLOADABLE E-BOOKS

For readers who can't wait for hard copy, we offer most of our titles in downloadable e-book format. These are available at **www.syngress.com**.

SITE LICENSING

Syngress has a well-established program for site licensing our e-books onto servers in corporations, educational institutions, and large organizations. Please contact our corporate sales department at corporatesales@elsevier.com for more information.

CUSTOM PUBLISHING

Many organizations welcome the ability to combine parts of multiple Syngress books, as well as their own content, into a single volume for their own internal use. Please contact our corporate sales department at corporatesales@elsevier.com for more information.

Securing Intellectual Property

Securing Intellectual Property

Protecting Trade Secrets and Other Information Assets

An Information Security Reader

Butterworth-Heinemann is an imprint of Elsevier
Syngress is an imprint of Elsevier
30 Corporate Drive, Suite 400, Burlington, MA 01803, USA
Linacre House, Jordan Hill, Oxford OX2 8DP, UK

Securing Intellectual Property: Protecting Trade Secrets and Other Information Assets

Library of Congress Cataloging-in-Publication Data
Application submitted

British Library Cataloguing-in-Publication Data
A catalogue record for this book is available from the British Library.

ISBN: 978-0-7506-7995-4

Printed in the United States of America
08 09 10 11 12 13   10 9 8 7 6 5 4 3 2 1

For information on rights, translations, and bulk sales, contact Matt Pedersen, Commercial Sales Director and Rights; email m.pedersen@elsevier.com

Publisher: Laura Colantoni   Acquisitions Editor: Pamela Chester
Development Editor: Matthew Cater   Project Manager: Paul Gottehrer

Code = 58741140

For information on all Syngress publications visit our Web site at www.syngress.com

Contents

Preface

According to the World Intellectual Property Organization, intellectual property refers to "creations of the mind: inventions, literary and artistic works, and symbols, names, images, and designs used in commerce" (2008). The organization makes a distinction between two separate types of intellectual property, "industrial" and "copyright." Typically, the former category of property is the kind owned by businesses (inventions, industrial designs, etc.), while the latter refers to artistic creations such as original writing or music. This book approaches the topic of intellectual property from an industrial perspective, focusing on the legal steps and preventative security measures that a business can take to protect itself from theft of trade secrets and other information assets.

Intellectual property theft can potentially happen in almost any business; however, certain entities are more at risk than others. A list from *CIO* identifies these as the following:

- Large, globally distributed organizations

- Small to midsize businesses in niche markets

- Companies with foreign partners or that sell directly in foreign markets

- Organizations with decentralized IT

- Military or government organizations that rely heavily on contractors and suppliers

- Industries like telecommunications that supply critical national infrastructure

- Organizations lacking executive sponsorship of security issues, technical enforcement of security policies, adequate security monitoring or process/preparedness for dealing with security breaches (*CIO* 2007)

Security has always been a major concern to businesses that have proprietary information, but as the instances of intellectual property theft rise from year to year, it is becoming more and more essential for businesses to stay abreast of the latest trends and technologies in the field. An effective security program is the surest way to protect a business from intellectual property theft, and the content in this book will help security managers to understand and address the dangers that face them.

Chapter 1, "Elements of a Holistic Program," discusses the various factors that a security manager must take into account when designing a security program. It touches upon the various types of security – such as personnel, physical, and cyber security – while also addressing the larger issues that apply to all types of security, such as organization, intelligence, and legal strategies.

Chapter 2, "Trade Secrets and Non-Disclosure Agreements," approaches trade secrets from a legal perspective, discussing the legal requirements of trade secret law, practices and agreements used for trade secret protection, and confidentiality provisions in contracts. It also includes a number of sample legal documents (such as a non-disclosure agreement) that businesses can use to protect their assets.

Chapter 3, "Confidentiality, Rights Transfer, and Non-Competition Agreements for Employees," focuses on the employee-side of protecting intellectual property, specifically with regard to technology businesses. Topics discussed include noncompetition provisions, use and protection of confidential information, and enforcement of intellectual property violations.

Chapter 4, "IT Services—Development, Outsourcing, and Consulting," concentrates on outsourcing work to an IT company, both from the perspective of the business doing the outsourcing, as well as the vendor. The chapter contains a number of forms to assist with protecting your intellectual property in this situation, including a Software Development Agreement form, a Software Consulting Agreement form, and a Web Site Development Agreement form.

Chapter 5, "How to Sell Your Intellectual Property Protection Program," marks a departure from the more legal focus of the earlier chapters, taking a practical look at how to explain the importance of your security program to upper-level management. Suggestions include assessing the probability of theft, the effect of it on the company, and the proprietary information that different departments may possess.

Chapter 6, "The Mysterious Social Engineering Attacks on Entity Y," is a case study that focuses on the subject of social engineering, which is the practice of obtaining sensitive information by deceiving the people that possess it. It explains how to avoid such attacks, and what to do when you suspect that you are the victim of one.

Chapter 7, "When Insiders and/or Competitors Target a Business's Intellectual Property," is a chapter that focuses on real-life intellectual property breaches. It describes a number of actual cases where insiders or competitors attempted to commit information theft, and the outcomes of these attempts.

Chapter 8, "When Piracy, Counterfeiting, and Organized Crime Target a Business's Intellectual Property," concentrates on the greatest threat to intellectual property: piracy and counterfeiting. It discusses both the technology of these activities as well as the effects these activities have on specific industries.

Chapter 9, "Physical Security: The "Duh" Factor," focuses on physical security, a topic which often gets overlooked in this day of electronic technology. It contains extensive information on how to assess and improve your physical security program.

Chapter 10, "Protecting Intellectual Property in a Crisis Situation," explains how to deal with a situation where you are vulnerable to intellectual property theft because of a crisis (such as a hurricane, earthquake, or other unforeseen event). This chapter focuses on the "Ten-Seven-Five-Three-One-Now" approach.

Finally, Chapter 11, "Top Ten Ways to Shut Down Hackers," offers a succinct but invaluable top ten list of how to keep your intellectual property safe. It addresses issues such as "shoulder surfers," the danger of wearing employee badges in public places, and how to check your company's surveillance gear.

A recent article published in *Wall Street & Technology* states that almost 16 percent of data breaches in 2008 were the result of insider activity – a number which is up from 6 percent in 2007 (Rodier 2008). Additionally, the U.S. Department of Commerce estimates that companies suffer a collective loss of $250 billion dollars every year due to breaches of IP – not including, of course, the cases where such theft has not been discovered or reported (Overby 2007). If the trends of the recent past are to continue, it is almost certain that this number will rise dramatically in years to come. Thus, this book is an essential resource for the security manager with the responsibility of protecting his or her business from intellectual property theft.

References

Overby, Stephanie. "Hacked: The Rising Threat of Intellectual Property Theft and What You Can Do About It." *CIO* (July 30, 2007), http://www.cio.com/article/126600/Hacked_The_Rising_Threat_of_Intellectual_Property_Theft_and_What_You_Can_Do_About_It?contentId=126600&slug=&

Rodier, Melanie. "5 Steps for Stopping the Insider Threat." *Wall Street & Technology* (August 2008), http://www.wallstreetandtech.com/advancedtrading/showArticle.jhtml?articleID=210004190&cid=RSSfeed_TechWeb.

World Intellectual Property Organization, 2008. What Is Intellectual Property? http://www.wipo.int/about-ip/en/ (accessed August 23, 2008).

Chapter 1

Elements of a Holistic Program

Introduction

In many environments, security as an element of business culture has been hit with the double-whammy—that is, it suffers from both an image problem and an identity crisis. Many people think of corporate security as the "guards, guns, and gates" guys and cyber security as those "snoops who read employees' e-mail."

Security often is seen as a controlling or constricting force within an enterprise. It is frequently thought of as something that gets in the way of business. And lacking either a real mandate or a bold vision, many people within security slip into a reactive mode and resort to playing whack-a-mole, thus contributing to the bad image and deepening the identity crisis.

Security also is harried from a pack of false memes, which hound it, as well as some structural impairment, which hobbles it.

False Memes Lead People the Wrong Way

For example, a false meme tells you that teenage hackers with purple Mohawks and skateboards are responsible for most network break-ins; they don't really mean any real harm or do much damage. That might have been true fifteen years ago, but it hasn't been true for quite some time.

Another false meme assures you that 80 percent of all serious cyber-crime is perpetrated by insiders, for example, by dishonest or disgruntled employees. Again, looking in the rear-view mirror, at a great distance, that might have been true years ago, but it is a dangerous assumption in today's world. It is not that the insider threat has been diminished; it is that the threat from outside has increased dramatically. Furthermore, the lines between insider and outsider have been blurred both by technology and business practice.

A third false meme (there are several others) states that "most industrial espionage is done by the turning of insiders." Like the notion about "insiders" being the cause of most problems, this meme about the turning of insiders is particularly dangerous because it is a half-truth. The turning of insiders was the principle method, and it still is a major factor, but the business environment has changed radically, and methods of collection, and those eager to collect, have changed along with it.

From the Industrial Age to the Information Age

Of course, just as the Agricultural Age did not drop away when we entered into the Industrial Age, the Industrial Age is still with us, but an added dimension, the Information Age, is laid over the top of the two earlier paradigms. We are up to our necks in what Toffler called the Third Wave, and it has brought with it tremendous opportunity and profound challenge.

Unfortunately, this Third Wave has yet to sweep away a lot of Second Wave thinking about the nature of security.

To understand what security should look and feel like in the twenty-first century, pull out a piece of black paper. First, draw a big circle on it, and write along the curve of the circle, "Global Economy." Next, draw a second big circle of the same circumference on top of the first circle, and then write along side of the curve of this second, superimposed circle, "Cyberspace."

Within these two dimensions, which share the same space, you cannot draw a perimeter for your enterprise. And certainly, if you cannot draw a perimeter, you cannot protect it. Of course, you could draw a smaller circle, or a square, within the shared circle of the global economy and cyberspace, and you could imagine that the lines of the smaller shape delineated your enterprise's perimeter, but you would be deluding yourself. The reality is that the smaller shape is permeated by both the global economy and cyberspace, both are inside of your enterprise, you cannot keep them outside, and they are integral to how we do business today.

This new world demands a new security paradigm. We think of it as a holistic vision of security.

We have described the bad image, the identity crisis, and the false memes, but what about the structural impairment? Just as intelligence suffers from stove-piping (i.e., unless intelligence can be cross-referenced and aggregated in many ways, and analyzed afresh from different angles, something very important will probably slip by), so does security; if personnel security, physical security, and information security are all stove-piped within an enterprise, each is less than it could be, and all could well be working at cross-purposes. Figure 1.1 shows how awareness and intelligence can help mitigate risk and threats within an organization.

Figure 1.1 Personnel, Physical, and Information Security Mitigate the Scope of Risks and Threats

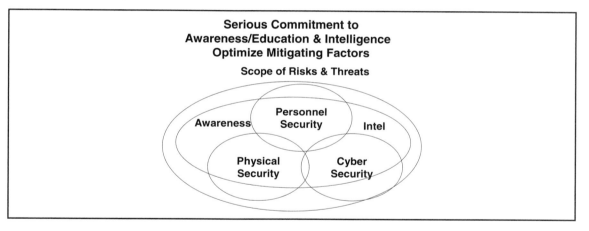

In life, in nature, in business, and in security, everything is interconnected, one way or another, just as the size of the glacier pack impacts the flow of the river, which, in turn, impacts the irrigation and reservoirs upon which human habitation has come to rely. In security, all the various elements interconnect for good or bad. If your most sensitive information is stored on an insecure server, your investment in physical and personnel security will be wasted. Conversely, if inadequate attention is paid to your physical security, then all your diligence in implementing personnel and information security controls could be for naught. Figure 1.2 shows how integration of physical, personnel, and cyber security helps narrow the scope of risks and threats within an organization.

Figure 1.2 Integrating Physical, Personnel, and Cyber Security

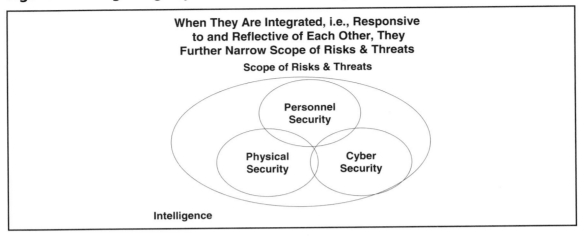

Each has to strengthen the other; each has to resonate with the whole (see Figure 1.3).

Figure 1.3 Serious Commitment to Awareness/Education and Intelligence Optimize Mitigating Factors

Here are some recommendations for a comprehensive program:

■ **Organization**: Where security reports within an organization is perhaps the most vital issue of all. Consider appointing a Chief Security Officer (CSO), who reports to either the Chief Executive Office (CEO) or the Chief Financial Officer (CFO). This person should hold the reins of personnel security, physical security, and information security, and should not be a stranger to the boardroom.

- **Awareness and Education**: Educate your workforce on an ongoing basis about the threats of economic espionage, intellectual property theft, counterfeiting, and piracy. Help them understand your expectation that they will protect the enterprise's intellectual property, and by extension, their own livelihood. Provide general education for the entire workforce, and specialized education for executives, managers, technical personnel, among others.

- **Personnel Security**: Implement a "Personnel Security" program that includes both background investigations and termination procedures. You need policies that establish checks and balances, and you need to enforce them. Know the people you are going to hire. Don't lose touch with them while they work for you. Consciously manage the termination process if and when they leave the enterprise.

- **Information Security**: Recruit certified information security professionals (e.g., CISSP, CISM, etc.). Adopt best practices, and establish a baseline. Utilize appropriate information security technologies, such as firewalls, intrusion detection, encryption, strong authentication devices, and the like. Pay attention to data retention and data destruction as well as data access.

- **Physical Security**: Do not overlook the "duh" factor. It is pointless to invest in information security, or commit to background investigations, if agents of an unscrupulous competitor or a foreign government can simply walk away with what they covet.

- **Intelligence**: You need both business and security intelligence. Know your competition, your partners, and your customers. Research the market environment. Keep abreast of the latest trends in hacking, organized crime, financial fraud, and state-sponsored economic espionage. You can outsource this expertise. But someone must be looking at both streams of intelligence, with the particulars of your enterprise in mind.

- **Industry Outreach**: Actively participate in industry working groups appropriate to your sector and environment. Talk with your peers about the types of attacks or threats they are encountering.

- **Government Liaison**: Leverage your tax dollars. Avail yourself of threat information from law enforcement, foreign ministries, elected officials, regulatory and trade organizations in your enterprise's country, and in those countries where you conduct business.

- **Legal Strategies**: Realize that even when right is on your side, a market may be lost to you, and protecting a portion of the global market is sometimes a viable survival strategy. Litigation is not the solution; it is confirmation that intellectual property theft has occurred. Work to protect your intellectual property and avoid the costs associated with litigation. Don't let a small legal mind make decisions about big legal issues. Get expert legal advice on intellectual property issues.

In sum, your security is in your hands. Employees tend to apply effort and intellect to the issue in portions commensurate with management attention to the topic of intellectual property protection. Employees line up smartly behind the leader providing direction, guidance, and support. Providing that leadership is essential to your firm's own continued economic viability in the global economy of the twenty-first century.

Chapter 2

Trade Secrets and Nondisclosure Agreements

Secrecy is the practice of hiding information from others.

—Wikipedia.

Introduction

For technology businesses, hiding information can be good. Does your business have technology, strategies, and other knowledge that you do not want competitors or customers to know? Can your business maintain its secrets? Can you get a remedy in court if your secret information is stolen? The subject of these questions is trade secret law.

Contents

In this chapter, we will cover:

- The legal requirement of trade secret law
- A comparison of patents vs. trade secrets
- The practices and agreements used for trade secret protection
- The risks from mishandled trade secrets
- Remedies when trade secrets are wrongfully taken or used
- Nondisclosure agreements
- Confidentiality provisions in contracts

What Is a Trade Secret?

As the name suggests, trade secrets are valuable information kept secret. But trade secrets are more than information—they are also a form of intellectual property. Indeed, they are the only way that you can "own" unpatented concepts and ideas. Under American law, trade secrets have legal protection, but that protection is far from complete. The law protects only against *wrongful* appropriation, disclosure, or use of trade secrets.

The law will protect your trade secrets only if you do. Because trade secrets are information, they can easily slip away. Trade secrets can be stolen in an instant by electronic transfer or can be carried out the door by departing employees. Trade secrets that are made public are destroyed, for example, by publication on the Internet. So your company's measures to protect trade secrets are critical for practical as well as legal reasons.

Trade secrets are a source of competitive advantage—but an other person's trade secrets in your possession are often a legal risk for you. If you use or disclose another's trade secret when you have a legal obligation not to, you can be sued and may be liable for large sums.

Basis of Trade Secret Law

Trade secrets are governed mainly by state law. There is a great deal of uniformity in this body of law. In 40 states, the main source of trade secret law is the Uniform Trade Secrets Act (UTSA). Even in those states that have not adopted the UTSA, the same basic rules apply either under other statutes or legal principles adopted by judges in their case decisions.

The term "trade secret" may bring to mind an image of a scientist in a white coat crafting complex chemical formulas. In reality, the definition of a trade secret is much broader. A trade secret can be any kind of information, technical or nontechnical, that fits the legal tests discussed below. There is no requirement that trade secrets be written.

To be a trade secret, your company's information must pass three tests:

- **Unavailability** The information must not be generally known or available. Information that can be found from an available public source is not a trade secret.

- **Value** The information must have actual or potential economic value. In order to prove that information is a trade secret, your company must show how the information—actually or potentially—confers an economic advantage in the marketplace over those that do not have it.

- **Protection** A company claiming a trade secret must prove that the company uses (and has used) reasonable measures to maintain its secrecy. This means that to prove a trade secret, your company must make an affirmative showing that at all times it has used and is using reasonably confidentiality procedures and protections.

Whether any particular information is or is not a trade secret is always a factual inquiry. It is a matter of proof based on the factors listed above. This makes trade secrets very different from copyright (where the particular copyrighted work is the basis of protection), patent law (which is based on a patent issued by a government patent office), or trademark law (which is based on particular trademarks and trademark registrations). In trade secret litigation, it is very common for the parties to dispute whether a particular piece of information is a trade secret at all.

Trade Secret Law vs. Contractual Protection of Confidential Information

In digital contracting, it is very common that contracts contain provisions to protect confidential information. Protecting confidential information contractually is very important for trade secret law, but it is not the same.

- Contracts bind only those that sign them. Trade secret law would bind a stranger to the contract. For example, a hacker that broke into your information system and took secret information would be liable under trade secret law.

- Breach of contract can cover (depending on how the clause is written) failures to protect confidential information that is without fault or purely accidental. Trade secret law protects only against wrongful violation (discussed below).

- Contractual definitions of confidential information are often broader than what is legally protected under trade secret law.

- These two bodies of law may overlap. For example, an ex-employee who uses confidential information without permission may breach both her employee agreement and also be liable under trade secret law.

■   Contractual protection of confidential information is a precondition to trade secret protection, because it is part of the "reasonable measures" that companies must use if they are to have legally protected trade secrets.

Technology as a Trade Secret

For digital technology companies, trade secret technologies can often be vital assets. Many different software technologies and techniques could classify as trade secrets if not generally known, for example, methods of data storage, data analysis methods, graphics display techniques, encryption and compression techniques, optimization methods, and so forth. The list is endless and always growing through creation of technology—but also always eroding as once-secret techniques become generally known.

A trade secret may exist in various forms and formats. Say, for example, that you have a new algorithm for efficient high-speed data transmission. Trade secret law would cover the algorithm itself, the flow chart that describes it, and the computer code that implements it. Each of these might be deemed as a trade secret.

Some trade secrets are more valuable than others. If you make a quantum leap ahead of the competition, if you solve a problem that others have tried to solve in vain, yours will be a much more valuable trade secret. From a practical point of view, you would be well advised to provide extra protection to the most valuable secrets.

Source Code as a Trade Secret

Many software companies do business under the propriety business model in which their commercial products are provided only in binary form. These companies treat their source code as a valuable trade secret. Most resist disclosing their source code to any customer or outsider. Disclosure of source code to trusted contractors will be under a form of agreement with clauses designed to protect trade secrets.

Many software vendors use source code escrow agreements as a means to provide customers access to source code *only if* the software vendor fails to maintain the software or goes out of business. Controlling disclosure is vital to maintaining the trade secret status of the source code.

Product Ideas—Flying under the Radar Screen

In the world of software, fundamental trade secrets may not last long. That is because clever programmers can often figure out how a rival company's software works. There is a saying in digital technology that "today's innovation is tomorrow's commodity." However, even short-lived trade secrets may be priceless.

A good example of a brief but extremely valuable start-up trade secret was webmail—the Web application that allows users to access e-mail online through a Web browser. Hotmail was the first webmail company, launched on July 4, 1996. Hotmail quickly obtained millions of users. As a result, Hotmail was sold to Microsoft in January 1998, just 18 months after launch, for $400 million—a smash hit deal even by the extravagant standards of the 90s Internet boom.

Hotmail's advantage was to get webmail first. After Hotmail was launched, its secret was out. Any sophisticated Web developer who saw the Hotmail service in operation could figure out how to build a competing service—but it was then too late. The key trade secret of Hotmail was having the *concept* of webmail before others knew it. As a result, Hotmail launched first, getting the jump on competitors that was the key to its success.

To protect product concepts and business plans, many start-up technology companies begin their business life in "stealth mode" or "under the radar screen." They swear all officers, employees, and investors to secrecy, and they try to keep even the basic outlines of their product secret as long as possible.

Confidential Business Information

Software companies also have nontechnical trade secrets that can be quite valuable. Examples are confidential customer databases, contact lists, prospect lists, mailing lists, lists of suppliers and contract programmers, product development and acquisition plans, cost and profit margin information, contract bids, and business strategy documents.

Confidential Information from Third Parties

Much of the most important confidential information used in your business may not be yours at all. You may have received a third party's confidential information under the terms of an agreement that requires you to keep the information secret. In that case, in accordance with your contractual obligations, you must take steps to protect that third party information, to use it only as permitted in the agreement, and otherwise to comply fully with the terms of the agreement under which you received the other party's secret information.

Limits to Trade Secrets

Trade secrets do not include information that is not really secret. For example, techniques or information generally known to skilled personnel in any technical field are not trade secrets—even if they were taught to an employee at great expense to the employer.

Sometimes in trade secret litigation, lawyers will try to make rather mundane techniques and informations look like well-guarded secrets—and opposing lawyers try to portray genuine secrets as common knowledge. Most often, the courts see through all this legal sleight-of-hand—but in a world where many judges have nontechnical backgrounds, sometime the courts get it wrong. This makes trade secret law an area where rights are often uncertain and contingent.

How Long Trade Secrets Last

Trade secrets last as long as the information remains secret and valuable. For some trade secrets—for example, the formula for Coca-Cola—that can mean a very long time. The longest lasting secrets are those that are not apparent from the products or services they are used to create.

Patents vs. Trade Secrets

Sometimes companies have a choice as to whether to patent an invention or to keep it as a trade secret. Not all trade secrets are potentially patentable—only those that meet the legal tests for patentability.

If an invention appears to be patentable—a company has to choose which route to protection it wants to take. Here are some of the factors to consider in making this choice:

- **Time to Obtain Protection** Patents take a long time to obtain—usually two or three years—but they last a long time—20 years from the application date. Some digital technologies become "old" and are "leapfrogged" by other technologies. So patenting really best fits technologies that can be expected to have continuing value.

- **Disclosure** Patents are public—they disclose technology. Most patent applications are published within 18 months of filing. There is a risk that after this disclosure, your competitors may figure out how to design around your patent but obtain the same general results. There is also a risk that the patent office will disallow or narrow the patent application. Where disclosure is dangerous, trade secret protection may be preferable.

- **Patenting by Others** In some cases if you chose trade secret protection, your innovation will be patented by some other company that independently invents it—in which case you could end up being the infringer. Your patent counsel can help you evaluate this risk.

- **Legal Protection** Legal protection under patent law is broader. Independent invention is not a defense to a patent claim. As is discussed below, trade secret law protects against wrongful appropriation only, and there are lawful ways to get around trade secret protection.

- **Expense** Patent filings are costly. The expenses of trade secret protection are those for the security measures that are used to protect secrets generally in your company; the marginal cost of protecting each additional trade secret is small.

The bottom line is that important technology advances need to be reviewed to determine which kind of protection is best. Consult with your technical staff and patent counsel and make the determination that best suits your market, technology field, and business strategy.

Can More Than One Company Have the Same Trade Secret?

More than one company *can* have the same trade secret technology. As long as the technique is not generally known in the industry, the trade secret can continue to exist in several companies. Unlike patents, trade secret protection does not provide the owner any ability to halt the use of technology by another company unless the other company obtained the trade secret from the owner by improper means or is using it in violation of a duty not to do so.

Care and Protection of Trade Secrets

Trade secrets are legally protected only if their owner uses "reasonable measures" to safeguard their secrecy. Unless you use reasonable measures to safeguard your new technologies, legal protection under trade secret law is lost. Your investors will expect that you will protect trade secrets. When you sell your company, you will be expected to warrant that you have used reasonable trade secret protections. Any innovative digital technology company should make trade secret protection part of its culture.

So what does the term "reasonable measures" really mean? In this context, "reasonable" means what a sensible person who was interested in keeping information would do under all the circumstances. So to some extent, the answer is context-driven; some business and some secrets demand more protection than others. Companies should be especially careful about core technologies that are the keys to their competitive advantage. A defense contractor is naturally expected to invest more on security of information than a software game development company. A company with three employees will need fewer formal confidentiality procedures than a business with 20,000 employees.

While there are these variations and degrees, there is a common set of security and confidentiality measures that are used in technology companies throughout the world. The following list of security measures are those commonly used. Not all of them are needed for every business, and this is not an exhaustive list of every measure that might apply.

One Person in Charge of Confidentiality Measures

A sensible basis for adequate trade secret protection is to put a single responsible person in charge of security and protection measures for the company—and in large companies, for each business unit. This will help you obtain implementation and follow up on a consistent basis.

Controls on Access to Confidential Data

The company must control access to confidential information within the company. The methods are straightforward:

- **Computer Access Protection** Where confidential information is accessed by computer, whether in a single machine or on a network, use password protection. Passwords should be changed frequently, and passwords for departing employees should be deleted promptly. For very secret information, you may want to consider biometric protections, such as fingerprint or retinal scan systems.

- **Need-to-Know Access** Access should be limited for directories where source code, product plans, customer lists, or other confidential data are stored. Access should be permitted on a need-to-know basis only. It is usually a mistake to let all employees have access to all data. There are many software tools that allow system administrators to control access to information.

- **System Protection** Computer systems that interface with the Internet or other networks (as most do) need protection by means of firewalls and intrusion detection systems. It is a good idea to hire consultants who do periodic "white hacking" penetration testing—so that you can find and fix points of vulnerability. You can also have security audits for your information systems.

- **Encrypted Transmission and Storage** Data are more secure if they are in encrypted form. This applies especially to transmission through open networks such as the Internet. When data are particularly valuable or sensitive, you may want to consider implementing encrypted internal storage as well. (Encrypted storage is an especially good idea for personal data including names, addresses, and social security numbers, because your company can face statutory liability for release of such data.)

- **Permanent Copies** Where confidential data are stored on tape, CD-ROM, or hard copy, access to the information should be controlled by lock and key, which sign out systems to record access. You may want to restrict use, storage, and access to particular locations.

- **Laptops and Storage Devices** One way that confidential information can be lost or compromised is to allow it to get into portable form in a laptop or flash drive. In some companies, there are strict limitations on putting company data on these devices. Others have procedures to require storage in such devices to be in encrypted form. Some companies forbid visitors to bring storage devices on site (even iPods) or into secure areas.

Entry Control and Badges

Physical access control is important.

- **Entry and Exit Control** It is a standard procedure at many high-technology companies to monitor who comes in and out. Visitors sign in and out, and should be issued "visitor" badges that they surrender on leaving. Visitors should always be escorted.

- **Employee Badges** As soon as the company is large enough that all employees are not known to one another, the employees should get numbered identification badges that include a photo. Systems to generate the badges are commercially available. In many companies, the identification badges also serve as keys to otherwise locked access doors.

- **Security Systems and Personnel** After-hours access should be controlled by a security system, and there should be an intruder alarm. Larger companies will consider hiring guards and having security cameras.

Confidentiality Legends on Documents, Code, and Other Data

Materials that contain (or may contain) trade secrets must be marked. They should have a clearly visible legend or notice. The legend alerts anyone who sees the document—employees and nonemployees alike—that trade secret protection is claimed.

Your confidentiality legend should normally be typed in all capital letters (in order to be more conspicuous) and read like this:

NOTICE: THE CONTENTS CONSIST OF TRADE SECRETS THAT ARE THE PROPERTY OF [NAME OF COMPANY]. THE CONTENTS MAY NOT BE USED OR DISCLOSED WITHOUT EXPRESS WRITTEN PERMISSION OF [NAME OF COMPANY].

Confidentiality legends should be used regardless of the form in which confidential information is maintained. For example, the legend should be placed conspicuously in or on:

- Every source code file (written into the source code, including at the top and the end)
- Every propriety database
- All laboratory notebooks or other records of research
- Product plans, plans, specifications, and so forth
- Customer lists, projections, market research results, and so forth
- Every printout or other hard copy of every type of confidential information

If in doubt, mark the information with the legend. Most often, you will do this electronically. It is also a good idea to get an old-fashioned rubber stamp reading: "CONFIDENTIAL TRADE SECRET: PROPERTY OF [NAME OF COMPANY]" and use it to mark documents, disks, and other media that contain trade secret matter.

While the use of a confidentiality legend is very important for secret information used within a business, the notice is even more important for information provided in confidence to someone outside. We have seen a judge deny trade secret protection to a graphics video board design based on providing a single schematic with no confidentiality legend to a potential business partner.

I recommend that each technology company configure their e-mail program (such as Outlook) at the company level so that it automatically adds a confidentiality message for each outgoing e-mail. For example, the following:

> *This e-mail message and any attachments are confidential and proprietary information of [NAME OF COMPANY]. If you are not the intended recipient, please immediately reply to the sender or call [NUMBER] and delete the message from your e-mail system.*

A note of caution: A confidentiality notice is important, but is not a substitute for a nondisclosure agreement (NDA) with the other party. Your unilateral assertion of confidentiality will probably not bind the other party—you also need to get the other party to agree to hold your information confidential.

Agreements with Third Parties to Protect Confidentiality

It is essential to use the correct form of NDA to protect trade secrets that are to be disclosed to third parties. In the following section of this chapter, I will discuss the goals and terms of such agreements, and there is a sample of a mutual NDA in Appendix 1 of this book. In any negotiations where there may be any disclosure of any confidential information regarding your business, you should get an NDA in place before any other discussions take place.

In addition, as mentioned above, it is essential to have confidentiality clauses in a great variety of contracts between a technology company and third parties, including business partners, independent contractors, and consultants that the company uses. You can find many samples in the agreement forms in the appendices to this book.

Confidential Undertakings by Employees and Contractors

Your company needs to obtain confidentiality undertakings from employees and contractors. These clauses are contained in the employee agreements of the type discussed in Chapter 3 of this book. It is a good policy to have each employee sign such agreements, not just technical and sales staff. These agreements should be signed by each officer and director and members of any advisory board.

Employee Guidelines

Every company should have an employee manual (a topic to discuss with your lawyer). Your company's employee manual must include the company's policies on confidentiality. That section will contain guidelines as to what sort of information the company considers confidential and how that information should be treated. It is a good idea to prepare and use similar guidelines for contractors.

Speeches, Paper, and Presentations

Many companies unwittingly lose trade secret protection when they allow scientists and engineers to publish and speak in public. Sometimes your technical staff will disclose information over cocktails in idle chat with their peers. It is important for companies to do their best to screen and preapprove any public discussion of their technology—and to impress upon all the need not to discuss secret technology with third parties. You may wish to assign an employee or employees the task of screening and approving public disclosures of technical information.

New Employee Orientation

When new employees or officers are hired, an explanation of the company's trade secret policies and protections should be part of their introduction to the company. On or before the first day of employment, they should sign the company's confidentiality agreement and receive a copy of the company's policy on protection of intellectual property.

New hires should be counseled not to bring with them or to use any information or materials belonging to another company, such as telephone directories, organizational charts, salary schedules, and the like, as well as technical and business information that were protected as confidential by that company. They should not be permitted to bring computer files from their former employer. You may make an exception for materials that are publicly available or for materials that the employee is bringing pursuant to the signed consent of an authorized officer of the former employer. A similar process should apply for your company's onsite independent contractors.

If you are going to discuss technical or other nonpublic matters with a prospective employee, you should have them sign an NDA before such discussions.

Exit Process

When employees leave or the services of independent contractor are ended, there should be an exit process, where, among other matters, trade secret matters are covered. Here are some pointers for this process:

- Be sure each departing employee or contractor returns his or her access cards, ID badge, keys, laptops, PDA or Blackberry, company flash drives, and the like.

- Disable the employee's access to computers, voicemail, and e-mail. Be sure that the appropriate usernames and passwords are deleted from all company systems.

- Make the employee return any documents or company material in his or her possession, including things kept at home (such as company files on his or her home computer or storage device), in his or her car, as well as such items in his or her office or work area. The employee's supervisor can help verify that this has been done correctly.

- Some companies archive the contents of the departing employee's computer records, including those on the server and on his or her workstation or laptop. Then you may erase the computer files to free up the storage area.

- It is a good practice to wind up the affairs of departing employees or independent contractors very quickly. If they stay on the job, they will have more opportunity to remove confidential data for use in the next job. You may want to check his or her recent access to computer systems; heavy activity may indicate that he or she has been improperly downloading files.

- An exit interview that covers confidential matters (and any noncompetition agreement) is recommended. In many companies, departing employees are asked to sign a written statement that they have returned all materials belonging to the company, and that they will maintain trade secrets and confidential information in confidence after leaving. During the exit interview, give the departing employee a copy of his or her employee agreement, which should remind the employee of their obligations, including confidentiality and (if applicable) noncompetition.

Nondisclosure Agreements and Confidential Disclosure

Aside from clickwrap agreements, perhaps the most common intercompany agreements in the world of information technology are NDAs. These are confidentiality agreements that companies sign before they talk. They are designed to cloak discussions in secrecy to allow parties to have freer discussions. You will find an example of a conventional reasonably balanced mutual NDA in Appendix 1 of this book.

It is a mistake to consider an NDA as "just a form." Most companies that deal with NDAs have their own favorite versions that fit their business—and are constantly adjusting and editing forms that come from other companies. Some of these adjustments can make a real difference. Many of the variations that you see in these forms are discussed below.

Some NDAs provide inadequate protection or may allow the receiving party to use the disclosing party's information. You should read these agreements from the other party very carefully. Many companies will not sign NDAs from other companies without legal review.

NDAs are not self-enforcing. You can enforce them only through litigation—and you can sue only after you discover the violation of confidentiality. Litigation is expensive and uncertain. So NDAs are imperfect protection. You should be careful about what you disclose to other companies even if an NDA is in place. Never "lift the kimono" more than you have to.

Of course, contractual provisions on confidential disclosure are not limited to NDAs. As noted above, many technology agreements have confidentiality provisions. These clauses also have variations. The considerations and analysis discussed in the following sections apply to the confidentiality clauses in contracts as well.

Mutual or Unilateral NDAs

There are some NDAs that are mutual; they cover both parties in their roles of "disclosing party" and "receiving party." Some NDAs are unilateral; they are a disclosing party's form of agreement that requires the other party to protect the disclosing party's confidential information—based on the assumption that no protection will apply to the other party's information.

We are particularly skeptical of unilateral NDAs. In most serious technical and business discussions, both sides have confidential information to disclose. Mutual NDA forms tend to be fairer, because they force the drafter to state rules that both sides must live with. Often, we will respond (with our client's permission) to a proposed unilateral NDA form by just sending my client's favorite mutual NDA form.

Defining "Confidential Information"

Definitions of "Confidential Information" in NDAs are often in this format:

> *"Confidential Information" means all nonpublic information provided by the Disclosing Party including, but not limited to, the following: [INSERT LIST OF EXAMPLES].*

When you are drafting or editing this kind of clause, be sure that this list of examples includes the type of materials and technology that you are actually likely to disclose. In addition, you should avoid narrowly drafted definitions of confidential information—because you might be waiving protection for anything that you leave out. (In this discussion, we use the term "Confidential Information"—with initial caps—to refer both to the defined term in an NDA and the information that it covers.)

What Written Information Is "Confidential Information"?

There are variations in the way that NDAs deal with confidential documents that are disclosed under the NDA:

- Some NDA forms are written so that documents are confidential information only if they are marked "Confidential" or "Proprietary." With this language, any contents of unmarked documents will be deemed nonconfidential and subject to unrestricted use by the receiving party.

- Some NDA forms are written so that any written information disclosed is deemed designated as "Confidential Information."

- Some NDA forms are written for that that any written information disclosed that the recipient "reasonably understands to be confidential" is deemed "Confidential Information."

Many high-technology companies tend to prefer the forms that require written information to be specifically marked confidential—because this makes it less likely that they will accidentally use information that is subject to a confidentiality agreement. On the other hand, if only marked information is deemed "Confidential Information," there is a risk that the disclosing party will accidentally fail to mark their disclosed information properly and lose protection.

If your company ever enters into agreements in which you need to designate written information as confidential, be sure to remember that this requirement applies to e-mail, instant messaging, electronic white boards, and every other form of electronic information exchange.

What Oral or Visual Information Is "Confidential Information"?

NDAs vary in the way that they treat information that is disclosed orally or visually. (An example of visual disclosure would be showing a PowerPoint presentation that is not provided in written form.) The concern here is that there is no record of the fact of the disclosure. Unless there is a mechanism for creating a record, the only evidence would be by the testimony of participants in the disclosure.

- Some NDAs are written to protect all oral or visual information that otherwise meets the Confidential Information definition.

- Some NDAs require the disclosing party to provide a written summary of its oral or visual disclosures in confirmation of the disclosure—typically within 30 days of disclosure. With this language, failure to provide the summary will waive confidentiality protection.

- Some NDAs include a written list of proposed discussion topics, which are deemed designated as confidential, and require a written summary of anything else.

If your company enters into agreements that require a written summary of confidential disclosure, it is important that you make sure that this task actually gets done. Unfortunately, many forget to do this, and much confidential information is therefore put at risk. It is a good idea to make one participant at the meeting in charge of such designations.

Carve-Outs from Confidential Information

NDAs virtually always have a provision (commonly called a "carve-out") stating what is *not* Confidential Information. Here is a typical provision:

"Confidential Information" will not include information that:

(a) was known by the Receiving Party prior to disclosure thereof by the Disclosing Party;

(b) was publicly available through no wrongful act of the Receiving Party;

(c) is disclosed to the Receiving Party by a third party legally entitled to make such disclosure without violation of any obligation of confidentiality to the Disclosing Party;

(d) is required to be disclosed by applicable laws, court order, or regulations (provided that the Receiving Party notifies the Disclosing Party and provides the Disclosing Party the opportunity to challenge or seek a protective order for the Confidential Information); or

(e) as the Receiving Party can demonstrate was independently developed by the Receiving Party without reference to any Confidential Information of the Disclosing Party.

This kind of provision is designed to remove "Confidential Information" status for information that the Receiving Party legitimately obtains by other means. These provisions vary, so you should always pay attention to them. Sometimes they include a requirement that each exception be "proved by documentary evidence"—and this may be unreasonable. Depending on the nature of the exception and the information, there may be situations where documentary proof of the exemption may not be feasible.

Prohibition of Disclosure

Virtually every NDA has provisions on nondisclosure of confidential information but they are often not absolute.

You should pay attention to provisions in the NDA that say how confidential information may be disclosed. Most forms allow no disclosure to third parties. Some allow confidential disclosure to accountants, advisors, or other third parties. Some impose an unqualified nondisclosure obligation, and some require only that the receiving party use "reasonable measures" to protect the disclosed information. You need to judge which level of protection is sufficient.

NDAs normally have provisions for return of confidential information either upon demand or the end of negotiations between parties.

Use of Confidential Information

NDAs should have restrictions on how confidential information can be used. Sometimes you see NDA forms that have restrictions on disclosure but not on use—a circumstance that a disclosing party should find unacceptable.

It is common for NDAs to have clauses that permit only evaluation. Some NDAs allow use "for the purposes of the relationship of the parties"— which strikes me as too vague and broad. If you disclose valuable confidential information, you will usually want to narrow its permitted use carefully.

Many NDAs for disclosed hardware or software expressly prohibit reverse engineering and provide for return of samples upon demand.

When Does Protection Time-Out?

Some forms of NDA are designed to be in effect permanently and to protect confidential information forever. Others have time limits—there are two kinds that may apply.

First is a time limit on disclosure—for example,

> *This Agreement covers disclosures made during one year from the Effective Date of the Agreement.*

Some NDAs have a limit on how long the obligation of confidentiality lasts. For example,

> *The receiving party agrees to hold in confidence the disclosing party's Confidential Information for five years from the date of disclosure.*

When entering into an NDA, be sure that the period of protection lasts as long as your secrets are likely to be valuable. When my client has a secret that is likely to be long-lasting, I recommend against *any* "time-out" of confidential information.

Risks from Others' Confidential Information

Exchanging confidential information may be a benefit because it facilitates deals and cooperation—but confidentiality carries danger as well. If your company discloses or uses another company's confidential information improperly, the disclosing party may well sue you—and seek money damages or seek injunctions to terminate the violation.

The problem is that in some cases, it may be unclear after the fact whether you did or did not misuse confidential information. Say, for example, that another company reveals to your company a technology in your field that your company did not then know—but which your company was very close to developing itself. Or say that the disclosed technology is new but it is an obvious extension of your company's current technology. In that circumstance, if your company releases a product that is similar to the disclosing party's product, you may be accused of improper use of the disclosing party's technology—and bitter litigation may follow.

Another risk is that you may inadvertently use another's technology. Sometimes a company's engineers and programmers discuss ideas and concepts informally among themselves without making it clear that they are subject to confidentiality restrictions—or they may simply not remember the context in which they learned about a particular technical approach. In this way, companies sometimes stray into use of the other's confidential information.

The bottom line is that obtaining disclosure under an NDA (or any other confidentiality clause) may create a legal vulnerability that you—and your technical staff—need to manage with great care.

Two-Stage Disclosure

To minimize the risk of receiving unwanted confidential disclosure, companies sometimes use an (admittedly rather awkward) two-stage disclosure. First, the would-be disclosing party has to supply an initial nonconfidential summary of the proposed disclosure—telling the other party the general nature of what it plans to disclose. Then if the other party agrees to accept the information, it would get the burdens of confidential disclosure. If the other party says "no," it will remain unburdened by confidential disclosure.

As you may imagine, this two-stage process for confidential disclosure is burdensome—and greatly slows communications. So this form of disclosure is relatively uncommon—we usually reserve it to critical high tech disclosures between competitors.

Watch Out for "Residuals" Clauses

Another way in which companies try to limit their exposure to the risks of receiving confidential information is by use of a "residuals" clause. The concept of "residuals" is information that is left in the unaided memory of the receiving party's head after the confidential information is returned. The residuals clause provides for the receiving party to keep the right to use residuals. Microsoft Corporation, for example, commonly includes a residuals clause in its form of NDA.

Here is a typical residuals clause:

> *Either party shall be free to use for any purpose the residuals resulting from access to or work with such Confidential Information, provided that such party shall maintain the confidentiality of the Confidential Information as provided herein. The term "residuals" means information in non-tangible form, which may be retained by persons who have had access to the*

Confidential Information, including ideas, concepts, know-how, or tech-niques contained therein. Neither party shall have any obligation to limit or restrict the assignment of such persons or to pay royalties for any work resulting from the use of residuals. However, the foregoing shall not be deemed to grant to either party a license under the other party's copyrights or patents.

If you are likely to be *getting* confidential information, a residuals clause can be very beneficial—if you are *providing* confidential information, a residuals clause can be very dangerous. Here are some key points to know about residuals clauses:

■ These clauses are in fact technology licenses. They permit permanent use of the residuals and trump a trade secret claim.

■ If a company duplicates your disclosed technology and relies on the residual clause in the NDA, you will be at a disadvantage in litigation. You will need to prove that the other company's employee did not remember your technology—and that is very difficult to do.

■ *Unless carefully worded, residuals clauses are broad intellectual property licenses.* This is because of the doctrine that when you grant permission for use of a technology, your permission, unless otherwise stated, covers all rights you may have. So even if you had a patent or copyright that would otherwise block use of the residual, the recipient of the residual is free to use it nonetheless, because you have given permission. To prevent this result, if you do use a residuals clause, you must use language like that quoted above: "*However, the foregoing shall not be deemed to grant to either party a license under the other party's copyrights or patents.*"

■ Residuals are especially dangerous when you have a secret innovative or unique technology or product. In that case, the concepts—rather than the code—may be the key to the value of your technology.

You need to consider carefully when use of the residuals clause is right for your company—and when it will be a threat. Note that the great majority of NDAs do not have this kind of provision.

Are There Oral Agreements for Nondisclosure?

It is *possible* to have enforceable oral agreements for confidentiality, but it is never advisable to rely on such agreements. While the courts have enforced such agreements on occasion, it is never smart to rely on an oral agreement to keep information confidential. The other party may deny that the agreement exists. There is also a risk that the court may consider that someone who relies on oral promise of confidentiality is not using "reasonable means" to protect its trade secrets. And, of course, it may be very hard to prove with specificity the terms of an oral confidentiality agreement. So our advice is always: Get it in writing.

Disclosure Agreements that Are the Opposite of NDAs

Some companies use form documents that you might consider a kind of "anticonfidentiality agreement." They are designed to protect against a claim of wrongful use. These agreements are commonly used in the video game business and have language such as this:

We may, from time to time, receive submissions of material similar to yours, or we may be developing similar products. You agree that we are not bound to treat as confidential your idea or any information that you may choose to disclose to us during the course of our evaluation whether or not marked as confidential or proprietary.

Our acceptance of your material for evaluation does not imply that we will market your material nor does it prevent us from marketing or developing other products that may be similar in idea or concept so long as we do not infringe your copyright or patent rights.

When You Negotiate a Deal, Should NDAs Be Superseded?

When the parties move from talking about a possible relationship to actually negotiating the business agreement between them, we think it is best practice to include a confidentiality clause in the business agreement that will supersede the NDA. We do not generally recommend agreements that have language that merely continues the existing NDA in effect. This is because most NDAs are written to facilitate discussions—not for an ongoing relationship. There are often new and different issues regarding confidentiality to be dealt with in the resulting agreement—and you are likely to miss these issues by just continuing the NDA in effect.

Confidentiality Clauses Generally

Many agreements have confidentiality provisions. The same considerations that we discussed with regard to NDAs should be considered when you craft any agreement that includes confidential information. Remember that restraints on misuse of your confidential information may be a key strategic and competitive factor in any agreement.

You should also pay very close attention to how confidentiality clauses in your various agreements may interact with other clauses—particularly clauses regarding limitations on consequential damages and damage caps. If you are not careful, you may find out that your agreement limits or even eliminates any money damage remedy for breach of confidentiality by the other party. Claims for breach of confidentiality obligations are often important exceptions or "carve-outs" from liability limitation clauses.

Violations of Trade Secret Law

Let us assume that you have protected your trade secrets by all the requisite reasonable measures. What protection then do you get under trade secret law? (Remember that this protection in addition to whatever remedies might apply under contract law.)

Trade secret law provides protection only against wrongful appropriation, disclosure, or use of trade secrets. The key word in that sentence is "wrongful." There are improper ways of obtaining and exploiting the trade secrets of another person that are illegal—and there are proper ways that are perfectly lawful under trade secret law.

What Is Illegal under Trade Secret Law?

Violations of trade secrets involve wrongful acquisition, use, or disclosure of another's trade secret. Here are some examples of trade secret violations:

- Obtaining secrets by industrial espionage

- Breaking into another company's computer systems and taking files

- Inducing an employee or former employee of another company to reveal trade secrets

- Receiving trade secrets from someone that the recipient knew (or should have known) is not entitled to disclose them

- Using or disclosing trade secrets in violation of your duty of good faith as a director or employee of a business

- Using or disclosing trade secrets in violation of an NDA or the confidentially clause of an agreement

All of these violations involve activities that the recipient should know to be improper.

What Is Not Illegal under Trade Secret Law?

Here are some examples of what is not illegal under trade secret law:

- It is not a violation to replicate a trade secret by independent invention.

- It is not a violation to reverse engineer another product—unless you have validly agreed not to do so.

Be careful about reverse engineering. Software and hardware contracts often contain broad prohibitions against reverse engineering, and these clauses are usually enforceable in the United States. (In the European Union, you may have a statutory right to reverse engineer for the limited purpose of making an interoperable product.) This means that reverse engineering of software in many cases will be illegal under contract law even if it is permitted under trade secret law.

What if Trade Secrets Are Disclosed?

If trade secrets are wrongfully disclosed and if the disclosure is limited, trade secret protection will usually not be lost. On the other hand, permitted publication or public disclosure will destroy any trade secret. Even illegal disclosure, if broad enough, will destroy trade secret status. If your former employee publishes your trade secret on the Internet or if it shows up in the *New York Times*, you can consider it gone. Your employee may be liable for damages, but you will no longer be able to get legal protection for the information under trade secret law.

Dealing with Violations of Trade Secrets

The most egregious violations of trade secret are theft and espionage—but more common by far is wrongful use and disclosure of trade secrets by former employees (and their new employers), contractors, or "business partners."

When you know or strongly suspect that someone has violated your valuable trade secret rights, you should consider taking immediate steps to stop the violation, including litigation, if necessary. Delay can be dangerous. If you do nothing, you risk letting your secrets circulate—and once they circulate, they are not secret anymore. Moreover, judges will likely rule later that if you did not care enough about your secrets to enforce your rights promptly, the secrets probably do not deserve protection. You should seek legal advice immediately.

Sometimes the holder of a trade secret gets an early warning that there has been a violation or probable violation—as, for example, when a key scientist or engineer quits and immediately goes to work for a competitor where he or she begins work on a competing product. Sometimes it is only long after the fact that the violation manifests itself—for example, when the competing product hits the market and an examination of the product shows that a trade secret was wrongfully taken or used.

To prevail in these cases, as the purported wronged party, you must identify the trade secret, prove it is valuable, prove that it is protected by reasonable measures, and show the wrongful removal, use, or disclosure.

In trade secrets cases, the wronged party will seek injunctive relief or damages or both.

- Injunctive relief means a temporary or permanent court order that the other party stops using the trade secrets. Where a former employee or contractor has taken trade secrets, the trade secret owner may also seek a court order mandating a separation between the employee or contractor and the new employee—or ordering the employee to work only in areas unrelated to a trade secret technology.

- The wronged party may also be entitled to money damages to recover its lost profits or the wrongdoer's ill-gotten profits.

Remedies Short of Litigation

Let us say that you find that your senior employee has left and gone to a competitor—and you fear that your trade secrets are going with him or her. What can you do, without the expense of litigation, to stop third parties from wrongfully delivering trade secrets to a new employer? There are steps that you can take (with the advice of an attorney), although none of them provide absolute assurance that your trade secrets will be safe:

Notice to Respect Trade Secrets. If the threat of a trade secret violation is moderate, a pointed reminder of the employee's obligations may suffice. The employer may give the employee a written reminder of his or her trade secret obligation as a routine part of the exit interview process. Then the employer can follow up with a letter to the former employee and his or her new employer stating the areas of technology involved and insisting that the confidentiality agreement be adhered to. In either case, it is best to supply both the employee and the new employer with a copy of the employment agreement signed by the employee so that the new employer will understand that a wrongful disclosure will violate a contractual duty of the employee.

Demand for Measures to Prevent Disclosure. If the disclosure risk is high, a more forceful letter is called for. This sort of letter is meant to be part of a strategy in which litigation is a possible outcome, but the preferred goal is a negotiated solution in which the former employer obtains reasonable assurance that trade secrets will not be disclosed. Such a letter might state:

- That procedures should be put in place immediately at the new employer's business to prevent use or disclosure of trade secrets.

- That employees at the new company must be instructed not to discuss the subject matter of the trade secrets technology with the employee.

- That the former employee should be assigned only to work areas and to projects that are technologically distinct from and physically separate from any work area that might want to use any relevant trade secret information.

- That the new employer confirms in writing that these safeguards will be put in place immediately and will remain in place for an agreed-upon period.

- That the former employee and the new employer confirm in writing that no trade secrets have been or will be revealed.

- That litigation may result if suitable assurances are not received. (Note, however, that you should never threaten litigation unless you are absolutely prepared to follow through on the threat.)

The employer needs to discuss an overall strategy with counsel before sending any letter concerning a suspected trade secret violation. When nonlitigation methods fail, you must seriously consider prompt litigation.

Is Taking Trade Secrets a Crime?

In a number of states, it is a crime to wrongfully appropriate the trade secret information of another. There is a similar federal law, known as the "The Economic Espionage Act." The federal act is best known for provisions on trade secret theft for the benefit of foreign governments, but it also makes intentional appropriation of trade secrets a crime if the trade secret is "related to or included in a product that is produced for or placed in interstate or foreign commerce." This would cover almost all commercial products sold in the United States.

Criminal prosecutions in trade secret cases are relatively uncommon. Most trade secret litigations are civil, not criminal. Criminal prosecutions in trade secret cases are most likely to occur when there is a truly egregious violation that causes major harm. Criminal prosecution is also much more likely if there is other criminal activity involved as well. For example, if there was an illegal wiretap or a break-in or bribe to steal trade secret materials, then a prosecutor might become sufficiently interested to take action.

Can Software Trade Secrets Be Licensed or Sold?

Where a company is selling technology, rather than just a software application, it is not unusual that trade secret techniques (or confidential know-how) are licensed. And trade secrets can also be sold by agreement. Licensing deals involving trade secrets are often similar in legal issues and in pricing structures to other digital technology licenses. Because trade secrets are vulnerable to destruction by disclosure, any such agreement must include carefully crafted confidentiality provisions.

Use of Counsel in Managing Trade Secrets

Trade secrets are often key assets in a digital technology business. You should be sure that they are protected by confidentiality measures and by careful contracting. Your attorney can help you assess and improve your confidentiality practices, can advise you on trade secret protection, can help you include trade secrets in your strategic plans, and can help craft agreements that protect and extend the value of confidential technologies. Where there are threats to your trade secrets by employees or others, you should contact counsel without delay.

Chapter 3

Confidentiality, Rights Transfer, and Noncompetition Agreements for Employees

Knowledge worker, a term coined by Peter Drucker in 1959, is one who works primarily with information or one who develops and uses knowledge in the workplace....

A Knowledge worker's benefit to a company could be in the form of developing business intelligence, increasing the value of intellectual capital, gaining insight into customer preferences, or a variety of other important gains in knowledge that aid the business.

—From Wikipedia on "Knowledge Worker."

Introduction

Your technology company needs clear, reasonable, and legally enforceable form agreements with your employees to secure intellectual property for the company, protect your confidential information, and secure protection against competition. Employee agreements help secure for your company the value that employees create.

These agreements are fundamental for every technology company and using them should be a routine part of the hiring process at your company. Venture capitalists and other investors will insist on their being in place—so will any potential purchaser of your business. We recommend that these terms and conditions be used, to the maximum extent possible, with *all* employees from the CEO to interns and that you get them signed before the first day of work for each employee.

The discussion of employee agreements in this chapter is focused on agreements that you would use in the United States for persons who are "W-2 employees," that is, persons who are classified as employees under federal and state tax reporting. For similar agreements in foreign nations, you will need local legal advice. For similar issues in consulting and contractor agreements, see Chapter 4.

You will find in Appendix 3 of this book a form of employee agreement for technology companies. The contents of these form agreements may require changes to adapt them to your company's situation. In addition, as is discussed in this chapter, there are state laws that may effect whether an employee noncompetition restraint is enforceable or unenforceable wholly or in part. For this reason, you should have your attorney advise you as to the right form (or forms) of employee agreement and any applicable state law rules.

Note on Terminology

We attorneys generally make a distinction between "employ*ee* agreements" and "employ*ment* agreements." They sound the same but are different.

- **Employee Agreement** This is a *form* agreement of the type that is the subject of this chapter. It covers topics such as the employee's obligations regarding confidential information and the company's ownership of the intellectual property. The document often has postemployment restriction against competition with the company and against hiring company employees. It is a document that is focused on employee obligations, not on employee rights.

- **Employment Agreement** This is a *negotiated* agreement (typically with a senior executive or lead technical employee) that includes employee compensation, title, responsibilities, minimum duration of employment, and benefits. An employment agreement may also include the subject matter of an employee agreement. Often an executive will sign a negotiated employment agreement and the form employee agreement.

The role of your legal counsel in these agreements is quite different:

- For the *employee agreement*, you use a lawyer to make sure you have the right form or forms in place. Thereafter, unless you need to change or update the form or you negotiate a special deal with an employee, you will use the agreement without further involvement of legal counsel.

■ For an *employment agreement*, you will use your lawyer to help negotiate and fine tune each agreement with each key employee. There are a lot of legal issues in these agreements, and you will likely need legal advice on each one. Negotiated employment agreements are beyond the scope of the discussion that follows.

Because these terms sound so similar, they are sometimes confused, and you may see inconsistent use of these terms.

About Employment Law Generally

There are many topics covered in this book, but the general field of employment law is not one of them. Employment is a fundamental relationship in our society and one that is much regulated. It is also a legal specialty at our law firm and at many others. Employment law covers compensation, taxation, social security, health insurance, retirement plans, discrimination, sexual harassment, layoffs, unemployment insurance, privacy rights, wage and hour law, and many other topics. There are also many documents relevant to employment that are not covered here, such as offer letters, employment manuals, ethical rules, employee e-mail policies, and so forth. In Wikipedia, the page on "Employment Law" has links to 75 subtopics.

It goes without saying that every employer needs to learn the applicable state and federal employment rules that apply to its business. Every technology company should discuss with legal counsel and its accountant the fundamentals rules of employment. You should consult counsel as needed when employment law issues arise. There are many laypersons' books on employment law that may help. The employee agreements discussed here are just one aspect—albeit an important one—of employment in the technology economy.

Contents of Employee Agreements

Let us now turn the heart of our discussion, the provisions that are in an employee agreement and the reasons that they are there. The main subject matter of employee agreements are: confidentiality, intellectual property rights transfers and—often—noncompetition and nonsolicitation provisions.

Confidentiality Provisions

Employee agreements always contain confidentiality agreements. Here is why:

■ Confidentiality has obvious advantages in competition and in negotiations with customers.

■ As discussed in Chapter 2, trade secret law protects your valuable nonpublic information only if you use reasonable efforts to keep it secret, including reasonable employee agreements.

■ When your company holds confidential information of other companies, you will breach your contract with the other party unless your employees protect it.

■ Public disclosure of information can often eliminate your ability to patent inventions, particularly outside the United States.

■ If you deal with public companies (or if your company is a public company), you may possess nonpublic information that, under the securities laws, is illegal to disclose.

Confidentiality needs to be part of the culture of each technology company—and the employee agreement is one important ingredient in accomplishing that.

Definition of "Confidential Information"

In employee agreements, confidential information is always defined broadly to include all nonpublic information regarding the company and its business affairs. Here is a sample provision:

> *Confidential Information means any information or data, whether in oral, graphic, written, electronic, machine-readable; or hard copy form or possessed by, used by, or under the control of the company, that is not generally available to the public. Confidential Information includes but is not limited to inventions, designs, data, source code, object code, programs, other works of authorship, know-how, trade secrets, techniques, ideas, discoveries, technical, marketing and business plans, customers, suppliers, pricing, profit margins, costs, products, and services.*

You may want to add to the long descriptive list in this clause those information items that are particularly important to your business. For example, if your company made voice recognition software, the list might include "speak interpretation and generation methods and algorithms." If your company made stock market analytical software, you might add "securities analysis methods and techniques." And so forth.

In many technology agreements, we put "carve-outs" or exceptions into confidentiality clauses—a listing of things that are *not* within the definition of Confidential Information. No carve-outs of this kind belong in employee agreements. The goal here is to keep in place the broadest definition. In case of doubt, the employee agreement should err in classifying information as confidential and subject to employer control. Some agreements add this additional provison:

> *Where the employee has any doubt whether information in his or her possession is confidential information, the employee shall request a determination from his or her supervisor.*

Regarding Use and Protection of Confidential Information

Employee agreements restrict the use of your company's confidential business information and forbid unauthorized disclosure. Here is a typical provision:

> *Employee agrees not to make any unauthorized disclosure of any Confidential Information. Employee agrees not to make any use of any Confidential Information except in carrying out his or her employment responsibilities.*

This general language is broad enough to cover third party information held in confidence by the company. Nonetheless many employee agreements contain provisions that expressly require the employee to treat third party confidential information as Confidential Information under the employee agreement:

> *Employee also agrees to preserve and protect the confidentiality of third party Confidential Information.*

Employee agreements require that employees return confidential information either at the employers' request or upon the termination or expiration of employment.

Confidentiality and Pre-Employment Communications

Employee agreements apply after hiring—that means they do not normally cover any confidential information given to employees *before* they were hired. If you are going to be discussing your technology and other confidential matters with the person that you are interviewing or to whom you have offered employment, the best practice is to have them sign your form of nondisclosure agreement before any confidential communications.

Provisions in Aid of Enforcement

If an employer learns that a former employee has taken confidential information after termination of employment in violation of the Agreement, the employer may send its lawyers to court to get an emergency court injunction. The injunction sought would normally be a court order that the former employee and the new employee cease immediate use of disclosure of the information. In some cases, the former employee may seek an order that the former employer not be permitted to work for the new employer in any role that would be likely to include use of confidential information.

Court orders of this kind are classified as "extraordinary relief." To get that injunction, the employer must demonstrate to the court that the harm is immediate (so that the matter cannot wait), that the harm to be stopped is irreparable (it cannot be fixed) and that money damages (also known as an "at law" remedy) are an inadequate remedy (recovering money would not solve the problem). To get a leg up on this relief, employment agreements usually have a clause such as the following:

> *Employee acknowledges that that immediate and irreparable damage will result to the Company and its business and properties if an employee breaches these confidentiality obligations and that the remedy at law for such breach will be inadequate. Accordingly, in addition to any other remedies and damages available, the Company shall be entitled to injunctive relief (without the necessity of posting a bond), and the employee may be specifically compelled to comply with his confidentiality obligations under this Agreement.*

These clauses will help the employer make its case, but they do not have any magic effect. The employer will still have to convince the judge that it really needs that injunction. Judges are obligated to rule on the facts and the law.

Why does the clause say that the injunction should be issued "without the necessity of posting a bond"? Sometimes an injunction turns out (when all the facts come out) to be unjustified. Judges frequently require a party that obtains an injunction to post a bond (which is a form of financial guarantee issued by a bonding company) to protect the enjoined party. If the injunction turns out to be wrongful, the judge will have the legal power and can award compensation from the bond to the enjoined party. This clause in the employee agreement is the employer's attempt to get the injunction without the cost of the bond. In spite of these words, judges would still have the power to require a bond as a condition of the injunction.

Capturing Intellectual Property Rights

Intellectual property rights generally include copyrights, patents, trade secret rights, and trademarks. A key function of employee agreements is to capture all of these rights that the employee may create for the employer. The normal way to do this is to define the "Work Product" that the employee will create and then provide for all rights in the Work Product to belong to the employer.

Here is a typical Work Product definition:

> *"Work Product" shall mean all items created or made, discoveries, concepts, ideas and fixed expressions thereof, past, present and future, whether or not patentable or registrable under copyright or other statutes, including but not limited to software, source and object code, hardware, technology, products, machines, programs, process developments, formulae, methods, techniques, know-how, data and improvements, which Employee makes or conceives or reduces to practice or learns alone or jointly with others that (1) are made, conceived, reduced to practice or learned during employment by the Company; (2) occur or have occurred during the period of, as a consequence of, or in connection with employment by the Company; (3) result from tasks assigned to Employee by the Company; or (4) result or have resulted from use of property, premises or facilities owned, leased or contracted for by the Company.*

This is another provision that you could tailor to your business by including in the list of items those technologies or categories of secret information that are most important in your business.

Next comes the provision that is designed to make the Work Product the property of the employer:

> *Employee agrees that any Work Product shall be the property of the Company and, if subject to copyright, shall be considered a "work made for hire" within the meaning of the Copyright Act of the United States (the "Act"). If and to the extent that any such Work Product is not to be a "work made for hire" within the meaning of the Act, Employee hereby expressly assigns to Company all right, title and interest in and to the Work Product, and all copies thereof, and the copyright, patent, trademark, trade secret, and all other intellectual property or proprietary rights in the Work Product.*

This text treats copyright differently from other intellectual property and specifically declares it to be "work made for hire." Any works generated by a W–2 employee is automatically "work made for hire" under the Copyright Act. So this language mandates a legal result that ought to occur by default. This language is thus a form of legal backup. It is designed to supply a "work made for hire" agreement if, for some unforeseen reason, the default rule does not apply. All other intellectual property rights are *assigned* to the employer.

Employee agreements commonly have provisions that make it clear that the agreement does not cover employee works and inventions that the employee makes on his or her own time and unconnected with work. This is a fairness provision. Here is common language:

For clarification, the term "Work Product" does not apply to any invention, work product, or development which meets all of the following three conditions: (1) Employee does the work entirely without use of Company's facilities, property or resources, (2) Employee does the work entirely on his or her own time, and (3) the development does not relate to the Company's business or research or to its planned business or research. However, employee agrees to disclose to the Company during the term of his or her employment in confidence each invention in order to permit the Company to make a determination as to compliance by Employee with this Agreement.

Special Rule for California and Certain Other States

There is a provision of California law that mandates that an employer include provisions in employee agreements rather similar to the last provision that we discussed. This is Section 2870 of the California Labor Code, and it applies to "inventions" that the employee makes unconnected with his or her employment. Here is a typical California employment agreement text that addresses Section 2870:

The provisions above regarding ownership of Work Product do not apply to Employee's inventions which qualify for protection under California Labor Code ("Section 2870"). As currently in effect, Section 2870 covers inventions for which no equipment, supplies, facility or trade secret information of Company was used and which was developed entirely in Employee's own time, and (i) which does not relate, at the time of conception or reduction to practice of the invention, to the business of Company, or to Company's actual or demonstrably anticipated research or development, or (ii) which does not result from any work performed by Employee for Company. Employee agrees to disclose to Company during the term of his or her employment in confidence each invention in order to permit the Company to make a determination as to compliance by Employee with this Agreement. Employee acknowledges that it is the Employee's burden to prove that Section 2870 applies.

As you can see from this text, Section 2870 allows the employer to require confidential disclosure to the employee of his or her inventions during the term of employment so that the employer can verify that Section 2870 applies. The wording of the provision closing follows the text of the statute.

There are very similar laws and required notices for employees in Illinois, Kansas, Minnesota, and Washington (state). See your attorney for the right form of employee agreement you have for employees who work in any of those states.

Cooperation in Rights Transfer

Employment agreements have provisions that require employees to cooperate in the transfer of intellectual property rights to their employer. These provisions also permit the employer to sign documents on the employee's behalf if the employer cannot locate the employee or if the employee is uncooperative. These provisions are needed because patent rights, under US law, vest in the inventor. Patent applications become the employer's property only when the employee assigns them. So these cooperation provisions come in handy in situations where the employee cannot or will not sign the necessary documents. Here is a sample text for this rather technical provision:

> *Employee will, during his/her employment and at any time thereafter, at the request and cost of the Company, execute all such documents and perform all such acts and provide such cooperation as the Company may reasonably require (i) to apply for, transfer, obtain, and preserve in the name of the Company (or its designee) any patents, copyrights or other intellectual property or proprietary rights and (ii) to assist in any proceeding or litigation regarding such intellectual property or proprietary rights.*

> *In the event that the Company is unable for any reason to secure Employee's signature through reasonable effort on any assignment or application or other document or instrument that the Company requires regarding intellectual property or proprietary rights, Employee hereby irrevocably appoints the Company and its duly authorized officers and agents as his/her agent and attorney-in-fact, to act for and on his or her behalf to execute and file any such documents and to do all other lawfully permitted acts to further the prosecution and issuance of patents, copyrights and other intellectual property or proprietary rights with the same legal force and effect as if personally executed by Employee.*

Documents and Records

Employee agrees also to have provisions to secure for the company the relevant documents and records that the employee prepares during the term of employment. Here is the typical language:

> *All written materials, records, data, and other documents prepared or possessed by Employee during Employee's employment by the Company are the Company property. At the termination of Employee's employment with the Company for any reason, Employee shall return all of the Company's materials, records, data, and other documents, together with all other Company property.*

Noncompetition and Nonsolicitation Provisions

Noncompetition provisions restrict ex-employees from working for your competitors. Nonsolicitation provisions restrict ex-employees from soliciting your customers for business or luring away your employees. We lawyers refer to noncompetition and nonsolicitation provisions together as "restrictive covenants."

Employees do not like restrictive covenants because they limit their freedom. However, these provisions are very commonly used by digital technology companies. Here are some ways that restrictive covenants can help your business:

- Restrictive covenants can lessen the impact of losing key technical and sales personnel.

- Investors in your business—and potential purchasers of your business—will expect you to have restrictive covenants in place.

- Restrictive covenants work together with confidentiality provisions. If your company's employee does not work for your competitor, your secrets will be safer.

State with Limitations on Restrictive Covenants

There is a widespread myth that the restrictive covenants are unenforceable—perhaps this is employee wishful thinking. Under the laws of most states, restrictive covenants are enforceable—although the employee will need to prove they are needed and fair. (The general tests for enforceability are discussed below.)

However, in one state, California, restrictive covenants in employment agreements are generally unenforceable. This is because of California Civil Code Section 16600, first adopted in 1872, that says: "every contract by which anyone is restrained from engaging in a lawful profession, trade, or business of any kind is to that extent void." In spite of the "every contract" language, California does permit restrictive covenants to the limited extent that the court finds them necessary to protect the employer's trade secrets.

The California limit on restrictive covenants is important because of the large number of digital technology companies that operate in that state. Because of this law, restrictive covenants are much less common in California than in other high-tech economy states such as Virginia, Texas, North Carolina, or Massachusetts. Many companies with national operations that have major operations in California omit restrictive covenants from their employment agreements nationwide.

There are other states that permit restrictive covenants—but limit them under state statutes in various ways. The limitations may include duration (how long the restriction can last) and what they can protect (primarily limiting them to protecting secret information). States that have statutes limiting restrictive covenants (as of the time that this is written in 2007) are Colorado, Louisiana, Hawaii, Missouri, Montana, North Dakota, Oklahoma, Oregon, Nevada, and South Dakota. If your business intends to use restrictive covenants in your employee agreements in California or these other states, you should ask your attorney to craft a clause that is likely to pass the applicable legal test.

About Consideration

When your company enters into a restrictive covenant with an employee, the agreement will be binding on the employee only if, under applicable state law, there is "consideration" for the agreement. "Consideration" is something of value given for a promise. The law of what constitutes sufficient consideration varies from state to state. Your attorney can tell you the rule that applies in the states where your business has operations.

Here is an overview of the rules that apply in most states:

1. When continued at-will employment is the only consideration for a restrictive covenant, the agreement must be executed when the employee is first hired as a condition of employment.

2. If the restrictive covenant is executed later (after hiring), then in most states, in addition to continued employment, the employer must provide the employee with *something extra*. The something extra could be a cash bonus (this is the most common), extra training, stock options, or another benefit—but it will count as consideration only if the employee would not otherwise have been entitled to the benefit. It is important that the consideration be specifically identified in the employee agreement. There are some states, however, in which continued employment without more consideration is sufficient.

Getting Employees to Sign

Some companies fail to get these agreements in place in the early days of their operations—and then find that key employees resist signing any employee agreement with a restrictive covenant.

We have found that a good way to deal with this is to tie signing the restrictive covenant agreements to option grants. If the employee will not sign the employee agreement, he or she gets no options. In our experience, most employees will sign with this inducement. It is good practice to have employee signatures witnessed.

Enforceability of Provisions

Even where restrictive covenants are generally permitted, the courts will enforce them only when justified. Two factors generally determine whether a restriction is enforceable: (1) the nature of the employment and (2) the reasonableness of the restrictions. This means that enforcement will never be automatic in court.

Nature of the Employment

The courts generally enforce restrictive covenants against only two types of employees:

- *Employees who have access to trade secrets or confidential information—usually technical and scientific employees.* The rationale is that the restraint preserves legitimate trade secrets. To enforce restrictions on this theory requires proof (1) that the employer actually has trade secrets, (2) that the employee knows the secrets, and (3) that the employer otherwise protects trade secrets with reasonable security measures.

- *Employees who have gained customer loyalty—usually sales staff.* The rationale is that the restraint allows the employer to protect its customer relationships. In this case, enforcement of the restriction requires proof (1) that customer contacts are important in the employer's business and (2) that the employee had significant customer contact on the job.

Both of these factors are matters of proof. When the employer wants to enforce a restrictive covenant against an employee, it will be the employer's burden to show that these factors apply.

Reasonable Scope and Duration

There is another important limitation on restrictive covenants. The courts enforce agreements only if they are reasonable in duration and geographic scope. This rule is a balancing test—pitting the employer's need for protection against the employee's interest in employment freedom.

- **Duration of Restrictive Covenants** Normally a one-year restraint is considered reasonable. In many states, when good reason is shown, two-year restraints are enforced. A three-year restraint is a stretch but will be allowed for good cause in some states. In general, the shorter the restraint, the more likely that it will be enforced.

- **Geographic Scope** The court will expect the restraint to be limited to a relevant area. Technical employees and sales employees may have very different relevant geographic areas. For a company with global competition, it may make sense to have a global restraint on a technical staff member's employment at a competitor. If a sales person has only a local territory, you may want to have his or her noncompetition restraint cover just the same territory. Some businesses have different forms for sales and technical staff members.

Here is the text of a typical noncompetition provision:

> *Except with the prior written consent of Company, during his or her employ-ment with Company and for a period of one year after that employment ends, Employee will not directly or indirectly run, operate, control, be employed by, hold an interest in or participate in the management, operation, ownership or control of any business if such business is in competition with Company [in the following geographic area: _____]. As used in this Agreement, "business" includes any corporation, company, association, partnership, limited partnership, or other entity. Notwithstanding the above, Employee will not violate this Agreement solely by owning less than one (1) percent of the publicly traded shares of a competing business.*

Getting these limitations correct is primarily a matter of thoughtful and careful drafting. If you craft provisions that do not overreach, you are more likely to be able to enforce them in court.

Noncompetition Clause

Here is typical language for nonsolicitation provisions that covers customers:

> Nonsolicitation of Customers and Prospects. *Except with the prior written consent of Company, during his or her employment with Company and for a period of one (1) year after that employment ends, Employee will not directly or indirectly, either for himself or herself or for any other business or person, solicit, call upon, attempt to solicit or attempt to call upon any of the customers or prospective customers of Company with whom Employee have had contact while employed at Company, and Employee will not accept any business from such customers or prospective customers of Company for his- or herself or for any employer during such period.*

When you hire a salesperson, do not be surprised if he or she says: "I own my contacts." You may need to compromise on your nonsolicitation language when hiring sales personnel. A common way to do this is to edit the text to exclude customers resulting from the salesperson's pre-existing contacts.

Here is typical language for nonsolicitation provisions that covers solicitation of other employees:

> **Nonsolicitation of Employees.** *Except with the prior written consent of Company, during his or her employment with Company and for a period of one (1) year after that employment ends, Employee will not solicit or have any discussion with any employee of Company concerning employment for any business other than Company, and Employee will not induce or attempt to influence any employee of Company to terminate his or her employment with Company.*

Automatic Extension of Restricted Period

Often the restrictive covenant will include a provision stating that if an employee violates her noncompete or nonsolicitation, the duration of the restrictions shall be extended by the length of the breach. This clause is designed to take away the benefit of any cheating.

"Blue Pencil"

If a restrictive covenant is too broad, in some states it will be unenforceable. In other states the judge will have the power (but not the obligation) to adjust or "blue pencil" the restriction. What this means is that a court will narrow the restriction and enforce it as rewritten. To encourage the court to save restrictive covenants in this way, many employee agreements include text like this:

> *If any restriction set forth in this Section is found by any court of competent jurisdiction to be unenforceable because it extends for too long a period of time or over too great a range of activities or in too broad a geographic area, it shall be interpreted to extend only over the maximum period of time, range of activities or geographic area for which it may be enforceable.*

If the judge does "blue pencil" the agreement, the judge will be deciding how much of a restriction is fair as applied to the particular employee under all the circumstances.

Enforcement of Noncompetition Agreements by Employers

What do you do if you think that your company's ex-employee is violating a restrictive covenant? This section will explore your options.

Do Not Delay in Addressing a Breach

If you discover that an ex-employee is breaching a restrictive covenant, call an attorney who knows software litigation without delay. Both the practical and legal remedies may evaporate if you wait too long. How long is too long? There is no fixed rule, but even a few weeks delay means that your trade secrets have been spilled everywhere and your legal case for an injunction could be dead.

Remedies Short of Litigation

What can you do, before starting litigation, to stop a former employee from violating an employee agreement? Generally speaking, the best bet is to send both the former employee and the new employer a demand letter insisting that the former employee and the new employer observe the restraint. Sometimes it will be sufficient if the new employer promises specified compliance, for example, that a salesperson will be given a territory different from that which is forbidden in the agreement. In other cases, there is no adequate remedy other than to separate the former employee from his or her new job at the new company.

Any demand letter should be written by your legal counsel or approved by your attorney before it is sent. Together with the letter, the former employer should send to both the former employee and the new employer a copy of the restrictive covenant. A demand letter will normally state that litigation will result if the adequate assurances of compliance are not forthcoming. Of course, a company should never threaten litigation unless it is prepared to follow through.

Preliminary Injunction

Like trade secret and employee agreement confidentiality clause cases (with which they are often combined), litigation on the basis of a restrictive covenant normally turns on a preliminary injunction hearing. For this reason, these cases may be relatively inexpensive as litigation goes. In most cases, the decision on the preliminary injunction (or an expedited appeal of a preliminary injunction decision) is effectively the end of the case, one way or the other. The party that won the opening round usually has a strong advantage in settlement talks.

The "smell" of the case plays an important role. If the employee has walked away with papers, disks or other property of the former employer, downloaded files, or has otherwise failed to leave clean, a preliminary injunction enforcing a restrictive covenant will be easier to get. Similarly if the employee was your company's top scientist and he went to a direct competitor, that will help get the injunction.

If the court issues a preliminary injunction, what will the injunction require? Normally the court will order, in quite specific terms, that the restrictive covenant must be complied with. The court has great discretion in fashioning relief, but it is common that the court will be guided by the terms of the covenant.

Obtaining Assurance of the Absence of Conflicting Prior Agreements

Prior to hiring an employee, you should do your best to ensure that he or she is not subject to any restrictive covenants with prior employers. Be sure to ask every prospective employee about this subject. Sometimes employees are not aware that they are subject to a restrictive covenant with a current or former employer either because they do not have copies of the written agreements that they have signed or, if they do, they do not understand the provisions. Ask about restrictive covenants when talking to references if they are former employers.

Employee agreements often include clauses that provide the employee's assurance that he or she is not breaching a prior employee agreement. Here is what this type of provision looks like:

> *Employee represents that entering into employment with the Company under this Agreement does not constitute a breach of any contract, agreement or understanding and that Employee is free to enter into the employ of Company. Employee promises to (a) remain in full compliance with the terms of any agreement with any previous employer or other party and (b) to refrain from using or disclosing to the Company any trade secret or confidential information of such previous employer or other party.*

What do you do if you find out that a prospective employee is subject to a legally enforceable restrictive covenant? If you hire the person, you may be sued for inducing the employee to breach her restrictive covenant.

If a job applicant is potentially valuable and if there is a problem with a contract that the applicant has signed with a past employer, you will need to consult with legal counsel. Counsel will do the requisite analysis—looking at the agreement itself, at the facts, and at the law—and determine the legal risk. Needless to say, this should be done *before* offering the applicant a job.

Chapter 4

IT Services— Development, Outsourcing, and Consulting

One of my favorite interview questions is, "How would you characterize your approach to software development?" My favorite answer came from a job candidate who said, "During software design, I'm an architect. While I'm designing the user interface, I'm an artist. During construction, I'm a craftsman. And during unit testing, I'm one mean son of a bitch!"

—Steve McConnell, Development Consultant, from IEEE Software, January/February 1998.

Introduction

There are many thousands of companies in the business of providing custom IT services, commonly known as "IT consulting." IT consulting is a technology service business; but, because its product is code, it is also an intellectual property business.

In this chapter, you will find a discussion of consulting in general, with particular emphasis on the methods and mechanics of development deals. This chapter looks at deals from both the developer's and the customer's point of view.

In This Chapter

This chapter covers:

- The business of consulting and development

- The development process, including characteristic risks

- The request for proposals (RFPs) and project planning processes

- Development agreements, including typical provisions and common negotiation issues

- Issues in offshore IT development

- More consulting deals (other than development agreements)

- Some legal issues in the operation of a consulting business

IT Consulting Business Model

Consulting companies depend on a cadre of highly trained and well-compensated employees who deliver professional services. Consulting companies usually pay these professional employees generous salaries and benefits. Consulting companies make their profits by charging even more for these employees. This means that personnel costs are high and fixed costs are substantial. (This is the reason that the cost-saving opportunities for offshoring can be very significant.)

Sales are all-important because consulting companies need to keep the "pipeline" full. Consulting companies lose money if they have their highly paid personnel "on the bench." Service companies therefore try their best to find large clients who will provide long-term projects—or projects that lend themselves to extensions and follow-up.

Business-oriented consulting is—and always will be—a field where demand fluctuates. Changes in technology stimulate the consulting market. Billions of dollars of consulting came from the introduction of enterprise information systems, client–server and Web architectures, and the deployment of networks, including the Internet. There have been IT booms driven by year 2000 compliance and more recently by the Sarbanes-Oxley Act. Recessions can reduce new business sharply. Consulting firms must meet the demands of the market and must be ready to grow or contract at any time.

Consulting is a fiercely competitive business. Consulting companies compete on price, service, reputation, and expertise. There is a premium on specialization.

Development Deals

Development has been a basic part of the IT industry since its infancy. As the quotation at the start of this chapter suggests, development is a tough business requiring many different skills. Without IT consulting, our knowledge-based economy could not exist.

This chapter discusses development deals in some depth. Development agreements are sophisticated contracts involving all the issues that affect IT consulting deals generally, such as the delivery of sophisticated IT-related services, payment matters, risk management, and intellectual property ownership. There are other types of IT consulting deals, and this chapter will touch on these as well.

Mention IT development and the first thing that comes to mind are projects for big business. Enterprise software development is indeed a major part of the information industry. Major IT service firms, such as Accenture, EDS, Computer Sciences Corporation, or offshoring firms such as Wipro, Infosys, or Tata Consulting Services, have thousands of professionals that span the IT spectrum. There are also thousands of smaller firms in IT consulting. Many software or hardware product companies have development arms to provide customized business solutions based on their technology.

At our law firm, we work on development agreements for enterprise software but we also do development agreements for many other types of software, components, and applications. Whenever one business needs to have another business build some software or a system, there must be a development agreement. The same development agreement issues apply to developing e-commerce solutions, networking software, middleware, messaging applications, games, entertainment, and any other software or IT system. Contracting for IT services covers projects that range from simple one-day consulting jobs to complex multimillion dollar, multideveloper development projects.

Development can meld with other deal types. In some cases, we combine development projects with distribution or marketing arrangements. Sometimes we merge development deals with strategic investments. If you are doing such a composite deal, you will need your attorney to create a hybrid of these various deal types.

The combination of a development project with mass-market distribution is a special case, which we call a "publication" arrangement.

Why Outside Development?

Let us begin with the business background of development engagements. Why do the customer companies do these deals? They do, after all, have a choice—which is to hire staff and do the development jobs themselves. So why do customers go outside? Here are the typical reasons:

- Companies perceive that developers are "experts" who will provide solutions faster and with less risk.

- Development projects are based on the use of third party software products put together with hardware, networks, programming, and configuration to create a solution. Companies want vendors that have existing expertise in the underlying products.

- Companies may see advanced technology solutions from expert developers as conferring a competitive advantage.

- Vendors may have prebuilt software modules that can reduce development time and cost and development risk.

- Companies often want to concentrate on their core technologies and business processes rather than investing time and attention in software systems.

In the contracting process, the key customer goal is likely to be getting a solution quickly and efficiently with low technical risk. Control of the intellectual property may also be a customer goal. The developer's main goal is usually the money but it may also want marketing opportunities, experience, and control of newly created intellectual property.

Scale of Development Deals and the Development Forms

Development engagements come in all sizes. Large deals are distinguishable from small deals on a number of levels including:

- Pricing and pricing structures

- The number of technical managers and the size of the programming staff involved

- The process and procedures necessary to manage the project

- The life span and technical complexity of the project including its innovative aspects as well as the degree to which existing third party technology is used

- The role of the completed application in the customer's business

What all of these factors translate into is a risk profile for the deal. Large deals with big price tags that involve a high degree of technical innovation and/or mission critical systems are much more risky to both the customer and the developer than smaller jobs.

At the conceptual level, the legal and business and contract issues for big and small development jobs are much the same. However, larger jobs have much more process and procedures (which we will discuss below) to manage complexity and risks.

In Appendix 4 of this book, you will find a "long form" of a development agreement that you may want to review. The long form is a starting point for a contract covering a major development project. Also included in the appendix are more general forms of consulting agreements that can be used in smaller development products. You can also find many examples of development agreements at legal sites such as www.findlaw.com and www.onecle.com; these examples will show you how varied these documents are in real life.

Development Can Be a Risky Business

There is no doubt that developers and customers strive for good results on budget and on time. Notwithstanding these worthy goals, study after study has shown that major IT development projects have a remarkably high rate of bad results. One 1997 study, for example, surveyed large enterprise IT managers and found that the managers consider over 60 percent of their IT development projects to be "unsuccessful." Moreover, three-quarters of projects reviewed in the same study were significantly late in completion, and more than half were significantly over budget.

Each IT development project gone wrong has its own tale of woe, but there are some common factors. Here, as a word to the wise, are some of the factors commonly cited as the causes of failure and disputes. You will see that many (but not all) of these problems come from inadequate planning at the start and poor controls.

- **Unclear Specifications** Creating thorough specifications requires time and money at the outset, so all too often projects are based on written specifications that are lacking in detail or vague. This leads to disagreements over the functionality and performance the developer was obligated to deliver.

- **Lack of Communication; Lack of User Involvement** Sometimes the customer's management has an unclear idea of what it wants—or wants something that differs from what the intended users want. The result can be a product that does not serve the customer's real needs and disappoints all.

- **Technical Risk** Large projects may have technical challenges where the level of effort required is simply unknown. New feature creation can be an iterative process of uncertain duration. If the project does not provide enough money and time, the project will run into trouble.

- **Aggressive Pricing and Scheduling** To secure contracts, developer's sales staff may base bids on unrealistic assumptions about the time and labor needed to complete the project. If the fixed price or estimate turns out to be too low, the developer will start asking for more money. That is when conflict can begin.

- **Lack of Monitoring and Control** Customers sometimes let projects go without close monitoring. Sometimes customers do not have the technical means to monitor progress. This can lead to unpleasant surprises when the problems finally emerge.

- **Poor Change Control** When changes are required in the course of a project, they should be documented. There needs to be a formal process to assess the impact of each change on project cost and its schedule. This is best done by means of a formal change order process. Unfortunately, some projects just "evolve," and changes are left undocumented. This leads to disagreements about specifications and schedules, as well as to developer demands to be paid for "out of scope" work.

- **Low Wages and High Turnover in Staff** In some cases, the developer may be cutting corners in staff salaries or benefits to keep costs down; the resulting high turnover rate can slow progress and compromise quality.

Experience shows that the bigger and more complicated the project, the more risk there is that things will go wrong. However, smaller projects are certainly not immune to problems. The loose specifications in smaller jobs can often lead to conflicts about what was supposed to be done. In either case, it is not unusual for failed IT projects to end up as a dispute in the hands of the lawyers.

Need for Planning and Risk Management

Good planning and writing sensible development contracts will not guarantee that there will be no disputes or failures, but these sensible measures can help reduce the number of problems and help manage them if they occur.

Before entering into any IT service agreement, each side should make an assessment of risk factors. Where there are special risks—whether it is a large quantum of technical risk, untried software components, an insufficient number of trained staff, a tight schedule, or other uncertainties, each side will need to devote more resources to risk management. In addition, both parties should monitor progress throughout the project. The customer may need contingency plans so that it can take action if the project is very late or fails altogether. Contract provisions need to be adjusted to compensate for perceived risks.

Because development deals can go bad, customers should understand clearly what contractual remedies will apply if the project fails. For the same reason, smart developers should always put clear risk limitations in development deals, including damage exclusion and limitation of liability clauses. (These contractual provisions are discussed below.)

Process Overview

Let us look at the stages of a typical significant software development project.

- **Needs Assessment** Every development project begins with the customer and its needs. The customer begins by assessing, sometimes with the assistance of an outside consultant, what it needs in terms of new or different products or services. Often the customer assembles an internal system acquisition team, which may include representatives of management, users, information services, and the legal department.

- **Acquisition Team** If the customer decides to go forward, the needs assessment team will likely become the acquisition team. The team may also consider whether to do the project in-house rather than hiring an outside developer.

- **Setting Goals** The customer needs to decide what the functionality and performance needs are and what the preliminary expectations are as to how long development will take and how much it will cost.

- **RFPs** To get the best combination of high skill and reasonable price, there is nothing better than competitive bidding. To start that process, the customer will often assemble RFPs—sometimes called an "invitation to bid"—to use in soliciting bids. Sometimes the customer will start with a "call for expressions of interest"—a preliminary document about the project used to identify developers that are interested in the project and who will be provided with the fuller RFP. The customer may retain an outside consultant to help prepare the RFP and to help evaluate responses.

- **Response to RFP** The developer becomes part of the process when it submits a written response to the RFP. Often the developer will assemble its own team of sales people, managers, and technicians who will put the response together.

- **Developer Selection** The customer reviews the responses and selects a developer.

- **Contracting** After the customer chooses a developer, the parties will negotiate a development agreement to govern the development process.

- **Development Services** The developer will perform the development services under the development agreement—hopefully to the customer's satisfaction. Development normally ends with acceptance of the final deliverables.

- **Postdelivery Services** The developer will normally provide postdevelopment services, such as ongoing maintenance and training and follow-on development work.

Lawyers are primarily involved in the contracting process—and, of course, in resolving any disputes. However, all the other phases of the process have significance for contracting and legal matters—the initial phases because they help define the deliverables and set the parties' expectations and the final phases because they determine success or failure.

Smaller projects will have similar stages—although needs assessment may be informal and the parties may not bother to use a formal RFP process to obtain bids.

Writing and Responding to RFPs

In the RFP process, the customer invites bidding on a project, states its requirements in a formal document, and seeks key information from the bidders. In some cases, particularly when a government entity is seeking bids, anyone who is qualified may submit a response to the RFP. More often, the customer chooses the developers that it wants to engage in the process.

Elements of an RFP—From the Customer's Point of View

Let us say that you want to retain a developer to supply development service for an IT project. Here are some pointers that you may want to consider in drafting your RFP.

Confidentiality is the first order of business. In order to explain your procurement requirements, you are likely to disclose confidential information about its business. Therefore, you will want to impose a requirement that the respondent not disclose your confidential information or use it other than to prepare a response. This is best done by requiring the respondent to sign a nondisclosure agreement (NDA) before you deliver your RFP. For more information on this topic, please see Chapter 3.

The RFP is designed to elicit key information that will enable you to choose a respondent that will provide the best value. A well conceived and written RFP will cover the following:

- **Background** State the reason for the project, including the current situation and the business problem that you seek to solve.

- **Your Goals** State the business and practical results that you expect to achieve.

- **Required Functionality** Explain what you want the resulting system to do. The more detail the better. Require the respondent to state that it will provide all expected functionality or explain any exceptions. If there are features that are not essential but "nice-to-have," consider adding those. Often this portion of the RFP goes on for many pages. You cannot be too inclusive or too careful about stating your needs in detail.

- **Importance** If the project involves a core or critical business function, this should be made very clear.

- **Technology Requirements** Explain the information system environment that the project needs to support and any decisions that you have made as to the technologies to be used in the project. Require the respondent to state that it can provide the required solution.

- **Developer Qualifications** Explain the particular qualifications and skills that you expect the developer to demonstrate in its response. You should also inquire as to the developer's (and that of its key staff members) experience with similar projects. And be sure to seek references to other customers for whom the developer has done similar work.

- **Development Team Size and Composition** Ask the developer to explain the project staffing and management, including the specific persons to be assigned. You may want to ask for recent employee turnover rates. Ask about any subcontracting that is contemplated.

- **Time Frame Expectations** State how long the project is expected to take. Require the respondent to state whether it can do the project in the expected time frame. Where timing is critical, this should be stated.

- **Budgetary Expectations** State the range of spending expected. Require the respondent to state its best price for performing the services. You will find a discussion later in this chapter on pricing structures. You may want to include the preferred pricing structure in the RFP.

- **Communications and Management** Explain how you want communications and reporting of progress to be managed.

- **Acceptance** Explain your expectations for implementation, testing, and acceptance of the project deliverables.

- **Maintenance and Support** Explain your expectations regarding continuing hardware repair and repair of the system, bug fixing, and the like.

- **Training** State what you expect the respondent to provide to train system users.

- **Risk and Risk Management** Ask the developer to evaluate the risks and explain how they can be mitigated. If you want an off-site disaster recovery system, make sure to mention it.

- **Security Needs** Explain your security requirements, both with regard to the development process and security features of the proposed project.

- **Legal Terms of Importance** Include proposed legal terms. Require the respondent to state whether it will agree to them, and if not, to indicate those that require negotiation. You may want to include insurance requirements.

- **RFP Process** State when responses are due, and when you will get back to the respondents. Explain the criteria for acceptance. Be sure to reserve expressly the right to reject all responses if you choose.

Responding to RFPs—From the Developer's Point of View

If your company provides IT services and wants to respond to an RFP, here are a few general observations on how to put together a winning response:

- **Be Aware of the Uses of Your Response** It is common for customers to ask that the RFP and your response be included as part of the final development agreement. Even if you are going to resist this (as most IT service companies do), it is a virtual certainty that much of the content of your response will go into the final contract. Therefore, you should not promise anything in the response that you would not want to promise in a contract.

- **Be Very Responsive** Be sure to address every point of the RFP in a way that demonstrates knowledge of both the business and technical issues and a capability to perform.

- **Provide a Detailed Response** State clearly what you can or cannot do. With regard to proposed features or functions, your response should explain if it is "fully supported," "partially supported," "not available," or "available at extra cost." Avoid general responses that leave in doubt what you are willing to provide. If further work is required to define the scope of the project, you should say so. If requirements are unclear, you should say so. If there are ways to get clarification before responding, you should use them. The goal is to avoid unpleasant surprises later on.

- **Avoid Sales Talk** Avoid sweeping and glib language in the response such as "instant response," "everything that you could want," "best performance in the market," and the like. There are problems with this kind of talk. First, it sounds slick and may be a turn-off. Second, it could cause legal risk if it is incorporated into your consulting agreement—and thus become a legally binding warranty. If the project ends up in a lawsuit, the judge and jury may weigh these over-the-top promises and representations against the actual results that you deliver.

- **Explain the Technologies That You Propose to Provide** Explain the preferred technology solutions and how they will be implemented. Use graphics as necessary to explain the architecture and designs you recommend.

- **Explain How You Bring Extra Value** Most projects are awarded based on value—which may or may not be the same as the lowest price. If your company provides additional value, explain why.

- **Subcontracting** If you are planning to use subcontractors, explain why. Note that you, as the prime contractor, will normally be legally responsible for the performance of your subcontractors—or their lack of performance.

- **Communication** Explain proposed communications and reporting methodologies. Explain how project setbacks or delays will be reported and treated.

- **Be Careful with Pricing** Be as responsive as possible regarding the expected price of your company's services and any goods that may have to be purchased. However, if you do not have enough information to state the final cost, say so. If there are contingencies that affect pricing, explain them.

- **Postcompletion** Explain postacceptance support for the project.

- **Legal Terms** If there are particular legal terms that are important to your company, be sure to say so. If you have standard terms that you want to use, you should include them.

- **Proof and Polish** Some companies lose out in the bidding process because they submit responses that are sloppy and filled with errors. Take the time to make it right.

Agreement

After selection of a vendor comes the negotiation of the development agreement. This is sometimes done under pressure—as both sides want to "get going." Sometimes the parties will start work while the contract is worked out under an informal MOU (Memorandum of Understanding)—a risky course for both sides.

In this section, you will find a discussion of the typical issues and provisions in development agreements. There are innumerable variations on development deals, of course—but from a lawyer's perspective these are usually variations on the same themes. This section is designed to help you see the issues and find solutions. The development agreement manages:

- What development work will be performed?

- How will the project be managed?

- What will happen if the project goes wrong or contingencies arise?

Each side should bring its technical, business, and legal resources to bear on this negotiation process. Both parties should be trying to minimize their risks and maximize their gains.

Getting the First Draft on the Table

There is an old adage in diplomatic negotiations: "The first draft on the table wins." This is an overstatement to be sure—but it is undoubtedly a negotiating advantage to have your form of agreement as the starting point for negotiation.

Most often, the party that gets this first draft advantage is the developer—because it does many deals of this type. However, customers that do a great many software or IT acquisitions often have their own acquisition form agreement—or sometimes key clauses that they want in agreements.

Smart developers begin with a "user friendly" form that is reasonably protective but fair. That is more likely to lead to a smooth negotiation and faster conclusion of the deal. Developers that look for perfect legal protection probably would not close many deals. On the other hand, developers that take unwise risks may end up in litigation—and likely reduce the value of their firm. For the developer, the key often is knowing what is a reasonable compromise and knowing how to "sell" the other side on its "must have" positions.

Structure of a Development Agreement

Development projects require contract provisions that provide for the management of many moving parts: complex tasks, complex specifications, third party tools, a team of professionals, and substantial sums of money over time to reach defined goals. For this reason, development projects usually require lots of documentation (discussed in more detail below) that specifies what is to be done and when and how it is to be accomplished. This task-oriented documentation normally becomes "schedules" to the agreement, placed at the end. The "body" of the agreement for the most part consists of the "legal terms" that interact with and govern the task-oriented content of the schedules.

One development job often leads to another. After systems are built, the customer often wants them enhanced, extended, updated, or integrated with other systems. For this reason, most development agreements are designed so that a single set of "legal terms" can be used with a variety of development projects. Such a form of agreement is sometimes called an "umbrella" agreement, because it "covers" a variety of tasks. In other cases, particularly for larger more complex projects, there will be a single highly customized agreement to cover a series of development tasks. Some large projects may have different contracts for different development phases or services.

Development Planning

There is a saying: "One who fails to plan, plans to fail." A large development agreement needs task schedules that explain in reasonable detail what is to be done. Even after the RFP process, the customer usually will have only a general idea of the functionality it needs, and the developer may have only a general idea of what it is going to supply. This means that there must be a planning process in place.

Development agreements for complex projects most often include provisions for a planning phase, designed for the creation of a development plan. The planning process can take days, weeks, or months, depending on the scale and complexity of the undertaking.

Sometimes the parties will sign a separate consulting agreement just to cover the project planning process—to be followed by the negotiation of a full development agreement. Alternatively, planning can be the first phase of a multiphase process under a comprehensive development agreement. From the customer's point of view, there are advantages and disadvantages from either course.

- If the customer negotiates the full contract first, it will spend time and money on contract negotiations covering the entire project before it has a clear idea of the project price and duration.

- If the customer has planning done first, it will spend money on planning without a clear idea of the legal and business terms under which the project will be built.

In either case, the customer normally gets to see the development plan first—and then decides if it wants to proceed with the rest of the development project. If the customer does not go further, the customer will have to pay for the creation of the development plan only.

A good planning process will generate much of the key project documentation that will be used to define the scope of the work. This documentation will often become a part of a detailed "statement of work," or "work order."

Here are some of the elements that might be in a development plan—whether in the form of one document or many. For convenience, we have arranged common development plan elements by subject matter below:

What Is to Be Delivered to the Customer?

- **Software Deliverables** The software deliverables for the project may be alpha, beta, and final versions of each module. The specification should state whether each deliverable includes source code and binary code or any software tools.

- **Documentation Deliverables** There should be a listing of documentation to be created and supplied, including any user document and system operator or maintenance documentation.

- **Data Conversion** If data are to be converted or processed from a pre-existing software application, the process for doing this needs to be stated.

Requirements for Providing the Deliverables

- **Specifications** Written specifications should include functional specifications (what the software will do) and technical specifications (how the software will be built). There may also be performance specifications (rate of transaction processing on a designated platform). These often are preliminary specifications—with detailed specifications to be created later.

- **Standards** There should be a listing of applicable technical standards for performance, interoperability, or quality. There may be applicable code development standards, such as naming conventions, rules on structure and modularity of code, and required formats.

- **Milestone Schedule** This is a schedule for the performance of tasks—generally in the form of a table listing dates and deliverables and the party responsible for each task. In many deals, selected milestones trigger payments to the developer.

- **Location** There should be a statement of the place (or places) that the services will be performed. There may be a listing of customer location workspace or development hardware to be made available to developer.

- **Team** There is normally a listing of the developer staff members to be assigned to the project.

Software and Data to Be Provided for Use in Development

- **Third-Party Products and Services** There will need to be a statement of third party products to be supplied (and it needs to be stated who will supply them). There may be a need for third party services, such as telecommunications lines or services for hardware installation or configuration. In some cases, third party services might include a subcontracting or off-shoring part of the work. Key limitations imposed by third party licenses should be made clear.

- **Pre-Existing Software** If the developer or the customer is providing pre-existing software code or products, those programs should be listed.

- **Data** In some cases, the customer must supply sample data and/or information about its data structures, equipment configurations, or business processes.

- **Access** The developer may require remote access to the customer's computer systems.

Oversight and Management

- **Management and Communications Plan** The parties will need a structure for meeting, progress and problem reporting, documenting decisions, and follow-up. There may be a process for escalation of problems.

- **Risk Management Plan** For complex projects, there should be a process for reporting problems and managing project risks, which includes delays, dependencies on third parties, quality issues, staffing changes, or other risk factors.

- **Quality Assurance** Depending on the product, there may be a plan for regular quality checking, reviews of software for functional completeness, error logging, and follow up with error correction. There may be periodic reviews to check conformity of product to specifications.

Price and Costs

- **Payments to Developer** The amounts and timing of payments to the developer (which may be subject to adjustment) should be clearly stated. Cost variables should also be clearly stated. Normally payments will be tied to the successful completion of designated milestones. Expense reimbursement and the reimbursement process should be explicit.

- **Third Party Payments** Estimates of payments for third party hardware, software, and services should be provided. The party responsible for making those payments—the developer or the customer—should be stated.

Acceptance

- **Acceptance Process** The acceptance standards and acceptance process, including any applicable testing, should be made clear.

Postacceptance

- **Training** Planning should include adequate training for administrators and users.

- **Maintenance** There should be planning for maintenance and support after acceptance. If the developer is going to provide maintenance and support, a fee schedule should be provided.

"Detailed Design"

Depending on the complexity of the project, the parties may agree on the creation of a "detailed design" document that refines and "fills in the blanks" of the original preliminary design documentation. In some cases, there may be more than one of these more detailed documents. Work may proceed in some areas while detailed design work proceeds in others.

Detailed design documents often lead to a change in the projected work. (It is usually an increase in the amount of services.) This can trigger negotiations about repricing of the project.

In each case, the development agreement will need to contain a process for customer "sign-off" of the design documents as they are created, including any change in price. The customer will want the option not to proceed or pay for development under documents that are not yet approved.

Here is typical language regarding such a provision:

In accordance with the Milestone Schedule, prior to beginning the development services, Developer will prepare a detailed design document ("Detailed Design") for the System that will be submitted to Customer at least two weeks in advance of a detailed design review meeting including Developer and Customer ("Design Review"). The Detailed Design will incorporate and comply with the Specifications and Requirements.

In the event that Customer approves the Detailed Design, Customer may provide Developer with written notice ("Design Approval Notice"). In any case, Developer may not proceed with the development services until Customer provides a Design Approval Notice.

Dealing with Informal Specifications

For small projects, it is often the case that neither the customer nor the developer wants to invest the time and money required to develop a detailed specification. What they use instead is a more informal "high level" specification that outlines the functionality of the desired system in a general way.

Development tools that allow for rapid development of applications and prototypes have caused a shift toward more informal specifications. This is especially true, for example, in Web development. These tools allow for iterative styles of development: the developer creates an initial version, gets customer feedback, and makes changes—until the parties agree that the application is as desired.

What is good about this informal specification methodology is that it can be fast and efficient. What is not so good is that it can cause uncertainty. And that uncertainty increases with the size of the project. Uncertainty makes it harder to contract on a fixed price and milestone basis. Informal processes are a better fit for time-and-materials billing. Fix price deals with soft specifications create more risk for developers and customers alike.

Project Management Provisions

Development agreements normally include provision for management. These can be simple or quite elaborate depending on the needs of the project. The types of provisions normally included are:

- **Representatives** The parties appoint administrators who communicate on their behalf regarding the project. These administrators are authorized to make decisions and receive notices. Sometimes roles are divided. For example, the parties may each have a "Contract Representative" and a "Technical Representative."

- **Reporting** There may be provisions for written reports on a weekly or monthly basis. Normally, the development agreement will specify the types of information to be reported, such as progress, delays, decisions made, and so forth. These may require specific testing procedures or quality reports.

- **Code Reviews** In some agreements, there are requirements that the developer makes the current version of the source code or each interim version of the executable files available for FTP download by the customer for monitoring and review. The customer may want the right to have the third party consultant download and review the work product.

- **Inspections** The customer may negotiate for the right to visit the developer's locations to verify processes for quality and security.

Personnel Assigned to Development

Because the people staffed on a project can be critical to its success, the customer often wants control over personnel assignments. This control can take many forms:

- The initial staff assignments to the project may be specified.

- There may be stipulations as to whether specified staff assignments are full time or part time.

- There may be prohibitions on reassigning key personnel to other projects for other customers.

- Additions to, or changes of staff, may be made subject to the customer's approval.

- There may be requirements that the developer promptly report staff turnover—and its impact on the project.

- There may be a requirement that persons who depart be replaced with personnel of "at least equal skill and experience."

Change Management Provisions

Most development contracts have provisions that manage requests for changes in the specifications and development tasks. This is required because any material change in the specifications or development tasks can impact the developer's workload and the scheduled completion of milestones and of the project overall. Of course, this means price adjustments. There are many ways to write these provisions, but the basic concept is always the same: any change order has to be reduced to writing, and it is effective only when signed by both parties.

If not managed properly in the development agreement, change requests frequently cause trouble. Often customers will ask for additional features without expecting to pay more. The developer will do extra work to respond to a request and expect extra pay. The result can be conflict. Litigation involving millions of dollars of disputes about liability for "out of scope" work (that is, work not covered by the specification) is not uncommon. Good contract language—combined with discipline in following the rules—can avoid this kind of problem.

Acceptance Procedures

Development agreements have provisions for the acceptance or rejection of deliverables. Here is how it normally works:

- The developer submits the deliverable.

- The customer is given a set amount of time to accept or reject the deliverable.

- If the customer takes no action in a specified amount of time, the deliverable is deemed accepted.

- If the customer rejects the deliverable, it must give a written statement specifying the reasons for the rejection. The developer is then given a set amount of time to cure the specified defects and resubmit the deliverable for acceptance under the same process.

There are some variations. For example:

- Some agreements provide for acceptance of deliverables only in writing.

- Some agreements require that key deliverables can be accepted only in writing.

- Some agreements provide that if the developer fails to cure the deliverable after two tries, the customer can terminate the agreement.

- Some agreements provide that if the developer fails to cure the deliverable after two tries, then *either* party can terminate the agreement. (This version—which we often recommend for developers—allows the developer to escape from the agreement if its staff is simply unable to meet the requirements.)

In some development agreements, the final deliverable (that is, the finished product) may have a different acceptance process than interim deliverables. For example, the final version may be subject to:

- A much more thorough testing process, including trial use by the intended users

- A longer time period for acceptance

- A provision that acceptance occurs only when the customer affirmatively accepts in writing (with a provision that such acceptance may not be "unreasonably withheld")

Payment Provisions

Probably there is nothing that is more bargained over in development agreements than price. And, of course, there are many different ways to write pricing provisions. Here are some common pricing mechanisms.

Milestone-Based

The most common payment structure for major development agreements is the "milestone-and-specification" structure. This is also known as "fixed price" although, of course, the parties can build in variables. Payment is based on "milestones" defined as acceptance of deliverables in accordance with the specifications.

We have seen development contracts where there are monthly payments that are not tied to a particular milestone—other than the final product. Obviously this kind of deal leaves the customer with much less leverage if the project is delayed or otherwise runs into trouble.

Structuring milestone payments is a mixture of skill, analysis, and negotiation. The customer will (if it is wise) have used competitive bidding to get a general idea of the market price of the project. (Some companies hire outside purchasing consultants to help in estimating likely costs.) The developer will have the advantage in understanding the approximate cost of meeting the milestones. The developer will want to be sure that pricing is high enough to leave a reasonable profit margin and to include a margin of error in case estimates are off.

Here are some of the goals that the parties may strive for in setting milestones:

- The developer would like significant "down money" (due on signing the agreement) as a "cushion."

- The developer may seek to include "easy" milestones in the early stages of the project.

- After its initial payment, the customer may want significant work done before major payments.

- The customer may bargain for a right to refund if milestones go wrong.

- The customer may want to "hold back" an amount that is due only after acceptance of the final deliverables.

Time and Materials

As the name indicates, this method of payment is based on the developer's level of effort—normally with different professional service rates for different classes of professional staff. From the customer's perspective, the time-and-material pricing method is risky because the price may get out of control. It is more typical to see this method for smaller jobs where costs are easier to track and control. In those rare cases where the unknowns predominant, the creation of milestones and a specification may be just too speculative, and time and materials may then be the logical pricing option for both parties.

There are many variations on time-and-materials arrangements. For example:

- The parties may work under an estimate, and may have arranged to suspend work if charges exceed a defined level.

- The parties may have negotiated a maximum price cap for completing the assignment, so that risk of exceeding the cap is significantly shifted to the developer.

- Many customers require expenses to be preapproved—and specify a procedure for expense reimbursement.

When the parties use a time-and-materials structure, the customer will want to be sure that it has the means to evaluate the developer's progress and verify the developer's time. Often the agreement will require the developer to deliver monthly or weekly reports to the customer and give the customer the right to audit the books and records of the developer.

A variation on the time-and-materials method—often used in state and federal contracting—is "cost-plus." This is a method under which the developer tracks and reports all its out-of-pocket costs (including labor) and adds an agreed markup to establish it billings.

Combinations and Variations

There are, of course, other ways to price development work. For example, one could have:

- Combinations of fixed and variable charges
- Provisions for relief from fixed pricing for "major unanticipated obstacles"
- Bonus payments for early completion
- Loss of retainage or reduced pricing for late delivery

Right Schedule

One issue that is a perennial problem in development deals is the time allowed to complete the project. Sometimes it is possible to estimate the amount of effort required with reasonable accuracy, because the task is routine. Sometimes estimating the effort is nearly impossible. For example, the team that wrote the first commercial spell checker could not have known in advance how many months of work would be required.

It is best that the schedule for delivery of new software be as realistic as possible. It is a common perception that software development is *always* late. Developers sometimes promise delivery when the customer wants it, fearing to tell the customer about probable delays. Lack of realism and candor in the beginning may lead to frustration and anger later on.

If there are delays, the timeframes can be extended by mutual agreement in writing. But if the customer is looking for an excuse to terminate the contract or force a price reduction, late delivery will often provide it.

Under contract law a modest delay in delivery is not always fatal. The courts generally hold that some minor tardiness in delivery is tolerable. However, where the fine print of the agreement states that "time is of the essence," any delay past the stated deadline will probably be ruled a material breach of the contract. Some software development agreements are written to provide the developer an express option to extend the time for delivery by a specified time if the development pace is slower than expected.

Developers who are late in their delivery run other risks. If completion of the software is behind schedule, the developer must incur payroll expenses for staff and contractors not provided for in the budget. In addition, delay in producing the software means delays in payment—and this too may cause financial strains on the developer. Customers hate it when developers come asking for more money—particularly when the product is late. Again the moral is that realism in time and cost estimates are important.

Intellectual Property—Ownership and/or License

Development agreements must provide for ownership and/or rights to use the intellectual property related to the deliverables or created in development work. There is no doubt that many companies negotiate intellectual property clauses without fully understanding what they have done. This is due to the subtleties of intellectual property law.

What Intellectual Property Is at Stake?

To understand the variety of intellectual property provisions, we need first to survey what intellectual property interests are likely to be in play. We can then look at who is likely to want—or to get—the various intellectual property interests. You may want to refer back to the chapter of this book on trade secrets (Chapter 2) as you read this discussion.

Copyright in the Software

In most development agreements, the intellectual property interest that we absolutely must manage carefully is the copyright in the code and documentation delivered by the developer. Copyright controls the right to make and sell copies of the program. Copyrights are created automatically.

By default the developer will own the copyright for code written by the developer's employees. Because the developer owns the copyright in the code by default, the customer will not get copyright ownership rights unless the development agreement expressly says so.

The developer that subcontracts work will need to be sure that it has arranged to get relevant intellectual property rights from its subcontractors; otherwise it cannot provide rights to its customer.

Patentable Inventions

In building "run-of-the mill" business applications using standard tools, there is probably not much likelihood that the developer will be making inventions (although you never know for sure). On the other hand, in developments requiring creation of innovative or cutting edge products, there is a reasonable likelihood that the developer may well have to do some inventing—and if so will create potentially valuable patent rights.

Patents, unlike copyrights, do not come into existence automatically—they are the result of an expensive technology review and application process. Unlike software copyrights, any resulting patent most likely would not cover the whole of the code, but rather a discrete invention. And unlike software copyrights, the coverage of patents is not limited to particular code—patents potentially cover any code or systems within the borders of a nation that constitutes a product or uses a method covered by the patent.

However, patents are like copyrights in that the developer will usually own patent rights it creates by default. (A joint invention would be jointly owned by default.) Due to this legal rule, the customer will not get the rights to inventions created in the development process unless the development agreement expressly so states.

Trade Secrets

In a trivial sense, confidential information is involved in every development deal. The customer's data and business processes are usually confidential. Certainly the source code to be delivered will be held in confidence by both the developer and the customer.

However, it is less common that the developer is providing a valuable trade secret of broader application—that is, a valuable processing method or software design that is not generally known. If that is the case, however, the developer's trade secret would need to be dealt with explicitly (and carefully) in the development agreement.

By default, the unrestricted delivery of trade secret information by the developer to the customer will permit the customer to use or disclose the developer's trade secret as it sees fit (of course, this means the loss of trade secret status). Moreover, most development deals require delivery of source code—which will disclose the program logic and therefore most likely fully reveal to the customer (if it takes the trouble to look) all the processing methods that constitute the trade secret.

Goals in Negotiating Intellectual Property Clauses

Ownership of intellectual property is largely a "zero-sum game"; any intellectual property ownership assigned to one party is lost to the other. So there is often bargaining about who will own what. Often each party begins with the assumption that intellectual property ownership is good, and that owning as much of it as possible is a worthy goal. Here are some other relevant considerations:

- If the developer's business model is to create and "resell" applications, it should try to retain ownership of the copyright to all or key portions of the code. If the developer's business model is to build intellectual property value in its business, it may want to retain patent rights in its area of expertise.

- A developer that sees its business as purely being a seller of programming services (with no ambition to be an intellectual property owner) may regularly give up intellectual property ownership just to keep the customers happy.

- The tenacity with which a customer will seek intellectual property ownership is frequently related to its core competency. If you develop accounting software for an auto company, the customer might not much care who owns the copyright. If you develop automobile engineering software for an auto company, the customer will likely insist on owning it. Companies in the IT and software businesses are often looking to acquire intellectual property rights to developed software.

- Developers find that many customers are not aware that patents are a potential outcome of development services. However, due to the publicity of "business method patents" and "software patents," it has now become more likely that customers will care about patent rights that the developer may invent.

- In some cases, the developer may be able to make a deal in which it retains the intellectual property in exchange for agreeing not to supply similar software to other customers for a specified period of time. Typical restraints are for periods from six months to two years. On the other hand, the customer might want to own the intellectual property *and* also impose a restraint against the developer providing similar solutions to others.

Common Means to Deal with Intellectual Property in Agreements

There is no end to the possible ways to deal with intellectual property rights in development agreements. Here are some of the most common methods:

Developer Owns/License Grant Clause

One common model—much loved by developers—is to make the developer owner of all intellectual property rights. Under this model, the developer simply licenses the deliverables to the customers. Here is a typical clause of this type:

> *Subject to payment in full of the Development Fee, the Developer grants to the Customer a perpetual nontransferable license to use the Software on computers and networks owned or controlled by Customer for its own internal business purposes, and make sufficient copies of the Software for such use. This Agreement grants license rights only.*

This clause is great from the developer's point of view, but may meet a number of customer objections:

- As noted, the customer may insist that ownership is needed for its business strategy.

- The license grant is very narrow, and a customer may well find it too constraining. For example, the license that is "nontransferable" might prevent the customer from transferring the license to a buyer of its business. The license "for its own internal business purposes" makes no provision for use of the software by the customer's subsidiary or "sister" corporations. The clause similarly makes no provision for sublicensing to a "spin-off" operation or for use by the customer's contractors, business "partners," or clients. There is no grant for the customer to modify the software. And so forth. The basic problem is lack of flexibility.

Some of these objections may be met by drafting a different kind of license grant. The developer can add license grants to address the customer's specific objections—or it can grant broad rights for copying, sublicensing, and modification. There are endless possible variations.

Work-Made-for-Hire Clause/Patent Clause

At the other end of the spectrum, one often sees "work-made-for-hire" clauses that grant ownership rights to the customer. Here is a typical clause of that kind:

> *The parties agree that all work product resulting from the Services performed by Developer hereunder (the "Work Product"), including, but not limited to, the Software, and documentation prepared by Developer, if any, shall be considered to be a "work made for hire" for the Customer, and to the extent not "work made for hire" are hereby assigned to Customer. In addition such work product and the intellectual property rights embodied therein are and shall be the sole exclusive property of Client.*

This clause sounds pretty comprehensive, but it is not quite what it seems. It covers copyright, but the clause may leave out patentable inventions. Although the phase "the intellectual property rights embodied therein" is very common, it may not be sufficient to grab inventions that the developer created during the development work. Here is why:

- One could argue that the rights to patentable inventions are not "embodied" in the work product at all. Patent lawyers will tell you that patents are rights to exclude others from a claimed invention and therefore are not really "embodied" in any technology. So this language is ambiguous at best with regard to covering patents.

- Moreover, the developer might have made inventions during the development work that are broader or different from the implementation in the "work product" or not used in the deliverables. These would not be covered by the clause.

- The language leaves unstated the duty, if any, of the developer to cooperate in patenting.

If the customer really wants these rights as well, it needs a clause that is broader. Here is the type of language that effectively grabs patent rights:

> *The parties agree that all Inventions developed by Developer in the course of the development services shall be the property of the Customer and not the Developer. "Inventions" shall mean and include any and all ideas, concepts, discoveries, designs, improvements, and creations, regardless of whether the same are patentable or protected under any Federal or State law, rule, or regulation or under the common law of any state. Subject to Customer paying Developer's reasonable out of pocket costs, Developer agrees to (i) execute an assignment or other document reasonably requested by the Customer in order to document, assign, and convey all Inventions arising from the development project to the Customer and for Customer to perfect its ownership rights and (ii) to cooperate in the registration, perfection, and enforcement of any resulting patent rights.*

Foreground Intellectual Property and Background Intellectual Property Clause

From the developer's point of view, there is another potential problem with the sample "work made for hire" clause quoted above—it may give too much away. If a developer designates the entire delivered software application as "work made for hire," it loses the copyright to the whole application. That language can give away the developer's pre-existing ownership of software.

Many developers have some pre-existing custom-made software code that they use as a "common code base" for a variety of solutions. Some developers are content to convey to their customers any code written "on the customer's dime," but they do not want to surrender ownership of their own pre-existing code.

One common way to deal with this issue is to divide the rights to be delivered into "background technology" and "foreground technology" or "background IP" and "foreground IP." The developer then transfers the "foreground" and licenses the "background" to the customer.

Here is typical language:

> *1. "Intellectual Property Rights" means any and all intellectual property rights including, without limitation, copyrights, trademarks, patents, and trade secrets.*
>
> *2. "Developer's Background IP" means all Intellectual Property Rights which are material to the supply of the Software and which are owned by the*

Developer and are in existence prior to or independent of providing the Services.

3. "Foreground IP" means all Intellectual Property Rights arising as a result of providing the Services including, without limitation, Intellectual Property Rights in the Software.

4. All rights, title, and interest in and to any Developer's Background IP shall remain the property of Developer. Developer hereby assigns to Client its entire rights, title, and interest in Foreground IP. Developer shall execute and aid in the preparation of any documents. Customer deems appropriate to document, secure, evidence, and perfect such rights.

5. The Developer hereby grants to Customer a perpetual, irrevocable, royalty-free, worldwide nonexclusive license (with the right to grant sublicenses) to use the Developer's Background IP for the purpose of exploiting the Foreground IP as Customer deems fit.

A note about this text: You can see in paragraph "5" an example of an extremely broad license of the Developer's Background IP. The grant is essentially unlimited. This contrasts with the rather narrow grant we saw in the "Developer License" example above. There are, as discussed above, many variations as to how broad or narrow these licenses might be.

Another potential issue to take note of: In this type of deal, the customer may not be able to easily sort out what is "background" and what is "foreground." The application as delivered will often be an inextricable mixture of both. As a practical matter, this means that the customer's use of the application will be limited by the license grant to the background technology. Some customers may ask that "background technology" be designated and separable to avoid this limitation.

Other Variations

There are many more ways that a developer and a customer might divide intellectual property ownership. Sometimes we divide the software into "reusable code" which will belong to the developer and code and data "unique to the customer's implementation," which will belong to the customer.

We can also divide ownership by data type, function, or software module.

- For example for a multimedia application, the customer might own the media files, while the developer keeps ownership of the applications that manage and play them (including any changes made in the development project).

- In a product used for management of mutual funds, the customer might own the code that represents particular management rules created at the customer's request, while the developer keeps ownership of the "rules engine" that makes them operate (including any changes during the project).

The ways to divide intellectual property ownership is limited only by the imagination of the parties (and the lawyers) doing the deal. You should be thinking about the format that would best serve your business.

Avoiding Jointly Owned Intellectual Property

Sometimes parties think that the best way to deal with intellectual property is to jointly own it. However, this is rarely the best solution unless great care is taken in setting forth each party's rights and obligations.

This is because there are counterintuitive default rules about the exploitation of jointly owned intellectual property, which differ for different types of intellectual property. For example, in the United States, joint owners of a *copyright* can each use the copyright without the co-owner's permission, but each must account to the other party (that is pay) 50 percent of the profits that he or she obtains from the copyright. The rule in the United States on jointly owned *patents* is that either can use the patent without an obligation to account to the co-owner. These rules vary from country to country.

The bottom line is: To handle joint intellectual property, you need to have clear rules in the development agreement as to who can do what with the jointly owned intellectual property. Although it is possible to handle jointly owned intellectual property, it is better and simpler just to allocate ownership to one party and have the other's use and exploitation regulated by a license grant.

When the Web Developer Is Also Providing Web Hosting?

Agreements for building Web applications are, for the most part, the same as any other form of development. The underlying technology is distinct, but the contract issues are the same. However, an extra issue may apply when the vendor is going to act both as the party that develops the application and the party that provides hosting—mixing two different forms of services. The development deal and the hosting arrangements can be in two distinct agreements or combined.

If the developer is planning to provide hosting or other Web functionality by means of the developer's own proprietary background and infrastructure management software (let us call this "background Web software") there may be a difference of opinion between the developer and the customer as to how the background Web software can be used by the customer.

- From the developer's perspective, its background Web software may not be considered "deliverables" at all. The developer may think of them as part of its "hosting service" and not a portable component of the application.

- Smart customers on the other hand want the hosted application to be "portable" from one hosting vendor to another. So this customer will want all background Web software: (i) to be deliverables, (ii) to be licensed to the customer with broad rights to copy and use, and (iii) will usually want them in source code form. The customer will also normally want the right to transfer such a license together with the rest of the Web application.

This issue can often be compromised by means of a carefully written provision that allows the customer to transfer the license to the background Web technology in connection with the sale of its business subject to carefully written confidentiality protections. The developer will have to decide whether it will provide source code or, perhaps, offer a source code escrow for any proprietary hosting software.

Subcontractors

If you are a developer, you need to be sure that you have contracts in place with your subcontractors under which they pass all intellectual property rights that they develop for or supply to your company. If you are not careful with documentation, the subcontractors will end up owning the intellectual property that they create—and you will have no way to deliver it to your customer. You should use a form of subcontractor agreement that has intellectual property ownership, confidentiality, and (if you want) noncompetition provisions. We have included a form of agreement with these various provisions in an appendix to this book.

Noncompetition Clauses

Customers sometimes want to include in development agreements a form of noncompetition clause. This kind of clause is designed to keep the developer from using expertise it developed "on the customer's dime" to benefit the customer's competition. A customer will typically ask for a non-competition clause when the developer has created a unique application—or at least one that is not generally available. Here is a sample:

> *Developer agrees that during the term of the Services and for one year thereafter, Developer will not develop or seek to develop any application or system with functionality similar to or competitive with the application developed for Customer under this Agreement.*

This kind of clause is often coupled with the injunction relief clause, which invites a court of law to stop any violation of this clause by means of an injunction, that is, a court order.

Provisions on Confidential Information

Almost every development agreement has a conventional mutual confidentiality agreement provision. The gist is that each party agrees not to disclose the other party's confidential information and agrees to use the other party's confidential information only as reasonably needed for the purposes of the agreement.

In many cases, the customer will not consider this clause good enough. The customer may want an additional provision stating that ownership of certain confidential information, particularly information relating to the deliverables or created during a project, will pass from the developer to the customer. Here is typical language:

> *The parties agree that data and information comprising or regarding the source code that Developer creates under this Agreement will become the exclusive Confidential Information of the Customer upon creation. Developer shall not disclose, use, or exploit such Confidential Information except to carry out its obligations under this Agreement or as Customer may expressly authorize in writing.*

This kind of clause as well is usually coupled with the agreement's injunction relief clause in language that asks the court to enjoin any breach by the Developer of this obligation.

Training and Support

In order for the customer to use a new sophisticated software or computer system, the customer's staff usually requires training. The developer's work may include preparation of training materials. Some agreements provide for "training the trainers"—that is the developer must train a group of customer employees who will train other employees.

Warranties

It is normal for development agreements to have warranty clauses in which the developer warrants that the application (after acceptance) "substantially conforms to the specifications" and makes available "maintenance" to fix logical errors in the code.

Pricing of maintenance for custom-developed software and systems is tricky. It is not like supporting commercial-off-the-shelf software, because:

- Custom software is more likely to be buggy at first. There is often a sharp demand at first for maintenance services that trails off over time.

- The developer usually does not have staff dedicated solely or even primarily to maintenance tasks.

For these reasons, developers often charge for maintenance for custom-developed software on a "time and materials" basis. Sometimes the customer gets a "warranty period" during which errors may be reported and fixed without additional billing to the customer. (Of course, this is built into the price of the project.) All of this is frequently the subject of negotiation. Usually a warranty period of this kind kicks in after acceptance. A typical period for one would be 60 or 90 days.

Disclaimers and Limitations

Development deals will almost always have risk limiter provisions. These include:

- Exclusions of implied warranties

- Limitations of remedies for "bugs" or "errors" to specified repair processes

- Exclusions of consequential damages

- A damage cap—often set at the amount paid to the developer

Date Processing (Y2K) Warranties

There was a time not long ago when every development agreement had elaborate (and a bit paranoid) warranties that the application to be developed would handle four digit date data (such as the year 2000) correctly. You may occasionally see these Y2K clauses, but they are becoming rare. That is because common development tools include full date functionality. It is also because the dire predictions of "Y2K" meltdown failed to materialize.

Open Source Provisions

Customers frequently ask for assurance that the application contains no software under any open source license. "No open source" restrictions will not fit all projects. In fact, more and more development project applications are being built with open source foundations and components and delivered to the customer wholly or in part under one or more open source licenses. If that is the case, the development agreement should make clear which open source licenses will apply and what software programs they will cover. Any company that receives such a program should be sure it fully understands the open source licenses involved.

Note that a customer that takes open source software commonly takes it with any infringement risks that may arise from using or distributing the program.

Intellectual Property
Warranties and Indemnities

The negotiation of intellectual property warranties in development deals has become more complicated due to the explosion of software and business method patents and the growth of intellectual property litigation. A decade or so ago, the odds of a developer accidentally infringing a third party's intellectual property were quite low. There is no doubt that the risks are higher now.

Developers and customers come at this question from different viewpoints:

- The customer will say: I paid good money for this application; I want the developer to stand behind its work. If the developer delivers an infringing application, the developer should take care of the problem.

- The developer's attitude is: I am paid for developing software, not for underwriting an intellectual property risk. I am certainly not going to run an intellectual property risk that might be much higher than the contract price. Besides the customer selected the functionality, so it should be responsible.

In determining a fair allocation of the intellectual property risk, it is important to distinguish between types of intellectual property:

- **Copyright** The developer cannot infringe a third party's copyright in a business application unless it copied the plaintiff's code. So normally it is fair to hold the developer responsible for copyright infringement, unless the customer selected the offending code.

- **Trade Secret** The situation with trade secrets is much the same. If the developer had access to a third party's trade secrets and took them for its development work, it should be responsible for this misdeed (unless it was the customer that wrongfully acquired the trade secret).

- **Patents** Patents are the tough cases. Most often, patent infringement in development is innocent—but it can lead to liability just the same. Moreover, depending on the nature of the patent claim, the potential liability—not to mention the costs of defense—can be much higher than the developer's profit margin. The patent risk has grown in recent years due to thousands of new software patents. When both parties are innocent of fault, the parties will have very different viewpoints on which party should bear the loss.

Who bears the risk of patent infringement is frequently the subject of hard bargaining and compromise. Here are some of the alternatives that developers can propose as alternatives to the unlimited indemnification requested by customers:

- The developer may propose that it bears responsibility only for "knowing" infringement. This "knowledge qualifier" will usually free the developer from indemnifying the customer, as long as it stays ignorant of the patents that might apply to its development task. We sometimes call this the "pure heart and empty head" standard—because, under this clause, the less you know about the patented technology in the field the better.

- The developer may propose that its liability for patent infringement indemnification be "capped" at an agreed figure. This is a shared risk proposal.

- The developer may propose a reverse indemnity—that is, indemnification by the customer if technology or functionality proposed by the customer leads to an infringement.

In the final analysis, this is a bargained-for risk allocation. You should be careful that your company puts limits on its exposure and does not "bet the company" on contracts.

Insurance

Insurance companies love software development firms, because they buy lots of insurance. It is not that they want to; their large customers *make* them buy it.

Most large companies that purchase development services will require that their developers obtain specified categories and amounts of insurance. The one that is most commonly required is "Errors and Omissions" insurance which covers losses due to the developer's negligent or erroneous services. If the developer's employees will be on-site at the customer's premises, customers may seek additional coverage as well—consisting of:

- **General Liability** This insurance covers personal injury and injury to tangible property.

- **Automotive** This insurance covers injury and damage caused by vehicles.

- **Worker's Compensation** This insurance covers claims of the developer's employees for on-the-job injuries.

Insurance provisions often include some rather technical requirements:

- **"Certificate of Insurance"** This is a written certification from the insurance company that the required coverage is in place.

- **Requirement That the Customer Be a "Named Insured"** This means that the customer becomes the direct beneficiary of the insurance coverage and, if need be, can sue the insurance company directly.

- **Requirement That the Insurance Be Primary and Not Contributory** This means the customer does not have to exhaust other insurance coverage first.

Developers should not be shy about faxing any requested insurance clauses to their insurance broker and making sure they have the required insurance coverage. Never guess.

Clause on Customer Nonsolicitation of Developer Employees

Developers fear that their employees will be hired away by the competition—this is one reason that developers want their employees to sign noncompetition clauses in states where they are enforceable. However, sometimes the "raider" is not a competitor but, in fact, the developer's customer.

This kind of problem arises when the customer begins to rely on the services of a particular developer's employee, and the customer believes that it can save money and get more control by inducing the employee to move from the developer's payroll to its own.

In order to deter "raiding" by customers, some developers try to include a "nonsolicitation" provision in their development agreements. Here is a sample:

> *During the term of this Agreement and for a period of one (1) year after termination, Customer shall not hire or solicit for employment (or for engagement as a contractor) any of Developer's current employees or persons who were employees during the preceding 12 months.*

There are many variations on this kind of customer nonsolicitation clause. For example:

- The provision can be made mutual—applying to both parties.

- The restriction can be written so that it applies only to employees that actually worked on the project in question.

- The restriction can be written so that it only applies to intentional solicitation.

- The restriction can have a "carve-out" (so that it does not apply) for hiring an employee that answers a mass-market recruiting request, such as an employee that answers an advertisement on the Web or in the local newspaper.

- The provision may be written so that the customer pays "liquidated damages" (often fixed in relation to the employee's compensation) for violating the restriction. For example, the provision might state that, in case of violation, the customer will be obligated to pay to the developer one-half of the purloined employee's yearly salary.

From the developer's viewpoint, these customer nonsolicitation clauses have an important drawback—no developer wants to sue its own customers. As a result, these clauses are not often enforced. They do serve to deter "employee raiding" by customers, but they are far from the perfect answer.

Termination

Development agreements normally contain termination provisions allowing either side to terminate the agreement for the other side's uncured default (known as a termination "for cause"). Where there are "umbrella" agreements covering more than one "work order," the customer may want the option of terminating only a particular work order or the entire agreement if the developer fails to perform.

Customers often want the right to terminate a development project or any work order for convenience (meaning with no stated reason). This is because there may be situations where the customer is unhappy with the developer, but does not have sufficient reason to terminate for cause. Developers working on a major project may resist such a provision—or they may want compensation for lost opportunity and shut down costs if the customer terminates for convenience. These provisions are often highly negotiated.

If the agreement is terminated before the development is finished, what happens to the partially completed computer code—and what are the customer's rights to it? Of course, the parties may make any provision they want for this situation—but the most common provision is that the developer delivers to the customer whatever software it has completed in exchange for partial payment of the contract price. Sometimes a customer will negotiate a provision under which it can get some or all of its money back if the developer fails to deliver early milestones in accordance with the agreement.

Where the agreement can be terminated early and provides that the customer will be entitled to keep possession of the code, the developer may want provisions that make clear that, in that scenario, the developer makes no warranty with regard to the quality or completeness of the code or has no maintenance obligations.

Dispute Resolution

As we mentioned above, large development projects have a troubled history, and for this reason are comparatively dispute-prone. While no one likes to dwell on negative outcomes, it is a good idea to build dispute management into every major development project. Here are a few suggestions:

- It may be a good idea to have a "dispute escalation" process—whereby matters in dispute must be discussed by senior executives before litigation starts.

- If the developer and customer are based on different jurisdictions, it may discourage litigation and encourage settlement if adjudication of disputes (whether by litigation or arbitration) is in a neutral location.

- Beware of "attorneys' fees" clauses that provide for an attorneys' fee award to the "prevailing party" in a dispute. While there is a certain appeal to this kind of "winner take all" provision, the downside is that these clauses tend to make parties feel more comfortable about starting litigation and may make settlement harder.

- Disputes over development projects may be well suited for mediation and arbitration.

Boilerplate Provisions

One clause to pay attention to is the assignment clause. The customer may want the right to prevent the developer's assignment of development contract—or any change of control of the developer if the customer believes that the change will impair the development project. On the other hand, customers often resist contract assignment provisions that would impair their own exit transactions.

About Offshoring

Enormous amounts of development are now done offshore. Many buyers of IT services get them directly from an offshore supplier. Many developers subcontract work offshore.

There is nothing different in principle between a contract with a US-based developer and one in a "lower-wage" country such as India, China, or Russia. The same planning, contracting, and development processes need to take place. There are some additional challenges and uncertainties associated with emerging countries, but thousands of companies have had favorable experiences when outsourcing development offshore. The price advantages in nations such as India are obvious (although price differentials are falling, due to wage inflation in foreign labor markets). The worldwide telecommunications infrastructure makes foreign suppliers accessible. While Bangalore is nine and half hours ahead of New York, managers there understand full well that they have to be available to talk to the Americans in the early evening.

Let us assume that—as a customer or developer doing subcontracting—you are actively considering having development done half a world away. Here are some factors (in addition to those that apply to development deals generally) to consider. Note that this is by no means an exhaustive list:

- **Right Tasks** Not all development tasks are suitable for offshore work. If the specifications are vague and completing the design requires frequent interaction with users, the offshoring effort may bog down or produce poor results unless the US party has staff onsite at the foreign location.

- **Knowing the Developer** It is important to deal with companies that you trust. That means that you should check references and get to know your vendor. You should be sure the offshore developer has the right technical skills and experience in similar projects. It is also a good idea to find out what you can do about the rate of employee turnover. One or more onsite visits at the vendor location in advance of any agreement are recommended.

- **Communications** Make sure that communications are good. This means that the developer should have good English language skills—unless you speak the developer's language.

- **Deal Exits** You should consider having "termination for convenience" provisions in any major agreement, so that you get out easily if things are not going well.

- **Confidentiality and Intellectual Property** You should be sure that confidentiality and intellectual clauses are tight and take reasonable steps to make sure the offshore developer has contracts in place with its employees to obtain all required rights and impose all relevant confidentiality restrictions.

- **Security** You should check both the physical security and the electronic and network security measures used by any offshore developer.

- **Your Management Resources** You need to be sure that you have the skills and staff in place on your side to generate tight specifications, and review work product. The management requirements are generally higher for offshore work.

- **Frequent Reviews** You should require frequent reporting and reviews of code, testing, bugs, integration, and so forth. For large projects, you will likely want to visit and speak with managers on site. If payment is on a "time" basis, you will need to do your own verification of whether projected savings are being realized.

- **Possession of the Code**   It is a good idea to obtain the most current build of the software frequently, say by daily or weekly FTP transfer. This will give you the ability to monitor the work—and to take it over if need be.

- **Discretion in Disclosure of Trade Secrets**   While there is no reason to consider foreign citizens more or less trustworthy than Americans, it is certainly true that tracking down stolen trade secrets is harder in Moscow or Shanghai than in Silicon Valley. So you may want to think twice about exposing your "crown jewel" source code. On the other hand, many companies conduct all of their product development offshore; in the final analysis, it is a business risk decision.

- **Regulatory Issues**   For some industries, there may be privacy law or export control law issues in offshore development. You should discuss these with your legal counsel.

- **Governing Law**   If possible negotiate deals governed by the laws of a US jurisdiction. Many deals with foreign developers are done under New York or California law.

- **Jurisdiction for Disputes**   It is often best to have disputes resolved by arbitration. This is because many nations do not recognize foreign court judgments but do recognize arbitration decisions. You may want to have the arbitration in a convenient US venue. Alternatively, you might consider a neutral site in a legally sophisticated city, such as London, Geneva, Singapore, or Hong Kong, as the site for arbitration.

Other Types of Consulting Businesses and IT Services

There are, of course, other types of IT consulting and IT services work beyond the development engagements that we have discussed above. Consulting and IT services can include routine maintenance for computer systems and service and "help desk" support for enterprise IT networks and computers. Some companies simply provide "programmers for hire" on a daily or weekly basis. In some cases, an IT service provider will engage in a type of "outsourcing" transaction in which it buys a company's computers, storage systems, and information systems and operates them over the course of a year for a fee—a deal that includes elements of finance, employment, and services. Some consultants provide advice on IT strategy and planning. There is really no end to the variations.

   This chapter could not possibly deal with all consulting variants. However, we have included in an appendix to this book a general form of a consulting agreement that you can think of as a container in which many consulting engagements would fit. As you will see by reviewing the form, the issues in consulting, in general, are the same as those that we discussed above in the context of the development agreements. In preparing consulting or IT services agreements, regardless of the variant, you will typically give attention to the following:

- Assessment of customer needs.
- Identification of services and/or deliverables.

- A process for customer acceptance or sign-off.

- Apportionment of any intellectual property created—although some simple engagements may not generate any intellectual property of significance.

- Confidentiality.

- Provisions for the upkeep and maintenance of computer code, if any are involved.

- Warranty disclaimers and remedy limitations.

- Indemnification in some cases.

- Dispute resolution procedures and other "boilerplate."

Because the issues recur, this chapter and the various sample agreements provided should be a good introduction to IT consulting agreements generally.

Legal Issues in Development and Consulting Businesses

In this chapter, we have emphasized the importance of good contracting to build value in a consulting business. Let us look at a couple of other legal issues that development, consulting, and IT services businesses need to keep in mind.

Employment Issues

It almost goes without saying that consulting companies need to pay careful attention to all the legal issues that relate to employment. Here are some issues that you should attend to if you own or operate a consulting company:

- Be sure that all employees sign employee agreements. (See the discussion of employee agreements in Chapter 3.) These should normally include noncompetition provisions in each state or country where these agreements are enforceable.

- Be very careful in classifying staff as contractors as opposed to temporary employees. Consulting companies can face tax and other legal problems if they classify workers as "contractors" when the law considers them to be employees. See your accountant or your lawyer about this important distinction.

- Consult legal counsel in case of any employment dispute and in case of any major reduction in force.

It is also recommended that you review your employment policies with a lawyer familiar with employment law in each state where you conduct business.

Building a Brand

Some consulting companies begin with just a few individual consultants or developers. Getting bigger means being able to sell the services of hundreds or thousands of professionals rather than those of just a few founders. To sell the services of a company rather than a founder requires building a strong brand. Some world-famous brands in this field are Accenture (formerly Andersen Consulting) and BearingPoint (formerly KPMG Consulting). Any brand worth using should be properly protected under trademark law.

Conclusion

If your company is careful in its development contracting, it can obtain expected results, make smart choices about intellectual property, manage risk, and build sound relationships.

Chapter 5

How to Sell Your Intellectual Property Protection Program

Introduction

Without executive commitment, your intellectual property protection program won't go anywhere. Without a meaningful, tangible executive mandate, the populace within the enterprise will blow you off. You may be the recipient of some pleasant indulgence and some seemingly sincere lip service in the initial phases, but sooner or later your program will end up in the dustbin of institutional memory. People will say, "Oh yeah, someone tried that once. Nothing ever came of it, why would we want to make that mistake a second time?"

No one is going to change corporate culture, or "make more work" for his or her team, unless it is unmistakably clear that this is the will of the chief executive and the message is being consistently and repeatedly pushed downward throughout the enterprise. In sum, this initiative has to flow from the top down; otherwise it is doomed to failure.

Our task is further complicated by the fact that no executive, whether C-level or at the entry level to the executive suite, is ever going to say, "No, security isn't important to us, we don't do everything possible to protect our intellectual property," publicly or internally. Board members, shareholders, clients, business partners, industry analysts, consumer advocates, perhaps even the public at large would soon be clamoring for their heads. No, executives will always list the security of the enterprise's people and intellectual property as one of their top priorities.

That means you are looking for something deeper. You are looking for a real commitment, a genuine understanding. You want to see the light switch go off, and you want that bright bulb to be seen from everywhere, from every cubicle, every assembly line, every test lab, and every conference room. Then and only then will you have what you desire: an integrated security program designed to protect the enterprise's lifeblood, the intellectual property.

In order to have a successful security program, both senior and mid-level management must understand the value of the security program and use this value as a differentiator in their outreach to clients, customers, partners, and vendors. So how do we get from zero support by any within the enterprise to acceptance and embracement of the concept by management?

You need a mandate with teeth in it, muscle behind it, and mechanisms to project this mandate. To get such a mandate, you have to deliver a stellar presentation with an irrefutable, irresistible pitch. The chief executive or the executive staff must come away from your pitch both informed and engaged. More importantly, they must come away from your pitch understanding what is required.

In this chapter, we will go through a five-slide presentation, one by one, and inspect the various elements of each slide, examining what goes into each of the elements and how one slide leads to the next.

The slide presentation aims to assist you in your own presentation to your corporation's leadership team, whether that is the executive suite, the board, or key principals, such as the CEO, CFO, and COO.

The immediate goal of such a presentation is to win executive commitment for your IP protection program. The ultimate goal is to change or enhance the corporate culture, so that every time employees speak of their activities, security of the intellectual property and of the enterprise as a whole, it is a "forethought" and not an afterthought. Employees will understand the overall value to the enterprise of having their research, development, manufacturing, sales, personnel, marketing, and the firm's products secured. To assist in this regard, as discussed in prior chapters, properly research and position the established body of policies and standards, as well as other resources, for them to rely on in the pursuit of an integrated, holistic security environment.

You are going to need to do your homework. You are going to have to take the concepts and principles outlined in this chapter, and the sample presentation they document, and turn it all into a pitch and a presentation that is properly calibrated to your corporate culture, accurately reflects the facts on the ground in your business environment, and offers a reasonable and achievable path to success. It is often said that when Wall Street looks at a publicly traded conglomerate, it is like looking at an American quarter horse and the prospects for the horse's success in the quarter-mile sprint. The reality is, your perspective must be that of the endurance race horse, prepared for the 50-mile ride. This journey through the process will entail both fact-finding and thinking outside the box. Success rarely comes pre-packaged.

The fact that you are able to have this conversation is a very good sign that you, the implementer, have a reasonable expectation of success; now you have to demonstrate that your expectations can be actualized.

If you follow the logic, the analytical process, and the argumentation suggested here, you will improve your chances significantly. Remember, as Thomas Edison said, "Hell, there are no rules here—we are trying to accomplish something."

Questions to Ask and People to Approach

There are five questions, or perhaps more accurately, five areas of inquiry which require exploration and development of answers. These are:

1.   What is your business differentiation from your competitors?

2.   Who do you have to protect your intellectual property and differentiators from?

3.   What are the probabilities in terms of likely vectors of threat, what would they target within your enterprise, and what would these adversaries have as their objectives?

4.   If they succeeded in their objective (theft, tampering, destruction), what would the consequences be to the overall enterprise?

5.   What countermeasures would be cost-effective and business-enabling, vice prohibitively expensive and disabling?

Notice in the second half of the title for this section, after "questions to ask," we said "and people to approach" rather than "and who you need to answer them." That is because it is unlikely that very many, if any, of the executives, managers, and individual contributors will have thought about what you are endeavoring to aggregate, analyze, and articulate.

The obvious business differentiators may be on the tip of everybody's tongue, but you have to go deeper and cast a wider net. It is not enough to know that your corporation has the best product in a direct comparison to the competition or that the firm's advertising agency assisting the marketing and sales entities is more professional, experienced, and in-tune with the target audience for the products being sold and developed.

You must put your closed-ended questions into the dust bin and focus on the open-ended inquiries to get to the items worthy of protection. You have to look for the undetected, the unseen, and the unconsidered to grasp the situation in an accurate manner.

You certainly need to ask executives about what differentiates the enterprise from its competitors, but also ask your engineers, your programmers, your operations people, your sales and marketing professionals, your human resources professionals, maybe even your customer service or procurement people. While it clearly depends on the nature of your business, it is paramount that your engagement is as all-inclusive as possible.

What differentiates your business could be how you make your product, what goes into it, who makes it for you, or where it is made. If, for example, your firm assisted a partner to enable the partner to make your product more efficiently, then perhaps that methodology is worthy of protection. Think of Henry Ford and his use of the assembly line in the automotive industry. Had he kept the concept and implementation of the assembly line "secret" would he have had competition on his heels as soon as he did? What other industries would not have evolved as quickly? It is a business decision to either protect or share methodologies.

What differentiates your product could be what you sell, how you sell it, who sells it for you. If you sell all your own products and have your own integrated work force, you may have greater control over the protection of your IP than if you used outside entities such as distributors, channel partners, vendors, or contracted sales forces.

What differentiates your product could be all of the above, and more. And it is this "more" which you must strive to identify.

All across the enterprise, there are people you will have to approach on your fact-finding mission who won't have thought much about the issues you are inquiring into beyond the cursory observation that they are good at what they do and are proud of their efforts and results. Therefore, they will have to be brought along; you will have to pluck it out of their heads or extrapolate it from their responses. What you are looking for is what differentiates your enterprise and its products and who would benefit from stealing it or causing it to fail.

You will also have to go outside the enterprise, to the World Wide Web, government resources, third party intelligence aggregators, industry analytic resources, individual subject matter experts, and more—particularly in regard to answering the second and third questions: who do you have to protect from and what bad could come from the successful compromise of the enterprise's intellectual property.

Let's look at each of these five areas of inquiry in more depth.

What Is Your Business Differentiation from Your Competitors?

What makes you different? Your people? Your processes? Your R&D? Your differentiation points are what you are declaring as worthy of protection.

> Human resources policies and procedures, such as hiring practices, could make your enterprise unique. What about your compensation regime? Retention policy and leadership development could also be a source of differentiation, as well as future personnel needs and projections.

> Research and development capabilities, level of investment, locale of investment, methodologies, personnel headcount, equipment allocation, and topics could be differentiators.

> Manufacturing as a whole could be a differentiator. If you outsource, how do you integrate the third-party's methodologies into your own? The Boeing Company had for years

dictated to its manufacturing partners how components would be built and how these components would be integrated into their aircraft—it was the company's differentiator. In 2007, Boeing introduced their newest aircraft, the Boeing 787 "Dreamliner," and with this introduction, Boeing also introduced a paradigm shift away from dictating methodologies to collaborative and consultative engagement.[1]

Marketing and Sales also have data worthy of examination and perhaps will be a differentiator as well. As noted previously, is your level of investment in advertising and marketing campaigns indicative of other metrics within the enterprise? Are your marketing efforts in a given market based on your competition's expected success in the market and designed to support your own success? How about your sales figures, margins, discounts, client lists? All of these individually or collectively could differentiate you from your competition and thus are worthy of addressing as a potential differentiator.

Who Do You Have to Protect These Differentiators From?

What are your points of vector, such as individual, competitor, organized criminal cartels, or state elements? Or is your enterprise threatened to some degree by all of them? The first step is to determine who would benefit from learning about any of these differentiators.

Individuals This vector is often characterized as the "insider-threat," but that is also a mischaracterization on the whole. That is not to say that the bona fide insider isn't in a better position to capitalize on your data, etc., but that individuals outside the enterprise can use the previously identified methodologies to garner your intellectual property as a force multiplier for their individual efforts. Take for example the situation in China, which according to 2007 statistics has identified 86% of all software as counterfeit.[2] This isn't just a theft of a company's intellectual property in the creation of the counterfeit, from the individual perspective, but it is the cost savings in going down this path as the individual as they prepare to enter the competitive marketplace—if an individual doesn't have similar infrastructure expenses as a similar enterprise, their cost of entry is reduced considerably. So we advocate looking from within and monitoring, auditing, and enforcing the need-to-know principal with your workforce, whether staff or contracted, but also being mindful of the individual not associated in any manner with your enterprise who may be looking for a quick point of entry into your market or the market of another.

Competitors It is unfortunate, but the world is not a level playing field with respect to free-market competitive engagements. And thus competitors will fall into two categories: those who will exploit any edge, legal or illegal, and those who will only engage in legal activities to take you and your enterprise to task in the market place. You must defend against both. The former will invest and engage at whatever level they believe is required to garner the desired results. The latter will engage and exploit anything you project or inadvertently provide via public disclosure and their ability to extrapolate. For example, it is totally appropriate to engage trade show staff in conversation and lead the conversation down any rabbit-trail to drill for details on a company's products. In this way, an ethical competitor may engage in ethical business practices advocated by the Society of Competitive Intelligence Professionals (SCIP)[3], whereas others may exceed this ethical brief and attempt to coerce information from your staff with financial inducements or other under-the-table arrangements. In both cases, your inappropriately protected data lands in the hands of your competitor.

Criminal elements These organizations have one goal—monetization. If there is a way they can manipulate your data systems to their financial advantage, through customer support, order mechanisms, or simply inducing an individual to share your intellectual property so that they may sell it to the aforementioned unscrupulous competitor, they usually will make the attempt.

State entity It is almost impossible to stop a state entity when the nation's resources have been allocated to compromise your intellectual property. That said, that does not mean that the boxing axiom does not apply—one does not lead with one's chin. You need to be on top of which state entities may be interested in your technology and why. For example, will your technology assist an indigenous firm who is your direct competitor? How is your technology being used by a geo-political competitor? It would surprise no one that during the Cold War, the former Soviet Union was very interested in the many commercial items used by the United States' military forces; that same level of interest is being played out today from the Chinese perspective. Take, for example, the case of Chi Mak and Tang Wai Mak, both accused and indicted for sharing their employer's data with the People's Republic of China (PRC)[4], data which would be of use to the PRC's military.

What Are the Probabilities in Terms of Likely Attackers, Targets, and Objectives?

Risk = Threat * Vulnerability * Impact

The Threat = Adversary + Capability + Intent

The Vulnerability = Opportunity, and the Impact = Asset Value

Ask yourself, "Who would want it?" For example, we make sandals. The probability that any government would want to take our sandals is low; unless we have come up with something like a way to make a plastic sandal that would be market-shattering, and then perhaps they would want that information. Maybe we need to protect our fancy machinery or chemical processes. If I am a milk bottler, then perhaps I do not have to protect myself so much from state power, I just have to have a general Hazardous Analysis Critical Control Point (HACCP) program and a clean environment that would allow me to protect from everything (six years ago only three people in the USA were teaching it). Then the real things I need to protect are my customer lists and my discounts. Or perhaps your HR activities project more than it may seem: Is your enterprise advertising an expansion into a given country via their employment advertisements, and thus signaling to the competition a move in research and development or an increase coming downstream in sales and marketing? This may benefit the competitor. Could it benefit the organized criminal elements? What of the individuals you will be hiring in this locale? Are they subjected to the same background checks as the rest of the enterprise? If not, then perhaps the criminal elements can manipulate your hiring practices so that they can monetize their inside knowledge. What of the state entities? Do they have an interest in who is hired by your enterprise?

If the Competition Obtained or Tampered with Your Intellectual Property, What Harm Would Be Done?

In mid-2007, counterfeit Colgate toothpaste was front and center in the news, with large quantities of the counterfeit product finding its way into the United States. Colgate appropriately warned the consumer of the existence of the counterfeit product, a product that actually damaged your teeth in contrast to the true Colgate product, and also provided the consumer a means to identify the true Colgate product. So, were these actions sufficient? Were these actions the full extent of what could have been accomplished given the circumstances? The situation begs several questions: How many consumers took the time to review the guidance? How many other consumers simply tossed out their Colgate and bought a competitor's brand? So in this example, it is clear that the monetization of the Colgate brand by unscrupulous criminal elements placed a stellar brand at risk. Could the company have done something different?

What if you sell a product used in the sophisticated arms purchased by a nation's defense forces, and an adversarial nation caused your product to malfunction or to act in a manner different than what you had envisioned? Are you protecting your research and development methodologies, checking and rechecking for unadulterated operability, or otherwise guaranteeing to your customer that what you sell operates as advertised and only as advertised?

What Security Measures Would Be Cost-Effective and Business-Enabling?

You must demonstrate that good security enables good risk taking. Your analysis has identified and articulated both business differentiators and risks that threaten to co-opt or otherwise nullify them, so now you have to offer ways to mitigate the risks. But just as importantly, the plan has to make business sense.

For example, in order to make this differentiator reasonably secure, it costs $5. If we don't do this, we put $1 million at risk. It is a clear business decision. It is worth a $5 investment to protect $1 million.

But if it takes a $1 million dollar investment in security to protect $10, then you have to make a business decision.

And once you make that decision, either way, all of your available resources designed to protect your intellectual property must line up behind this decision. Even if it may not be the right one from your perspective, the fact that your security regime is present allows for the risk taking by the business elements, and a business decision is a business decision. There is no room for standing back and second-guessing or undermining that business decision. If the enterprise has decided that it is worth taking the risk for the good of the business—for example, if we are successful, and we believe we will be, we will be able to jump ahead of our competition—then all your security resources have to align to protect the enterprise within the new paradigm that has been created by the business decision to move forward in spite of the risk. You can't just walk away from it and say, "I am done now." The security regime designed to protect the enterprise and its intellectual property is always in a dynamic state and thus must be flexible enough to step forward as a full partner as the business dynamics adjust to the marketplace.

So you have to think through these issues ahead of time. You cannot wait for the executives to do the math for you. You have to do it for yourself first, and then demonstrate it to the executives. By doing so, you accomplish two vital feats: not only do you solve the problem of how best to protect that particular differentiator, or collection of differentiators, you have also demonstrated that security, personified by you and your efforts, is a business enabler, not a business impeder, and that security protects profit instead of draining it away.

Let us go through each of the five figures in this chapter and explore what they are meant to communicate and the desired effect they are meant to achieve. Let's now discuss Figure 5.1.

Figure 5.1 Intellectual Property Protection Program—the Agenda

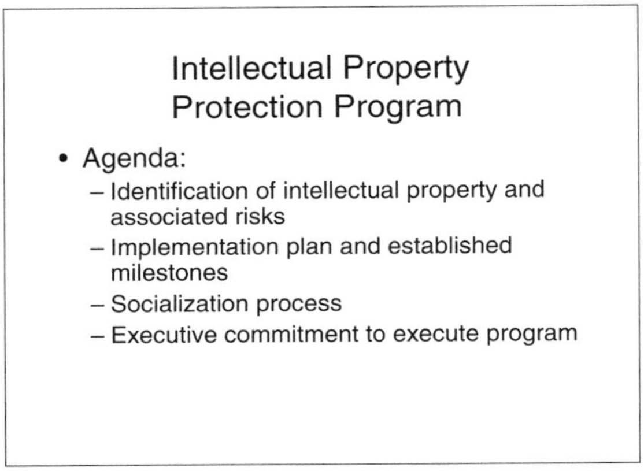

Intellectual Property
Protection Program

• Agenda:
  – Identification of intellectual property and
    associated risks
  – Implementation plan and established
    milestones
  – Socialization process
  – Executive commitment to execute program

Notes on Figure 5.1

The overall protection program for a corporation's intellectual property starts with a confirmation of what the information, processes, etc. are and where they reside within the corporation's footprint, and also identifies the risk to that same property. This is your agenda—it fulfills the first tenet of executive briefings: you are identifying and presenting the cadence of the briefing and the content of the briefing. Your executive should now be well prepared to actively listen. Now let's discuss Figure 5.2.

Figure 5.2 Intellectual Property Identification and Risk Identification

> ### Intellectual Property Identification and Risk Identification
>
> - Intellectual property locales
> - Identified risks
> - Implications of loss
> - Business value of protecting intellectual property

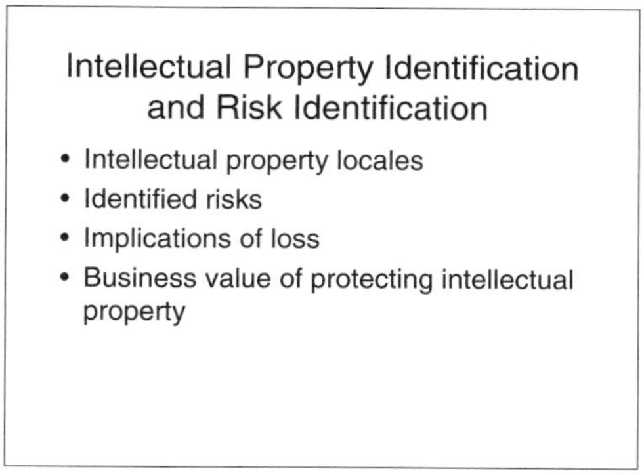

Notes on Figure 5.2

First you must identify the locales where intellectual property may reside:

Executives and Board Members

You may wish to highlight, for example, those topics which are discussed in the board room, such as meeting agendas, board meeting minutes, compensation committee minutes, and more.

You may also wish to highlight the information your executive team would have natural access to, but which may not be accessible by the rank-and-file of the company. Some examples of these types of data would be discussion on potential mergers and acquisitions, changes in the strategic vision of the company, new partnerships, geographic expansion plans, direction of the firm in out-years, and more.

Research and Development

Consideration should be given to identifying exemplars such as new product designs, unregistered inventions, pending patents, awarded patents, new innovations, researched dead-ends, research successes, new materials, new developmental and testing methodologies, schematics, and so on. In addition, the individuals who make up the company's research and development department may also be potential holders of intellectual property, to include their unique and irreplaceable base of knowledge.

Manufacturing

Your manufacturing entity has unique methodologies and materials. In addition, the enterprise's supply chain, from start to finish, includes partners, vendors, and sub-contractors. Additionally, finished goods, unfinished goods, goods storage, raw materials, and so forth should be considered for review as possible sources of the firm's intellectual property.

Sales and Marketing

Information resident in the sales and marketing arena may include the firm's go-to market plan, pending and historic bids, profit margin and discount margins, inside and outside sales methodologies and organizations; public relations campaigns, and reseller networks, to include channels and distributors.

Additional areas of potential interest could be corporate branding (present and future), conference and trade show presentations and participation, client lists, customer lists, and order sheets.

Specifics located in the competitive intelligence group may include product comparisons, marketing guidance, and results of table-top exercises which detail the results of the hypothetical competitor strategy comparison exercise. For example: How would Accenture beat out Ernst and Young in a head-to-head competition for a given bid? How would your enterprise fare in a head-to-head with your primary competitor?

Human Resources

Areas retaining intellectual property within the scope of human resources may include the firm's hiring processes, files/databases containing personal identifying information, employee health issues, performance evaluations, vacation schedules, individual salary compensation, EEO files, benefits, and so on.

Additionally, knowledge of the firm's processes, such as how the background investigation process works, what is included, how cases are adjudicated, etc., may allow an individual to craft a scenario to beat your processes.

Operations

Data found within the operations entity of most companies would include costs, margins, budgetary data, information technology infrastructure, business continuity plans and test results, physical security, information security policies, transportation, equipment procurement (to include channels used), problem mitigation methodologies, data destruction protocol including degauss and shredding regimes, and contractor identification (if one is used).

Risk Identification

Risk can come at you from only two vectors—inside and outside. Inside risk is almost completely in your control, whereas outside risk is almost completely out of your control. Each of the identified intellectual property items should be charted with all known inside/outside risks. In both cases, data/information leakage is a very real risk; inadvertent publication of confidential information can occur in both inside and outside environments, data can be physically stolen, electronic surveillance can be done of your personnel and facilities. One methodology that may be of assistance is rating the risk to intellectual property based on geography, as detailed in Table 5.1. It will allow you to rank your intellectual property in order of risk.

Table 5.1 Risk Levels 1-5

Risk Level 1-5	Factors
1 = Lowest	Little or no technological threat: first generation public switched telephone network, with limited national infrastructure, some protection to intellectual property rights exists and laws do not hinder the ability to protect yourself
2 = Low	Low technological threat: developing national infrastructure, competitors present, minimal protection to intellectual property rights, laws and regulations which may preclude the ability to protect yourself are not present
3 = Moderate	Moderate technological threat: developing national infrastructure, competitors present in force, foreign official presence potential threat, moderate protection to intellectual property rights, laws concerning the ability to protect yourself are present but not enforced
4 = High	Advanced technological threat: developed national infrastructure, competitors present in force, foreign official presence confirmed by nations with track record of assisting competitors, intellectual property rights, protection is the norm, laws and regulations may preclude the ability to use Cisco technology to protect yourself
5 = Highest	Confirmed advanced technological threat: advanced national infrastructure, competitors present in force, foreign official presence confirmed assisting competitors in this locale or domestic official presence known to pose intellectual property threat, intellectual property rights protection regime exists, but is problematic, laws and regulations preclude the ability to use Cisco technology to protect yourself

Implications of IP loss

When you lose your intellectual property, the potential ramifications should be identified for inclusion in your presentation, to show the cost to the enterprise, which is not always fiscal loss. Knowing what you need to protect, the risks involved, as well as the ramifications of losing the intellectual property, allows you to respond to market opportunities with speed, strength, and agility.

- Research & Development
  - Loss of competitive advantage
  - Loss of market leadership
  - Litigation probability
- Manufacturing
  - Counterfeit risk

- Loss of customer confidence
- Sales & Marketing
  - Loss of customers
  - Brand reputation
- Human Resources
  - Loss of employees
  - Brand degradation
  - Potential legal quagmire

Now let's move on to Figure 5.3.

Figure 5.3 Plan Execution Road Map

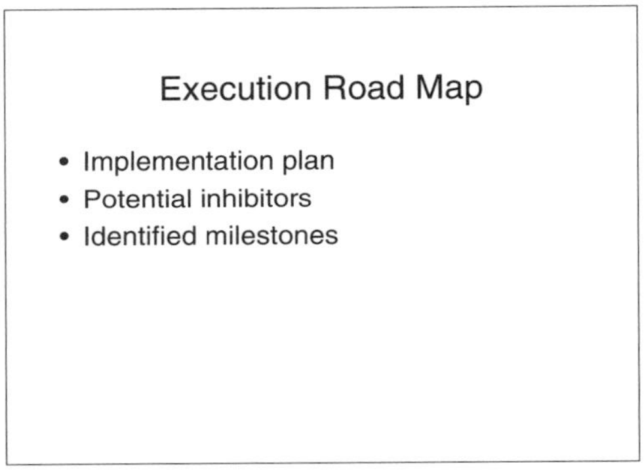

Notes on Figure 5.3

Implementation Plan

Discuss where the rollout of the plan will occur, the cadence, and so forth. It is important to know where you start, where you will finish, and how often you are going to review and repeat the educational processes and audits.

Potential Inhibitors

Identify internal points of resistance to change in intellectual property protocol, potential competitor action which may cause you to adjust your intellectual property protection schema, events which may render your plan moot, and environmental (global), political, or legal factors which could derail your plan, such as partner, vendor, or contractor failures.

Identified Milestones

Socialization schedule: When are you going to message to whom, where, and how, and obtain audit and feedback

Identified timeline points for review of process and rollout and redirection opportunities

Expected budget, burn-rate, and potential costs not included in the burn-rate analysis

Headcount required; identification of key personnel, dedicated and shared resources, and conflict resolution regime for acquisition of shared resources

Logistical considerations, if any

Partners, vendors, and/or other outside resources required to achieve success

We'll now discuss Figure 5.4.

Figure 5.4 Socialization of IP Protection Program to the Enterprise

```
┌─────────────────────────────────────────┐
│                                          │
│       Socialization of IP Protection     │
│         Program to the Enterprise         │
│    • Senior executive messaging           │
│    • Group level messaging                │
│    • First line manager messaging         │
│    • Feedback process                     │
│    • Measuring, adjusting and re-messaging │
│                                          │
│                                          │
└─────────────────────────────────────────┘
```

Notes on Figure 5.4

Using the aforementioned awareness platform, share the upside and downside of each individual engaging in the protection of the firm's intellectual property within each of the various business areas.

Demonstrate the value of the intellectual property to be protected in a monetary unit of measure and a man-hour unit of measure, and be sure to tie into this portion of the presentation the identified milestones and expectations.

Create a core message, which will be retooled, oriented, and calibrated for each of the various business units by the executive and management team so as to ensure the message resonates with the receiving audience—the firm's individual employees.

Ensure that there is available an employee and executive feedback methodology so as to allow a sharing of results across the enterprise to adjust, redirect, or message anew as appropriate.

Identify the required policies to be created, via recommendations, position papers, and formal policy evolution—this is a linear thought process.

We'll now discuss Figure 5.5.

Figure 5.5 Executive Staff—Execute Commit

Executive Staff – Execute Commit

- Executive
  - Backing
  - Messaging
  - Policy and exception policy defined
  - Review at milestones and course correct.

- Business value statement

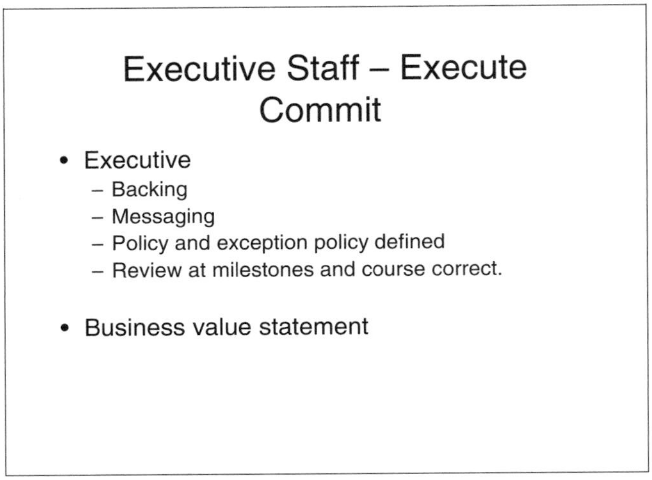

Notes on Figure 5.5

Executive Commitment

Backing—stakeholders identified—be it the CEO, COO, CIO, etc.

Overview of the sharing of messaging amongst the different identified strata by the appropriate executives

Policy identification and policy exception process

Business Value Statement

Good security of the intellectual property risks enables educated risk taking with respect to business opportunities with the knowledge and expectation that the security apparatus will align behind the business unit taking the approved risk.

Notes

1. www.thenewstribune.com/front/topphoto/story/105380.html

2. "Piracy from China: How Microsoft, Ralph Lauren, Nike and Others Can Cope." SeekingAlpha.com. April 9, 2007. http://retail.seekingalpha.com/article/31723

3. www.scip.org/

4. http://cicentre.com/Documents/DOC_Chi_Mak.html

Chapter 6

Case Study: The Mysterious Social Engineering Attacks on Entity X

Introduction

Social engineering, the practice of conning people into sharing sensitive information, be it in everyday person-to-person interaction, or via cyber interconnectivity, is a real security threat that has evolved in sophistication and broadened in scope over the decade we have been both writing about it and training people how to thwart it. Unfortunately, in most organizations, countermeasures against social engineering have not kept pace, and thus the adversaries to the enterprise continue to stretch their lead and put in danger the intellectual properties of those ill-prepared corporations.

Most organizations acknowledge it as a problem, but treat it as a nuisance rather than a very serious issue. Accordingly, most organizations do not invest any, let alone, enough in the one real countermeasure—effective and empowering security awareness and education for all employees as well as extra training for those in sensitive positions or positions of extreme trust (e.g., executives, executive assistants, human resources staff, and help desk personnel). We want to stress "effective" and "empowering," because just having a program is not enough. To be effective it has to be compelling and show your employees, in meaningful ways, that they have a stake in security and that the enterprise security depends upon their efforts. It also has to empower these employees instead of simply scaring them or leaving them with the sensation that they are being talked down to by the "security people."

And as these three news stories on a scandal that erupted at Hewlett-Packard in the fall of 2006 illustrates, it is not only hackers or competitors, but also your organization's executives and investigators in their hire that have to be considered as potential risks if not direct threats, literally originating from the inside of the organization:

Investigators hired by Hewlett-Packard to find a media leak used sensitive information to access phone-company computers and get the calling records of nine reporters without authorization.…The revelations came a day after complaints by a former member of HP's board of directors forced the company to file a statement with the U.S. Securities and Exchange Commission (SEC), acknowledging that investigators hired by the board had fraudulently accessed the private telephone records of board members and reporters. The private investigators fraudulently used the identities of the victims to get the necessary login credentials to access online telephone records without authorization, according to media reports.… (HP-funded hacking included reporters' data, Security Focus, 9-8-06)

Not only did investigators impersonate board members, employees and journalists to obtain their phone records, but according to multiple reports, they also put an HP director and a reporter for CNET Networks Inc under surveillance. They sent monitoring spyware in an e-mail to that reporter by concocting a phony story tip. They even snooped on the phone records of former CEO and Chairwoman Carly Fiorina, who had launched the quest to identify media sources in the first place. And in a twist that might seem preposterous if it happened in a movie, The New York Times *reported that HP consultants considered hiring spies to pose as clerical or custodial workers at CNET and* The Wall Street Journal. (Hewlett-Packard scandal gets wider and weirder, The Age, 9-21-06)

The news has once again highlighted a growing problem plaguing the telecommunications industry called "pretexting," a scam where unauthorized individuals pretend to be someone they're not to obtain personal information. Private investigators and con artists have been using this technique for years not just to obtain phone records, but also to get access to bank records, credit card information and other sensitive information. The telecommunications industry came under fire nine months ago when news reports pointed to Web sites where customer records could be openly purchased. The news prompted several phone companies, including Cingular Wireless, Sprint, T-Mobile and Verizon Wireless, to sue brokers selling customers' phone records.… (Security breaches are wake-up calls to phone companies, CNET News.com, 9-11-06)

Fundamentals of Social Engineering Attacks

There are two types of social engineering: *technology-based deception* and *human-based deception*. In both cases, the perpetrator relies on the natural human tendency to trust, as the means by which they manipulate the individual into engaging in a demonstrable activity, which may otherwise not be in the normal course of events for that individual. The perpetrators are always well prepared, and engage in preliminary data collection to support their "engagement" with the individual whom they wish to manipulate into a desired action or actions.

Let's start with a classic example of human-based deception.

Throughout the 1990s—the formative years of the Internet and information security—hackers had taken on an almost mystical aura. To satisfy the appetite composed mostly of curiosity, which could easily evolve into fear, an important community event was the "Meet the Enemy." This event was a teleconference between hackers dialing in and an assembly of information security professionals on-site. In the years before Jeff Moss's Defcon and Black Hat conferences came to dominate the space, "Meet the Enemy," moderated by the great Ray Kaplan and hosted by the Computer Security Institute, offered the only public forum for real dialogue between the black hats and the white hats (and yes, the gray hats, too).

On one legendary evening, one of the hackers who had called gave a live demonstration to substantiate his boasts about his social engineering prowess:

He dialed up a phone company, got transferred around, and reached the company's Help Desk.

Hacker: "Who's the supervisor on duty tonight?"

"Oh. It's Betty."

Hacker: "Let me talk to Betty." (He's transferred to Betty's extension)

Hacker: "Hey Betty, having a bad day?"

"No, why?"

Hacker: "Your systems are down."

"My systems aren't down, we're running fine."

Hacker: "All of my monitors here are showing that you are completely offline. Something is really wrong."

"We didn't even show a blip, we show no change."

Hacker: "Sign off again."

She did.

Hacker: "Betty, I am going to have to sign-on as you here to figure out what is happening with your ID. Let me have your user ID and password."

At this point, this senior supervisor at a Help Desk for a major telecommunications company told the hacker her user ID and password.

Hacker: "I'm signed on as you now and I can't see the difference. Shoot, I know what it is. Let me sign off. Now sign yourself back on again."

She did.

Hacker: "I know what it is. You're on day-old files. You think you're on-line but your not. You're on day-old files. Do me a favor, what changes all the time? The PIN code. Pull the PIN code file, just read me off the first ten PIN codes you've got there and I will compare them."

As she started to read off the first pin code, the hacker hung up on her.

Turning back, virtually to the audience of information security professionals, which included some stunned personnel from the telecommunications company he had just attacked, he bellowed out "I told you I could…"

Of course, human-based social engineering isn't just attempted over the telephone; it can be accomplished via e-mail, online chat, or any other communications medium. In the above example, the goal was obtaining a userid/password, pin codes, and other means to access an enterprise's infrastructure. Once in the infrastructure, recognized by the information systems as a trusted-insider, the enterprise's intellectual property is put at risk.

The many ways social engineering attacks have evolved over the years has been the development of technology-based approaches (e.g., using e-mail messages or Web sites that masquerade as some communications from or sites belonging to vendors, service providers, or clients known to your users).

In one illustrative case, Yahoo users received e-mails from an individual falsely identifying himself as a Yahoo employee. The e-mail informed the Yahoo users that they had won a fast modem from Yahoo. To receive their free gift, the recipients simply had to provide their name, address, telephone number, and credit card number, in order to cover the cost of shipping. Before Yahoo detected the con and sent out a bulletin to its users, numerous people had fallen for it. This was the earliest form of what is now known as "phishing."

Social engineering, whether human-based or technology-based, is used to gain user or administrator passwords to break into networks. It is also widely used to collect personal information for identity theft (e.g., "phishing") as well as for tricking users into clicking on booby-trapped e-mail attachments with malicious payloads (e.g., the "I Love You" worm).

How much identify theft could have been thwarted if even just the largest employers had instituted effective and empowering awareness and education programs that explain what social engineering is and how to thwart it for their work forces? How many hundreds of millions of dollars in fraud losses could have been avoided? How much anguish in people's personal lives? How much intellectual property that had been properly secured, would not have been unsecured and revealed.

But social engineering isn't just used by hackers to gain network access or fraudsters to commit identity theft.

It would be folly to simply focus your defensive efforts on thwarting the conversations that happen via technological communications mediums. Person-to-person interaction can be extraordinarily damaging. When an adversary obtains the userid/passwords they are perhaps able to gain entry to your enterprise, but they are oftentimes discovered shortly thereafter due to their lack of knowledge in moving about the infrastructure and inadvertently setting off alarms and alerts, which enables the enterprise to lockdown and inspect. But what of the adversary, who successfully obtains the userid/passwords and then sits on them, invests the time to then collect the necessary data to knowledgably transit the enterprise's infrastructure in an unalarming fashion.

This theorem begs the question, how? Through painstaking observation and interaction with your employees, much can be accomplished without suborning an employee's loyalty to the enterprise. Some examples:

- Restaurants in proximity to the enterprise building: team meetings, after-work libations, visiting employees dining, all of which provides opportunity for the skillful to listen and learn. If it was only listening, when the artful adversary engages your employees in conversation, the elicitation begins. Scientists, engineers, and developers, individuals who are more skillful in their respective technology than in social discourse, are prime targets, as like most of the populace of the world, they too are pleased when listened to and heard. The innocent employee guided through the conversation by a malevolent interlocutor can and unfortunately often will provide more information than they should.

- Monitoring of "roommate wanted" advertisements. In the initial minute of conversation the adversary can determine if the population of the abode with the vacancy comprises personnel from within the enterprise of interest. If yes, they pursue; if not they move on to the next advertisement. What happens with a "yes?" The adversary's cohabitation with the employee provides unlimited opportunity to view your employee's remote work habits and interactions. When the bond of trust is established, the conversations and comparisons of respective technologies can and will occur.

- Monitoring of the Public Relations announcements detailing wins, new technologies, new hires, and so forth, may provide the adversary with leads to individuals or simply locations where the adversary may be able to engage some elementary surveillance to determine where employees can be engaged.

These are just a few of the many avenues available to observe, elicit, and listen about how the enterprise operates and put together a more expansive brief, to enable the exploitation of the illicitly obtained userid/password.

The human-to-human aspect, unfortunately, doesn't end there. What of the employee who has been suborned? A willing and collaborative employee can boost, exponentially, the success ratio of the determined adversary in as much as they are on the other side of the technological barriers; they are knowledgeable of the infrastructure and the navigation procedures. Perhaps more importantly, once armed with the adversary's needs they can utilize their access to dig and sift through the various nooks and crannies of the enterprise.

The individual is one of the nexus of the entrée to your enterprise, whether or not you wish to acknowledge such. We urge you to involve yourself and empower your managers to involve themselves in investing and knowing in the work-life balance of your employee base, train in the art of listening and inquiry so as to better increase the odds that your employees know how to react and act when confronted with that unscrupulous adversary, offering inducements and attractive alternatives in the hopes of inducing them to break their trust with your enterprise.

Please realize that there are no shortages of unscrupulous organizations willing to break all the rules to gain competitive advantage over their competitors in the marketplace. And that motivation constitutes the greater threat, as both the Hewlett-Packard scandal and the following case study show.

The Mysterious Social Engineering Attacks on Entity Y

Someone called an office in a major northern European city, assuming the identity of an actual employee of Entity Y, and tried to elicit employee contact list information for an office in another northern European city. But the request was turned down.

NOTE

Please consider "Entity Y" an appellation ascribed to an aggregate of enlightening events and insightful experiences gained in our work with some of the global giants. And remember, as in the disclaimer often stated at the beginning of novels or movies, any resemblance to any actual person or organization is purely coincidental.

Several days later, a caller, using the same false identity, obtained the coveted contact list from an Entity Y office in Eastern Europe, from an employee who believed they were speaking to the identified employee.

A month later, an unsuccessful attempt is made to elicit client lists from an Entity Y employee in the Western USA.

Three days later, impersonating an employee from the UK and claiming a laptop malfunction, someone called an Entity Y office in Canada and requested complete contact information for the same Northern European office targeted in the initial attack.

The caller claimed to be working on an engagement with an actual client of Entity Y and requested that the information he needed be e-mailed to a private e-mail account. One of the first tangible clues.

The next day, someone impersonating an Entity Y employee from the UK called an Entity Y office on the Mediterranean. He claimed his laptop was malfunctioning and requested complete contact information for same Northern European office as well as one other in the Northern European region.

Two days later, in the Balkans, a second Entity Y employee succumbs to the elicitation and provides the caller with an Excel spreadsheet with the requested information. Again, from an employee who believed they were speaking to a colleague.

The next day, the attacker calls back and requests further information. But this second solicitation is rebuffed, as the employee has reflected on the totality of the provision of the spreadsheet.

The next day, someone, again impersonating an Entity Y employee, called the Northern European office directly, saying she was on assignment in Central Europe and requested the client list. The request was refused.

The next day, an Andean office received a telephone request for information on personnel in an office in a major North American city. This elicitation was successful.

In the ensuing weeks, similar calls eliciting confidential information were received in numerous Entity Y offices in Africa, the Balkans, the Baltic, North America, and Asia Pacific. There were over 30 documented incidents, targeting dozens of offices on six continents. Several of them were successful. All of the callers impersonated Entity Y employees, all of the callers claimed their laptops were malfunctioning, and all of the callers sought specific, targeted information about various groups and individuals within Entity Y and its clients.

Who were the attackers? What were they really looking for? What was their ultimate objective?

The counterintelligence component of Entity Y's global security team launched an investigation. The investigation showed that the adversary targeting Entity Y on a global basis, had done its homework and covered its trails. The telephone numbers used to call into Entity Y were non-traceable. The e-mail addresses provided, ostensibly as a personal e-mail address of a colleague, were found to be throw-away Web-based e-mail accounts. The callers were both male and female, with South African and/or British accents.

The investigation did not identify the adversary and the leads developed were insufficient to warrant and justify bringing in law enforcement entities, as all that Entity Y really had were individuals calling into their enterprise, identifying themselves as employees, and requesting the provision of information. What would law enforcement suggest? Perhaps, make Entity Y personnel more aware of elicitation and manipulation techniques that come at Entity Y via the telephone.

So let us focus on the countermeasures that the global security team recommended be undertaken.

Bulletins were sent out only to human resources personnel in the initial stages of the investigation but then later on, when there was no longer any reason to remain discrete, the bulletins were sent to all employees, thus ensuring 100 percent of the workforce were cognizant of the activity being experienced elsewhere in the enterprise and were thus on their guard.

The bulletins were to be disseminated to all personnel via e-mail and posted on all Entity Y intranets in a high-visibility spot.

A letter from the Global HR Director was proposed. This letter was to be issued simultaneously, providing context, pointing to the bulletins and the linked instructions. This letter was to underscore the importance of following the security team's admonishments. Like the bulletins, the letter was to be disseminated to all personnel via e-mail and also be posted on all Entity Y intranets in a high-visibility spot.

Regional conference calls with HR managers were to be held by the responsible HR leaders, in coordination with the global security team. The global security team was to provide presentation materials, brief the conference call participants on the nature of the elicitation attacks, explain the proper procedures for dealing with such encounters, answer questions, and discuss related issues.

The ongoing attacks underscored the importance of all offices adopting the available awareness and education resources (e.g., an e-learning module, an electronic newsletter, a new hire orientation presentation, annual on-site events), since these resources provided guidance, suitable for general audiences, on how to deal with such attacks.

The global security team also vowed that the next generation of awareness and education resources would include a workshop for human resources and Help desk personnel, as well as executive support staff, which would go into elicitation attacks and countermeasures in greater depth.

Guidance for the Workforce

The following instructions were developed by Entity Y's global security team:

How to Recognize Elicitation

Here are some common elements in recent incidents:

- The callers have identified themselves as Entity Y employees. The names they use are real employees. Sometimes these employees are out of the office on holiday or client work, but sometimes they are not.

- The caller usually claims to be working on a client project, and the client they name is actually an Entity Y client.

- The caller asks for a listing of Entity Y employees in either a particular office or a particular business line. The caller will make an excuse as to why they cannot get the information, usually that he or she is in an airport and is having computer problems.

- The caller will ask that someone e-mail the list to him at both a valid internal Entity Y address and an external Web-based company like operamail.com.

- The callers have all been male, with a British or South African accent.

- Any time you are faced with a caller, usually without a valid caller ID, who asks for internal information of any kind, you should be suspicious of elicitation.

How to Handle the Caller

Here are some instructions on how to handle suspicious callers:

- Do not give the caller what he asks for.

- Do not give the caller any indication that you know what is happening.

- Be evasive about how and when you can provide the information. Make an excuse for not providing the information immediately (e.g., "I have to get onto another call right now – you know how it is").

- Be friendly and open, as if nothing is amiss. Imply that the information will be forthcoming.

- Ask for return voice contact information. Ask for the caller's mobile number and his point of contact at the client. If the caller will not provide this information, it confirms that he is attempting to elicit information from you. If he provides the information, it does not mean he is not making an elicitation attempt.

How to Report the Incident

Here are some instructions on how to report suspicious callers:

- Immediately report the incident to your regional HR director and the global security team.

When reporting the incident, please provide the following information:

- The time and date of the call.

- The specific information the caller requested.

- Any background noises you may have heard.

- A description of the caller's voice.

- Any information the caller gives; employee name, client, phone numbers, and so forth.

Perhaps you find it hard to believe that your co-workers, friends, or family members could fall for such cons. But social engineering is very effective. The psychological techniques are powerful and technologies are getting increasingly sophisticated.

NOTE

See Appendix 9, which contains the U.S. Department of Justice questionnaire that may be used to report a loss of intellectual property within the United States.

General User-Oriented Guidance on How to Detect and Defeat Social Engineering

Here is a more generalized checklist developed to provide personnel with some ways to detect and defeat social engineering attacks:

- Be alert for the telltale signs of a social engineering attack. Is the caller reluctant to provide contact information? Is the caller rushing you to provide the information they have requested? Is the caller name-dropping (i.e., using names of important people or even family members)? Is the caller trying to manipulate your emotions (e.g., fear, sympathy, ambition)? Has the caller made any small mistakes (e.g., misspellings, misnomers)?

- Remember, an individual using the telephone as the instrument of engagement and social engineering methodology is always going to be playing on your emotions: The attacker might play on your fear, by using intimidation; or conversely the attacker might play on your desire to help others, by appealing to your sympathy, or even on your ambition, your desire to get ahead, by impressing an important caller.

- Verify the identity of callers. If you are suspicious and you cannot immediately identify them, insist on calling them back. If it is a legitimate call about security or some other sensitive issue, they will understand and appreciate your caution.

- Do not answer unexpected or unusual requests for sensitive information unless you can verify the caller and the caller's legitimate need. Don't answer questions about other employees, particularly IT personnel, unless you can verify it is an authorized request. Do not provide information on your system or your own level of access (e.g., ID and password). Do not answer "questionnaires" or provide business information such as sales figures, marketing plans, and so forth, unless you can verify it is an authorized request.

- Don't just shrug it off, sound the alarm. Report any suspicious encounters that you suspect may indeed be social engineering attacks immediately to the appropriate authorities within your office or to the security office. It may be part of a pattern, but a pattern cannot be discerned without the sharing of experiences.

Chapter 7

When Insiders and/or Competitors Target a Business's Intellectual Property

Introduction

By definition, an insider can come in many forms, be it an employee, a member of the management team, a corporate board member, a vendor, a third-party contracted manufacturer, or a collaborative partner in a joint venture.

The newspapers are replete with countless examples of the damage an insider can do to a business.

The following is a selection of some particularly insightful cases, which serve to illustrate the various motivations of the offenders, as well as the damage done to the enterprises they undermined.

Lightwave Microsystems

Let us begin with the case of an employee at a privately held firm (Lightwave Microsystems), who occupied a trusted position within that company, that of Director of Information Technology, and who acted alone in his attempt to illegally share Lightwave's intellectual property. The individual, Brent Woodward of Oakland, CA, chose to exercise his venial needs, as well as obtain some solace via revenge when faced with circumstances that he believed were unjust—two very powerful motivators in an individual contemplating a malevolent act.

In late 2002, the owner of Lightwave Microsystems, a California firm, announced that the company would cease operations due to the firm's inability to make a profit, but Lightwave Microsystems was not without value—it owned patents and had evolved trade secrets that could be sold. (Lightwave was subsequently purchased by NeoPhotonics of San Jose, CA.) When faced with the prospect of unemployment and upside-down stock options, Woodward made copies of the company's trade secrets from the firm's backup tapes and created a plan to sell these secrets to a competitor. He would feather his own nest monetarily and get revenge for the abruptness of his CEO's actions.

No one at Lightwave Microsystems detected the unauthorized copy activity. Why would they? Woodward's access was both natural and unencumbered. Furthermore, as Director of Information Technology, it was Woodward's responsibility to protect this very data—to discover, neutralize, and mitigate any and all attempts to steal Lightwave Microsystems' intellectual property.

Admittedly, Woodward's methodology was very sophomoric, but worthy of sharing nonetheless. He created an alias name, "Joe Data," and also set up a Web-based e-mail account, lightwavedata@yahoo.com, from which he executed his crime. Woodward contacted JDS-Uniphase's (JDS) chief technology officer and offered to provide Lightwave Microsystems' data to JDS in return for a significant sum of money.

JDS did the absolute right thing: the firm immediately contacted the U.S. Federal Bureau of Investigation (FBI), and at their request, JDS consented to the monitoring of communications between JDS and "Joe Data," which was to occur via e-mail. The FBI, with a consensual monitoring permit provided by JDS, was able to observe the controlled negotiations between JDS and "Joe Data," as well as trace back these communications via the user's Internet protocol address to the e-mail service provider, Yahoo. The trace activity showed "Joe Data" was connected to the Internet from within Woodward's residence. This discovery enabled the FBI to execute a valid search warrant of the residence, which produced sufficient evidence to ultimately bring about Woodward's arrest. Ultimately, he was charged with one count of theft of trade secrets under 18 U.S.C. § 1832.

In August 2005, the United States Attorney's Office for the Northern District of California announced that Brent Woodward had pled guilty to the aforementioned charge. Though he could have been sentenced to ten years imprisonment and fined US$250,000, he received a $20,000 fine and was sentenced to two years in prison, plus three years of supervised release.

Though Woodward found that his vengeful attempt to obtain an illegal bonus to be very expensive in the end—in both defense fees as well as penalties adjudicated—it is important to note that Woodward was acting by himself, and for himself, and thus had no interests other than his own venial needs. What would have happened had Woodward offered the purloined data to a less ethical competitor? Perhaps that competitor would have taken the data and set up the equivalent of a parallel universe. Would the value of Lightwave Microsystems' intellectual property sold to NeoPhotonics have been jeopardized? What of NeoPhotonics, the purchaser of Lightwave Microsystems' technology? If the unscrupulous competitor had taken the trade secrets and capitalized on the technological advances, what recourse would NeoPhotonics have had to recoup their investment/payment to Lightwave Microsystems? Litigation would only be an option IF Lightwave Microsystems knew the intellectual property had been stolen. And this would have come to light when? The purchaser wouldn't have admitted to having purloined the intellectual property, and Woodward certainly wouldn't have advertised his sale. Only during the unscrupulous competitor's developmental, manufacturing, and/or marketing/sales processes would there have been the possibility that the technology acquisition might be revealed.

The best course would have been to initially establish a defense against Woodward's action. Lightwave Microsystems should have had in place multiple audit trails and either human or machine tracking of all users, including the super-user, so that a warning could have been sent that anomalous behavior had occurred.

America Online

Let's now move on to another case in which greed was the motivating factor, inducing an employee to steal his employer's private data. In April and May 2003, American Online (AOL) software engineer Jason Smathers, utilized a colleague's access codes to surreptitiously log on to the AOL server. Then, posing as the colleague, he used his colleague's access to acquire information from each of the then 30 million AOL customers. The data stolen by Smathers comprised 92 million records, which contained the personal identifying information of those 30 million customers. The data included e-mail addresses, screen names, ZIP codes, customer credit card types (not numbers), and telephone numbers associated with AOL customer accounts. Smathers sold the stolen AOL data to Sean Dunaway of Las Vegas. Dunaway paid Smathers US$27,000 for the addresses, and then utilized them to advertise his own online gambling Web site. Dunaway later resold the AOL data to online "spammers" for approximately US$52,000. Clearly, he was an early adopter of the concept of spamming.

The Department of Justice (DOJ) prosecuted this case under the (then new) federal law Can-Spam (Controlling the Assault of Non-Solicited Pornography and Marketing Act). Smathers had pled guilty in February 2005 to the crime. In October 2005, he was sentenced to 15 months in prison and fined US$84,000—triple what he had garnered through the sale of the data. Smathers clearly knew the data had value, but he grossly underestimated the value of the information. Though the DOJ recommended to the presiding judge that Smathers be barred from the software profession, the judge noted Smathers' cooperation in the investigation and believed that his cooperation and Smathers' contrite behavior warranted leniency. Smathers noted to the court that AOL had said his theft and subsequent sale had cost the company at least US$400,000—and potentially millions of U.S. dollars.

At first glance, it would seem only AOL and their 30 million subscribers were exposed to unwanted spam. So where's the damage? The user can simply press the Delete key and get on with life. After all, spam is received by virtually every Internet user, and a variety of companies now specialize in filtering spam so only "good" e-mail arrives in their inbox. However, the loss of revenue to AOL was the loss of time each user experienced while deleting those unwanted e-mails—and time has value. But why was a crime that was committed in 2003 not prosecuted until early 2005? A very good question.

The delay in prosecution is largely due to the fact that until mid-2004, Smathers was still an employee of AOL and had not yet been identified as the source of the data breach. While AOL knew they had a problem and were cooperating with law enforcement, Smathers' use of a colleague's administrative logon was an effective method of bypassing the AOL corporate security apparatus. Smathers' colleague did have authorized access to the data, whereas Smathers did not. Had the colleague perhaps protected his passwords better (there is no evidence to suggest the unidentified colleague colluded or provided Smathers with his login passwords), this crime might never have occurred.

But the real damage may still be looming. What of the collation of e-mail addresses, usernames, and user telephone numbers? What malicious use could this data be to e-mail phishers or unscrupulous telemarketers? The answer: Priceless. That was 2003. Fast forward to 2007 where some spammed e-mail has evolved into what is known euphemistically as *phishing*.

AOL is advertised as a "family-friendly" environment—one where the customer doesn't have to be a technological marvel, nor think in bits or baud, to enjoy the pleasures of the Internet—and AOL works extraordinarily hard to exclude the seedier side of the Internet. AOL admitted to having spent at least US$400,000 as a result of this incident, but the downside may be much greater as they continue creating software to mitigate the loss of customer data, while simultaneously working to regain the trust of their customer base.

According to the Privacy Rights Clearinghouse, in 2006 alone there were approximately 100,453,730 cases of personal identifying information revealed to those without a need to know. These revelations occurred in government entities, retailers, educational institutes, and consulting firms (www.privacyrights.org/ar/DataBreaches2006-Analysis.htm).

Casiano Communications

Let's look at another instance of personal greed—this in a separate industry where a worker was accused of stealing the intellectual property of his employer and setting up shop as a direct competitor. In mid-October 2005, Casiano Communications, Inc. (CCI), arguably the most prominent publisher within the Caribbean basin with respect to Caribbean business and travel literature magazines, filed suit against a former employee, John Bynum. The suit alleged that Bynum stole intellectual property from CCI—specifically, CCI's databases, which Bynum then forwarded to his personal e-mail account from CCI's computers. According to the CCI complaint, Bynum stole client and advertiser information, violating CCI's Electronic Mail and Company Resources and Equipment policy, which is a condition of employment with CCI.

San Juan, Puerto Rico Superior Court issued a temporary restraining order against Bynum that required him to cease and desist from utilizing, transmitting, selling, or reproducing any form of database or other trade secrets obtained during the course of his employment with CCI. The injunction granted CCI the right to seize all materials contained in any computers, disks, or other information-technology items in the personal possession of the defendant. CCI alleged that Bynum had been selling a database of key island (Puerto Rico) business contacts to companies to market their products and services.

Again, this is an example of personal greed, motivated as much by circumstances as opportunity. It is not beyond the pale to assume your employees know who your competitors are and how to reach out to these firms to sell your intellectual property should the opportunity present itself and the competitor be unscrupulous enough to accept it (unlike the Lightwave Microsystems case).

Corning and PicVue

A case that hit the public eye in 2005, and that was settled in 2006, has these very circumstances present, where an opportunity presented to a low-level employee, coupled with the identification of an interested party, created a temptation for instant financial gain that was simply too great for a weak-willed employee to ignore.

This was the case of Corning Incorporated and PicVue Electronics, the latter a Taiwanese corporation. On October 20, 2005, the Department of Justice charged Jonathan Sanders, an employee of Corning's Harrodsburg, KY, plant, with the theft of trade secret material belonging to Corning. Specifically, material pertaining to an "overflow down draw fusion glass-making process used to produce Thin Filter Transistor (TFT) Liquid Crystal Display (LCD) flat panel glass."

In the DOJ complaint, it is alleged that Sanders began his theft of Corning's IP in December 1999 and continued to perpetrate the crime through December 2001. Sanders allegedly took, without authorization, trade secret material belonging to Corning and subsequently sold that same material to PicVue Electronics Ltd., a Taiwanese corporation. This case of Economic Espionage, not only involved PicVue Electronics, the corporation, but also the former president of PicVue.

When arrested, Sanders waived his right to a preliminary hearing, was indicted, and pled guilty. He was sentenced to 48 months imprisonment and ordered to pay a fine of US$20,000 on April 18, 2006.

He told the FBI that he found blueprints containing the Corning trade secrets within a Corning warehouse in 1999. The blueprints were within a container of sensitive corporate material awaiting destruction. He said he simply took the blueprints instead of destroying them.

In December 1999, Sanders then traveled to California and met with PicVue's company president, Jacob Lin, as well as Yeong C. Lin, a consultant to PicVue. Sanders claimed he only described the fusion draw process, and did not show the drawings to the PicVue president nor his consultant. Subsequent to this meeting, Sanders was allegedly offered a job by PicVue, but declined the position.

Then around September 2000, Yeong C. Lin, the consultant, informed PicVue that Sanders was now offering Corning's blueprints/drawings via an oral description. PicVue authorized the payment of US$30,000 and wired the funds to a California bank account, where apparently the PicVue consultant took control of the funds. The consultant then enlisted the aid of a college roommate, Danny Price, who carried US$25,000 to a meeting with Sanders outside of Atlanta, GA, so as to obfuscate the connection between PicVue and Sanders.

Sanders met with Price as planned, outside of Atlanta, and accepted the money from Price. In exchange, he provided Price with the Corning blueprints he had stolen from the corporate sensitive data destruction bin. Price apparently gave the documents to consultant, Lin, who met with PicVue engineers in California. The PicVue engineers took digital pictures of the blueprint documents and transferred the images to a digital storage device. The engineers hand-carried the digital storage device back to Taiwan, and the blueprints were then, allegedly, destroyed.

Two months later (November 2000), engineers from PicVue traveled to Kentucky and met with Sanders directly to discuss the blueprints he had sold to PicVue. Sanders claims the conversations were centered on providing clarification to PicVue on details contained within the blueprints.

PicVue representatives then traveled to the offices of Saint-Gobain glass, Niagara Falls, NY in September 2001 to purchase a part specific to the fusion process. Given the prior commercial relationship between Corning and Saint-Gobain, the latter recognized the utility of the part as being only applicable to the fusion draw process and alerted Corning to the possibility that their trade secrets had been compromised to PicVue.

Corning representatives visited Saint-Gobain's offices, reviewed the specifications provided by PicVue and concluded that Corning trade secrets were involved. Corning contacted the FBI, who opened an investigation October 2001.

In this instance, Corning apparently had a set of procedures in place to destroy company confidential documents, but it would appear no mechanism existed to ensure that documents put into the "to-be-destroyed" bin were, in fact, subsequently destroyed. Again, the company was ignorant of the theft of their intellectual property until the recipient—PicVue, in this case—approached one of the few firms in the world able to create the parts necessary to make the purloined documents effective in the marketplace. If there is a bright side to the entire episode, it is the strength of the relationship between Corning and Saint-Gobain, which brought this illegal activity to light, not internal procedures.

Let us assume you have appropriate checks and balances in place to protect yourself against the opportunistic and greed-driven employee. What defense do you have to protect yourself when the theft of your technology is premeditated by individuals who are the leaders, and literally in the driver's seat of one of your main competitors? Can't happen, you say? Think again.

Avery Dennison and Four Pillars

Let's now review the well-documented and publicized instance of intellectual property theft that was encountered by Avery Dennison, the firm that makes labels, and by extension, the firm that spends a great deal of money on the research and development of adhesives. Unbeknownst to the company, they had had their intellectual property stolen from them from 1989 through 1997. The theft of their IP was literally a textbook example of the methodical harvesting of a firm's technological advances and research by a competitor.

Avery Dennison, whose headquarters is in Pasadena, CA, is one of the United States' largest manufacturers of adhesive labels, and retains intellectual property for these formulas. The firm's adhesives and methodologies give Avery Dennison their market advantage within the global adhesive label market. Because of this, a competitor, Four Pillars Enterprise Limited of Taiwan, specifically targeted Avery Dennison's research facility in Concord, OH.

Four Pillars is a manufacturer of pressure-sensitive products in Taiwan, with market share both in the United States and the Far East. Prior to 1989, the Four Pillars CEO had identified his competition and had noted the competitive advantage held by market-sector leader Avery Dennison and so had set out as a corporate goal to capitalize on Avery Dennison's advance research in adhesives. A very determined individual, he was successful in stealing the formulas for Avery Dennison's adhesives—some might say very successful.

Successful that is, until 1997, when one of his Four Pillars' employees applied for work with Avery Dennison, and during the course of the interview(s) revealed that for the preceding eight years, Avery Dennison's adhesive formulas were being provided to Four Pillars by an employee of Avery Dennison.

Avery Dennison had not previously detected this theft of their IP. The firm took the correct action and contacted the FBI, and together with Avery Dennison, the two contrived a sting operation to identify the employee who was supplying Four Pillars with company secrets. The sting operation was fruitful and identified Mr. Ten Hong Lee—a.k.a., Victor Lee—a U.S. citizen and senior research engineer at Avery Dennison's Concord, Ohio research facility, who was stealing the intellectual property of his employer.

Lee was confronted and admitted his guilt, confessing to having stolen the formulas and methodologies of his employer from 1989 to 1997. He was later persuaded to act as a cooperative witness for the Department of Justice (DOJ), who wished to prosecute this theft of the intellectual property of a United States corporation by a foreign national, under the powers of the Economic Espionage Act (EEA) of 1996.

The ensuing investigation revealed Lee—who received his undergraduate degree at the National University of Taipei, his Masters degree in polymer science from Akron University, and his Ph.D. in chemical engineering from Texas Tech—had been invited to Taiwan by the Industrial Technology Research Institute to give a lecture at one of their conferences. While there, he was asked to present a technical lecture to Four Pillars by the company's technical director.

During this visit to Taiwan, Lee was enticed to covertly enter into a relationship with Pin Yen Yang—a.k.a., P.Y. Yang—President and CEO of the Taiwanese firm, Four Pillars Enterprise Company, Ltd as a "secret consultant." For this, he was paid $25,000 for his first year. Lee, Yang, and Yang's daughter, Hwei Chen Yang—a.k.a., Sally Yang—conspired to provide the Yangs with Avery Dennison's intellectual property and business methodologies. In exchange, Lee would be paid substantial sums of money—to be deposited with Lee's relatives, who were residents in Taiwan.

Following the discovery by Avery Dennison, the covert relationship continued under FBI scrutiny until early September 1997, when Lee provided to the Yangs proprietary information of Avery Dennison origin during a meeting monitored and controlled by the FBI in a room within the Holiday Inn located in Westlake, Ohio. Lee indicated on the video coverage of the meeting to the Yangs that the papers he was providing were the intellectual proprietary property of Avery Dennison. The Yangs acknowledged such, and following the meeting, the Yangs were observed cutting, with a knife, the headers and footers off the documents provided by Lee. Subsequently, the Yangs were arrested by the FBI as they attempted to board a plane and return to their corporate headquarters with the data.

The relationship between Lee and the Yangs' Four Pillars was a clear case of "economic espionage." During the prosecution of this case, it was learned that Lee was paid more than $150,000 over a period of eight years in exchange for sharing the intellectual property of his employer, Avery Dennison. In 1999, U.S. District Court Judge Peter C. Economus convicted both Yang and his daughter for stealing trade secrets and also convicted Four Pillars on economic espionage charges. Yang was sentenced to six months of home confinement and fined $250,000; his daughter was fined $5,000 and received a year's probation. The firm, Four Pillars, was fined $5 million for accepting the pilfered trade secrets. Lee pled guilty to wire fraud and defrauding his employer.

Avery Dennison's discovery of Four Pillars' illegal activity was due to a serendipitous event, the employment application by a former Four Pillars' employee and this employee's willingness to share information concerning Four Pillars' recruitment of an Avery Dennison employee for the sole purpose of compromising the intellectual property of Avery Dennison. In this instance, Four Pillars personnel targeted an individual with whom the Yangs could relate to on the basis of ethnicity, leveraging Lee's desire to help a fellow-countryman. The Yangs stroked Lee's ego, giving him "recognition" for his intellect, and providing him with remuneration in a covert manner—thus, keeping his skullduggery out of the view of the tax authorities, Avery Dennison lenders, or others who may question the increase/addition in Lee's income.

The Yangs' investment of approximately $150,000 resulted in an approximate $30 to 50 million loss to Avery Dennison. It is worth noting that Yang and his firm, Four Pillars, were acting in their own self-interest and not at the behest of any other entity.

Four Pillars ultimately appealed their conviction to the Supreme Court, hoping for a reduction in the sentence, but the convictions were upheld in October 2002. Four Pillars continues to be an active firm, involved in adhesive and label manufacturing

Lexar Media and Toshiba

Let's move on to one of those ticklish situations that every company that has ever collaborated with another company encounters: *Is this a win-win scenario, or am I placing my company in a situation of inordinate risk?* The answer could be yes—*It could be a win-win situation*—but you must keep your eye on your property and monitor your partner's actions as well.

Now, let's review the litigation undertaken by Lexar Media (as of June 2006, a wholly owned subsidiary of Micron Technology) and their successful lawsuit in which they claimed the theft of their trade secrets by a foreign competitor and the competitor's U.S. subsidiaries.

In late March 2005, a California Superior Court jury found Toshiba Corporation (a Japanese company) guilty of the theft of trade secrets from Lexar Media and assessed damages of $381.4 million and punitive damages of $84 million for a total of $465.4 million. Lexar had alleged that Toshiba had utilized Lexar's trade secrets in Toshiba's product line, which included NAND flash chips, Compact Flash cards, xD-Picture cards, and Secure Digital cards. The jury agreed and the issuance of punitive damages by the jury indicated that the jury found Toshiba's actions to be oppressive, fraudulent, and/or malicious.

Toshiba petitioned the court in April 2005 to recognize the jury's award as an advisory verdict and asked that the monetary damages be reduced, while Lexar petitioned the court for an injunction against Toshiba so as to prevent the sale of any Toshiba products that incorporated Lexar's intellectual property. On October 14, 2005, the court ruled that the jury findings were not advisory but in fact final. The court also declined to issue an injunction against Toshiba. Lexar's Executive Vice President and General Counsel, Eric Whitaker, noted that Lexar will continue to pursue patent infringement litigation against Toshiba, and remains confident that once patent infringement has been confirmed, that an injunction against Toshiba preventing the sale of their products will be forthcoming. Then in April 2006, Lexar filed a petition with the U.S. International Trade Commission (ITC) to initiate a Section 337 investigation in which Lexar asked that Toshiba's NAND flash memory chips be barred from import into the United States. According to an ITC press release, in May 2006 the ITC voted to institute an investigation of certain flash memory chips, flash memory systems, and products containing the same. In October 2006, Toshiba and Micron (having acquired Lexar) reached a settlement, the details of which were omitted from the public Securities and Exchange Commission filings of November 2006.

A tremendous amount of legal wrangling was involved in the proceedings, and while a settlement occurred, it begs the question: How did it get this far? According to Lexar, in mid-1996 Lexar Media was created by employees of Cirrus Corporation, and its business plan centered on technology created by Cirrus. Prior to the creation of Lexar, Cirrus and Toshiba had been involved in discussions (1994 to 1995) on how Cirrus would collaborate with Toshiba in creating flash memory controllers in support of Toshiba's preferred flash memory technology. Upon creation of Lexar, discussions between Toshiba and Lexar increased in depth and frequency. Toshiba and Lexar's Toshiba—Toshiba America and Toshiba America Electronic Components (TEAC)—were given access to Lexar's intellectual property under a Non-Disclosure Agreement (NDA) signed on December 1, 1996, which had a five-year expiration date.

Following the signing of the NDA, in-depth discussion between the parties ensued, and Toshiba invested US$3 million in Lexar in May 1997. They also placed a member on the board of directors of Lexar. Throughout 1997, Lexar continued to share intellectual property with Toshiba. In April 1998, Toshiba and Lexar entered into a partnership so as to be competitive in the flash memory market. The joint relationship apparently prospered throughout 1998 and most of 1999. On October 6, 1999, Toshiba and SanDisk announced in a joint press statement that the two firms had entered into a joint agreement to develop and manufacturer Gigabit Scale flash memory. Interestingly, the Toshiba board member apparently missed the October 5, 1999 Lexar board meeting. Lexar felt that their "partner" had sold them out to their main competitor in the flash memory market—SanDisk. Not only had Toshiba been a partner in numerous joint development projects, but Toshiba's presence on the Lexar board of directors provided Toshiba with all the strengths and weaknesses of the firm.

The Lexar board requested an explanation from the board member representing their partner Toshiba. The board member provided assurances that the agreement between Toshiba and SanDisk did not involve Lexar technologies. The board member continued with his assurances, noting the publicized agreement between Toshiba and SanDisk involved a separate division within Toshiba than that involved with Lexar. Less than seven months later, SanDisk and Toshiba announced in a joint press statement that the two had signed a US$700 million deal to create a joint fabrication facility in Virginia to produce multilevel cell (MLC) flash memory chips. Lexar believed that their intellectual property, specifically the multipage write technology was being used in this, and that without this technology, the MLC flash memory initiative would not be financially viable.

Lexar believes that Toshiba and its subsidiaries have incorporated into their product line intellectual property which, when disclosed by Lexar to Toshiba, were not only considered proprietary trade secrets of Lexar, but also were covered under the subsequent NDA. Though suspicious, it was not until Toshiba published in 2001 the technologies used in their MLC smart memory application that proof was evident to Lexar that their IP had been used.

In this instance, Lexar was able to prove what they suspected when Toshiba published the technical specifications of the Toshiba product line. What makes this case especially noteworthy is the apparent brashness on the part of Toshiba. Toshiba had a seat on the board of the company whose intellectual property they would be purloining. In addition, Toshiba had a number of joint development projects, during which Lexar's intellectual property was fully disclosed to Toshiba, and which Toshiba then leveraged for their own benefit in their own product line.

So, would Lexar not have lost their intellectual property had they chosen their partners more carefully? Probably yes, but did they have a choice in choosing their dance partner? Lexar was a spin-out and a startup and thus required a rock-solid partnership to reduce the unremunerated burn rate and shorten the distance to profitability. The preexisting Lexar/Toshiba relationship at first appears to have given Toshiba the impetus to take advantage of the startup's perceived lack of attention to the protection of their intellectual property, when in reality the importance of the intellectual property was not lost on the Lexar executive team, being that they did pay attention and did notice it, albeit after the theft had occurred and the IP had been incorporated into a competitor's product.

SigmaTel and Citroen

Which brings us to two situations of alleged IP theft involving companies from two separate industries—automotive and audio entertainment devices. So what's the similarity? Both companies allege that their patented methodologies were copied by a competitor located within China and then marketed within the Chinese market—thus, the companies in each case apparently ended up competing against their own product designs, manufactured by companies that had little or no research costs associated with the development of the product design, allowing the companies to market the product for a cost considerably less than the company owning the patent. So, is that the price of doing business in China? The government of China claims to be improving their intellectual property rights protection methodologies, but they have a long row to hoe. There will be repeated instances where individual corporations will be victimized. Unscrupulous business practices will always arise when intellectual property protection is lax.

In January 2005, SigmaTel, a developer and manufacturer of audio devices, filed suit against Actions Semiconductor Company of Zhuhai, Guangdong, China (Actions Semi), alleging that Actions Semi's integrated circuits, which are within Actions Semi's MP3 players, infringe upon multiple patents related to SigmaTel's portable audio devices. SigmaTel followed in March 2005, with the filing of a complaint with the U.S. International Trade Commission (ITC), requesting that the ITC initiate a Section 337 investigation on Actions Semi. In the ITC complaint, SigmaTel identified the specific patents that they believed had been infringed upon and requested that the ITC grant a permanent exclusion order, banning the importation into the U.S. of the infringing products and issuing a cease-and-desist order halting sale of these same products. The ITC opened an investigation, and the trial began in November 2005.

Actions Semi claimed no infringement of SigmaTel's patents had occurred. In September 2006, the ITC found that Actions had infringed upon SigmaTel's patents and rendered judgment in favor of SigmaTel. The ITC issued a limited exclusion order protecting SigmaTel in the U.S. market from Actions Semi's importation of products that were found to contain certain identified components. Thus, SigmaTel had their U.S. market protected.

The second case, which occurred in October 2005, involves Citroen's joint venture in China: Dongfeng Peugot Citroen Automobile. Citroen alleged that Shanghai Maple used Citroen's core chassis technology in producing a series of Shanghai Maple models. According to the Chinese press, Shanghai Maple claimed their automobiles were created from their own designs. Citroen, however, claimed their patent on "special chassis technology" had already been filed with the world IP rights organization and had not been licensed to Shanghai Maple. Shanghai Maple, a subsidiary of Geely Automobile, claimed no knowledge of any infringement, stating that they had never received any documentation from Citroen.

Interestingly, the unlicensed use of technology apparently is not an unusual occurrence within the Chinese automotive manufacturing sector. In May 2005, General Motors Daewoo alleged that Cherry QQ copied its "Spark" sedan design and so demanded 80 million RMB (approximately US$10 million) as compensation for patent infringement. Prior to the GM/Cherry suit, Dongfeng Honda and Toyota Auto sued Hebei Shuanghuan Auto and Geely Auto for similar reasons.

Truly remarkable is the perspective of the deputy engineer from within the China Automotive Technology & Research Center, Zhang Zhenzhi, who noted in the *Shanghai Daily News*, "It's inevitable for domestic automakers to imitate other advanced technologies, no matter from other domestic companies or foreign firms. But in the future, we would be able to better our designs after getting more experience on developing our own autos." To the untrained eye, it would appear that loss of IP is expected and will continue to be accepted within the nascent Chinese auto industry.

In both of these examples, the company whose technology has been illegally used did all of the right steps to protect their intellectual property—for example, filing patents, and so on. But in the end, they found themselves caught up in an embryonic legal system, oftentimes described as a litigation quagmire of quicksand where it is all but impossible to effectively litigate patent violations. In SigmaTel's instance, they took appropriate measures to protect themselves within one of their prime markets—the United States. The fact that they prevailed in the ITC trial speaks volumes, especially given that the overt threat to SigmaTel's market share in the U.S. was successfully mitigated. That said, the injunction, levied against Actions Semi, affects only business within the U.S. and has no effect on the Chinese or European market. While in Citroen's instance, it boils down to what they would call in prohibition-era Chicago—*gettin' the business*—where the deputy engineer from within the official Chinese Automotive Technology & Research Center viewed the apparent "borrowing" of IP as the norm—something to be expected of young companies, and something to be tolerated by the more established new-to-China foreign firms.

3dGEO – China

In 2004, Chinese citizen Yan Ming Shan, 34, of Daqing, China, pled guilty in federal court to a one-count indictment that charged him with the unauthorized access to the computer programs of 3dGEO, where he fraudulently obtained proprietary source code and other software. Shan was sentenced to two years imprisonment.

According to the DOJ press release concerning this case, from April to September 2002 Shan worked for 3dGEO Development, Inc., a Mountain View, California company that develops software used in the survey of land for sources of natural gas and oil. 3dGEO employed Shan under an agreement with one of its customers, PetroChina, a Chinese company with a division named DaQing Oil, which arranged for its employee to travel to California for training on 3dGEO's software. FBI agents arrested Mr. Shan in September 2002 as he attempted to board a flight to China. Ever since, he has been held in custody as a flight risk, pending trial.

Interestingly, in an interview with 3dGEO's president, Dimitri Bevc, which occurred shortly after the arrest of Shan, Bevc said the episode highlighted a dilemma for the company, which was seeking to secure its intellectual property but also expand its business in Asia. "There's incredible demand from Chinese firms that are hungry for technology," said Mr. Bevc. "But we are built on our own intellectual property."

Bevc continued, saying he was afraid his company was being punished in the Chinese market-place. In addition, with the pending payments from PetroChina for work already completed, Mr. Bevc said his company's Chinese sales prospects had been drying up. "What we heard back was … that 3dGEO did something wrong" by taking action against Mr. Shan, who served most of his sentence while awaiting trial, and has since returned to China, Mr. Bevc related.

When Piracy, Counterfeiting, and Organized Crime Target a Business's Intellectual Property

Introduction

Previously, we discussed the vector posed by the "Insider and Competitor" and the "State Entity." The greatest and most insidious threat to one's Intellectual Property (IP), however, involves counterfeiting and piracy, and often times, these activities are sponsored by organized crime.

The threat to IP from backroom thieves who produce counterfeit and pirated products is absolutely the most pervasive threat to the global economy as a whole. The U.S. Chamber of Commerce (Chamber) estimates that counterfeiting and pirated products account for 5 to 7 percent of the global economy, costing the United States alone over 750,000 jobs, and socks U.S. industry for a loss of sales in the area of $250 billion. The Chamber has directed its efforts, via trade missions and educational programs, toward China, Brazil, South Korea, and Russia with the goal of encouraging enhanced enforcement of IP protection laws within. In addition, the Chamber on each of these countries offers an IP protection toolkit. In 2005–2007, the Chamber, working together with various law enforcement entities, not only initiated the STOP (Strategy Targeting Organized Piracy), but has continued to expand the footprint (www.uschamber.com/ncf/initia-tives/counterfeiting.htm).

In most instances, the motive to pirate or counterfeit is simple: "economic greed"—to manufac-ture and sell goods without the overhead and costs incurred by the rightful owner of the IP. Thus, they are able to bring a product to market that is manufactured, marketed, and sold at a fraction of the cost borne by the original manufacturer. Innumerable examples exist; we offer a selection, across many industrial sectors. Additionally, given the infrastructure necessary, it is not surprising the most robust enterprises have ties to organized criminal networks.

It is not only the Chamber that recognizes the ties between piracy and counterfeiting and organized criminal elements. In the U.K., the "Alliance Against IP Theft" (Alliance) has produced a 40-page primer, "*Proving the Connection – Links Between Intellectual Property Theft and Organised Crime*," on the issue, detailing the deleterious effect on the U.K. economy and the clear and unambiguous involvement of organized criminal elements. The primer's case studies identified organizations with points of origin in Russia (mafia), South Asia (multiple countries), China (triad organizations), and Ireland. All of which served as points of origin for either the fiscal wherewithal to affect the manufac-ture, distribution, and sale of pirated and counterfeit goods in the U.K., or the initial point of origin of the bogus goods. The Alliance puts the value of these illegal items at over £9 billion (www .allianceagainstiptheft.co.uk).

We took the liberty of reviewing the available data on intellectual property regimes which are, in our opinion, not up to par in the area of intellectual property protection, both with respect to the existence of laws and/or the ability or willingness to enforce those laws that do exist. Figure 8.1 was derived from available data found in the 2007 BASCAP (Business Action to Stop Counterfeiting and Piracy) report, the 2007 BSA (British Software Association) Piracy data report, the U.S. Trade Representative's 2007 301 report, and our own analysis. This chart identifies the ten lowest-rated countries with respect to a regime designed and enforced to protect intellectual property.

Figure 8.1 The 10 Lowest Ranked Countries with IP Regimes

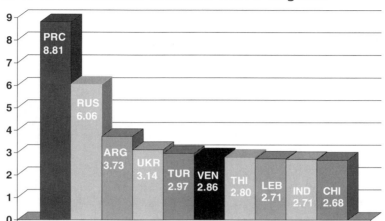

Using much of the same data found in both the 2007 BASCAP and the 2007 BSA Piracy data report, coupled with our own analysis, we have created our own read on those countries we believe have earned the honor of being the Top Five countries with an intellectual property protection and enforcement regime in place and in use (see Figure 8.2).

Figure 8.2 The Top Five Countries with IP Regimes

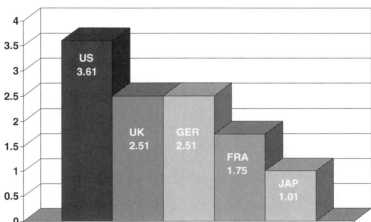

According to the United Kingdom's National Criminal Intelligence Service (NCIS), organized crime is defined as:

- Collaboration of a minimum of three people

- Criminal activity which has, or is intended to be, continued over a prolonged period

- The commission of serious criminal offenses which, taken as a whole, are of considerable importance

- Being motivated by the pursuit of power or profit

- Operations that are international, national, or regional

- Crime using violence or intimidation

- Criminal activity using commercial or business-like structures

- Crime that engages in money laundering

- Criminal activity that exerts an influence upon politics, the media, public administration, judicial authorities, or the economy (www.allianceagainstiptheft.co.uk/Proving-the-Connection.pdf; p. 12-23 of hard copy)

- Software piracy

While software piracy costs the global economy financially, it also costs countries jobs, according to a study commissioned by the Business Software Alliance (BSA). The 2007 global study notes that in 2006, piracy rates in 13 countries had increased over the prior year. Leading the list are Armenia, Azerbaijan, Moldova, and the rest of the Commonwealth of Independent States (CIS), where it is estimated that between 94 to 96 percent of all software purchased is a pirated copy. While the top 20 countries with a high rate of software piracy are comprised mostly of developing nations, the list also includes China with a rate of 82 percent, and Russia, which tails close behind at 80 percent. By comparison, the United States has the lowest rate at 21 percent. The 2006 study opines that a 10-point drop in piracy in the Asia-Pacific region alone would generate $135 billion worth of additional economic growth and create approximately 2 million new jobs. The 2007 study of the 2006 piracy situation notes that losses from piracy rose by more than $5 billion, a 15 percent increase over 2005.

But enforcement remains an issue. Let's look at a typical case of enforcement, in the Philippines where the manufacture and sale of pirated software is not uncommon. In October 2005 in Cebu City, two persons were arrested for IP rights violations—the two were charged with attempting to sell pirated software, valued at approximately nine million Filipino pesos (US$160,000+). One of the individuals was identified as a U.S. citizen and the other a Filipino citizen. The pair is facing fines of between 50,000 and 1.5 million Filipino pesos (approximately $900 to $25,000) and incarceration of one to nine years, if convicted. It should be noted that, according to the Filipino press, no individual has ever been convicted of software piracy in the Philippines. The fiscal deterrent is minimal, though the incarceration may be sufficient to catch the attention of an individual contemplating entry into the criminal milieu; the track record of the legal process tends to negate these deterrents. It would appear that these are token arrests and enforcement efforts, and not directed at the large wholesale piracy efforts.

As the aforementioned study indicated, piracy of IP is a problem within Brazil and not a priority of the Brazilian government. To punctuate this fact, on the October 18, 2005 flight from Moscow to Brasilia, President Lula's presidential aircraft showed a pirated DVD-version of *Filhos de Francisco*, a film released in Brazil in August 2005 and not yet available on DVD. This, coupled with Brazil's declaration in mid-2005 to the pharmaceutical world, "cut your drug price or we'll take your IP," makes Brazil an interesting conundrum for companies contemplating doing business in this market.

The incongruous perspective presented to the international community needs addressing. Perhaps to adjust this perception, the Brazilian National Council to Combat Piracy and Intellectual Property Violations announced that between November 2004 and November 2005, Brazil has seized counterfeit and pirated goods valued at approximately US$87 million—a 130 percent increase over the amount seized in 2004. The Brazilian's claim, "*the main entryway for contraband is the Brazilian borders with Paraguay, in Foz do Iguaçu, in the state of Paraná.*" Brazilian government officials claim that "barriers" set up in the region have reduced importation of counterfeit goods by approximately 60 percent. This would suggest that tightening a country's borders may reduce the inflow of illicit goods and thus reduce the opportunity for the sale/purchase of pirated/counterfeit items.

Technology Counterfeiting

Counterfeiting isn't limited to software. Take the example of the network gear manufacturer, D-Link. D-Link's intellectual property was being successfully pirated/counterfeited within the Indian market. In late August 2005, a number of D-Link products were found in New Delhi's Nehru Place market area by Indian law enforcement officials from the Criminal Bureau of Investigation (CBI) (some of the seized products included Ethernet switches [model DS1016D and DES 1024D]). Interestingly, D-Link's distributors in India have a remarkable degree of understanding as to why customers would willingly purchase fake products, as customer support is unimportant. According to Pankaj Surekha, proprietor of Surekha Compunet, a D-link distributor, "D-link has a very tiring and time-consuming replacement process, which at times distracts customers from the brand. Hence, the company should revise and minimize the replacement cycle to help customers retain long-lasting faith in the brand."

Perspective oftentimes is determined by where you stand, and in this case, it would appear that the distributor is advocating a more streamlined process on the part of the manufacturer that may lead potential customers to make their buy-choice based on robust product support—something that is lacking when a pirated product is purchased.

Korea technology manufacturer Samsung has been victimized repeatedly. The crimes range from outright theft of their IP to the counterfeiting of their cutting-edge product lines. In November 2005, four current and former Samsung employees pilfered the blueprints and documents for a new mobile phone design and were caught by Korea's National Intelligence Service (Korea's Counterespionage organization), who discovered the group attempting to spirit the files to China mobile phone manufacturers. Samsung notes that its investment in the design project was 25 billion RMB (approximately $25 million). Had the quartet been successful, Samsung may have taken a market hit of approximately 500 million RMB (US$500,000) in the handset market, and it stood to lose almost 8.8 trillion RMB (approximately $8.8 billion) worth of intellectual property on their entire line of technology products which were included in the data trove. What company can withstand a fiscal loss valued at over $8 billion due to their blueprints and documents being stolen?

Samsung has a "policy" in place that prohibits employees from sharing data outside the company or retaining or copying such data for personal retention. That said, one of the individuals arrested was discovered sharing approximately four gigabytes of computer files. These files included documents, blueprints, program source code, and circuit diagrams of mobile phones. This individual used multiple technological avenues to affect the transfer of data to his co-conspirators by using DVDs, e-mail, and wireless connectivity between laptops to successfully transfer the data outside of Samsung.

It begs the question, especially in this day and age of Sarbanes-Oxley (SOX) enforcement, if this were a U.S. firm, what liability would the corporate hierarchy hold for lax protection of their intellectual property? And which corporate officer would the shareholders hold liable?

Perhaps as interesting is the lamentable fact that in the United States the likelihood of this type of event being serendipitously discovered by U.S. governmental agencies is slim. This country's own privacy laws prohibit random and pervasive monitoring of private communications.

It is just as interesting to note that the Korean NIS has the capability and exercises their counter-espionage capability within the Economic Espionage milieu in support of Korea's industrial base. A separate report from the Samsung Economic Research Institute on the topic of stolen Korean technologies indicates that 39 percent of all technology stolen from Korea is destined for China.

Korean manufacturers of mobile phones and other electronic devices such as MP3 players have noted that approximately 70 percent of the products manufactured by LG and Samsung available in the Chinese marketplace were counterfeit products. In their effort to thwart counterfeit activity, a Hong Kong–based company, Marksman Consultants Ltd., has conducted surveys and investigations, working closely with the Chinese law enforcement entities. According to Joseph Tsang, Chairman of Marksman, "One big problem: Too many scammers have ties to local officials, who see counterfeit operations as a major source of employment, and pillars of the local economy. Two or three of our raids have failed because of local protection."

The Apparel Industry

But piracy isn't limited to the technology or software industries. The apparel industry is also victimized. Counterfeit shoes are commonplace in the open markets of Southeast Asia. Adidas, the German sports clothing conglomerate, recently filed a lawsuit against three separate Chinese companies for IP violations.

- **Aile Clothing and Shoe Company** Adidas alleges that Aile is using the three-stripe design on shoes manufactured by Aile, which violates Adidas' three-stripe trademarked logo.

- **Beijng Jianlijia Aile Sports Good Shop** Adidas alleges that this firm is selling goods that violate the Adidas trademark.

- **Beijing Ruiguan Sports Goods Company** Adidas alleges that this firm is selling goods that violate the Adidas trademark.

Adidas requested three million RMB (approximately USD 370,000 in compensation) from the three companies for violating Adidas' logo and trademarks.

The apparel and fashion goods industries are a ripe target as well. In early November 2005, the Assistant U.S. attorney for the District of Massachusetts and the U.S. Immigration and Customs Enforcement in New England, along with the U.S. Internal Revenue Service, announced the arrest and indictment of four individuals charged with trafficking in more than USD 1.4 million worth of counterfeit goods. The ten-count indictment details how the four used 13 separate self-storage units within a storage facility located in Revere, MA as their base of operations (ten of the units were for storage, two were show rooms and one was the manufacturing facility). When raided, the units contained 12,231 counterfeit handbags; 7,651 counterfeit wallets; 17,000+ generic handbags and wallets; and counterfeit labels and medallions in sufficient quantity to turn more than 50,000 generic handbags and wallets into copies of the originals. The following trademarked brands were copied: Louis Vuitton, Kate Spade, Prada, Gucci, Fendi, Burberry, Coach, and additional bags and wallets of other manufacturers. In addition, numerous other items were also contained in the storage units, including scarves, belts, umbrellas, sunglasses, duffle bags, hats, visors, garment bags, coats, shoes, necklaces, bracelets, rings, and earrings bearing counterfeit marks owned by these and other victim companies. The indictment places the value of the "counterfeit" goods at approximately USD 1.4 million, and USD 6.0 million had the goods been authentic.

The sales methodology used by this group of counterfeiters, according to the indictment, was to sell their items at flea markets or "purse parties" in the Revere, MA area. Indeed, it is alleged that they held more than 230 purse parties throughout Massachusetts. The goods they acquired were purchased from both legitimate generic goods manufacturers and illegal suppliers of goods in New York. According to ICE, "The public needs to know that when they buy a counterfeit purse at a house party or on the street, their dollars are ultimately helping to finance large-scale counterfeiting organizations. And every time they buy a knock-off purse, they are contributing to legitimate companies losing billions of dollars in revenue to counterfeiting every year."

In 2007, the government of Italy's domestic intelligence service, SISDE (Servizio per le Informazioni e la Sicurezza Democratica, Italian for *Service for Information and Democratic Security*) accused Chinese hackers, apparently operating with the acquiescence of the government of China, of the wholesale theft of industrial methodologies associated with the apparel and fashion goods industry. While the Chinese government denied all allegations, the Italian government was adamant that the Chinese were purloining the intellectual property of the Italian firms so as to enhance the production and bring the Chinese knock-offs closer to the quality of the real Italian merchandise. A news piece notes how SISDE's alarm has been echoed by reports from the Chinese desk of Italy's special anti-Mafia investigative directorate.

The Entertainment Industry

Now we'll discuss the pervasiveness of IP theft that occurs with artistic products produced by the entertainment industry. In late 2005, a judge in Hong Kong sentenced a Hong Kong resident, Chan Nai-ming, to three months in jail for the copy and distribution of three motion pictures via the Internet. Chan operated under the Internet alias "Big Crook" and apparently did not charge for the films that he availed to the Internet community. Chan utilized the BitTorrent software program to conduct his Internet file sharing. This case is the first that resulted in a jail sentence for the online piracy of motion pictures in Hong Kong. Hong Kong customs investigators determined that between 30 and 40 individuals had accessed Chan's computer to obtain illicit copies of the copyrighted materials. The fact that Chan did not charge for the films was not found to be material.

While in Sweden in mid-2005, it became illegal to share music and films over the Internet, the Swedish anti-piracy group Antipiratbyrån (APB) found itself being disciplined by the country's Data Inspection Board for breaking privacy data rules in its hunt for illegal file-sharers.

In their exuberance to locate and identify individuals who were sharing, illegally, music and film files over the Internet, they hired a paid informant within the Swedish ISP Bahnof to provide the Internet protocol addresses of "file shares" from within the Swedish ISP's network. The Data Inspection Board noted that an individual's Internet protocol address is considered private; the manner in which the information was collected was illegal. Subsequent to the discovery of a paid informant within Bahnof, the ISP fired two employees, including the paid informant for the APB.

In late 2005, again in Sweden, a judge sentenced Andreas Bawer, a Swedish citizen, to approximately USD 2,000 in civil penalties but no jail time for the illegal online distribution of a pirated motion picture. The court found that Bawer had violated Swedish copyright laws by making a Swedish movie available via the Internet for others to download. The software used by Bawer was not identified, and it is believed that Bawer had only copied one film and was not a large-scale provider of films via the Internet.

In mid-summer 2005, the Motion Picture Association of America (MPAA) declared losses to the motion picture industry to be approximately US$1.9 billion, due to Internet-driven film piracy. The MPAA continued, detailing how the overall piracy of films in other formats was identified as being valued at approximately USD 3.5 billion. One would expect that the MPAA would be in search of large wholesale pirates, but then the MPAA, on behalf of the major studios, filed 286 lawsuits against individuals whose names were provided by the 30 bit-torrent site operators that were shut down earlier in 2005.

These prosecutions, while totally appropriate, are truly small potatoes. Put differently, the prosecutions against "individuals" aren't difficult, because the individual doesn't have the fiscal capabilities to compete with the MPAA or industry proper. It can be argued that it would be more appropriate for the MPAA to invest its investigative funds to identify those organizations with robust infrastructures that produce thousands of copies.

In closing, and as noted in the press release from the Business Action to Stop Piracy issued on the heels of the May 2007 Group of Eight (G8) conference, counterfeiting and piracy costs businesses to lose a total of over USD 600 billion to counterfeiters each year.

Juxtapose this against the October 2005 DOPIP Security Counterfeit Intelligence Report that noted more than 341 separate incidents involving goods valued at more than USD 1 billion, and involving more than 54 separate countries. Not surprisingly, the top ten brands counterfeited were Adidas, Nike, Louis Vuitton, Microsoft, Chanel, Gucci, Prada, Fendi, Manchester United, and Puma. The report also noted that there appears to be evidence of a link between copyright and trademark infringements and more serious crimes. The report, continued that in 37 percent of the cases, counterfeiters were found to be involved in drug trafficking and use, 20 percent carry weapons, 11 percent commit other frauds, and 26 percent carry out other crimes such as assault, extortion, murder, theft, immigration violations, money laundering, identity theft, and robbery. Increasingly, a more violent type of criminal is being attracted to this activity as profit margins become larger, and penalties and chances of being arrested are relatively low (http://i-newswire.com/pr50468.html).

This vector is on a near vertical growth path, and until governments and industries unite in both reactive and proactive steps, the criminal elements will always have the upper hand and the loss of intellectual property will continue.

Chapter 9

Physical Security:
The "Duh" Factor

Introduction

If you have ever debriefed a hacker, or an industrial spy, or even a penetration tester working for the good guys, you will know that the first attempt any of them make is to simply walk through a door, whether at the front or the back of the facility. Well, perhaps they will dumpster dive prior to the direct assault. But certainly, an attacker, whether intent on breaking into your information systems, stealing your trade secrets, or demonstrating how easy it is to do either, will always probe your physical perimeter before either going cyber (e.g., gaining unauthorized network access or planting a Trojan to collect data) or even psychological (i.e., using social engineering techniques).

That's why we call physical security the "Duh" Factor. It is so easy to overlook or take for granted. And when you do, you invariably get burned. That's when people slap their foreheads and cry out, "Duh!"

Are You Owned?

How the Pros Do It

When we asked an industrial security penetration tester what his approach would be to conducting a penetration test specifically targeting intellectual property and trade secrets, one consultant responded:

"I would physically target hardware, laptops, servers, and backup media… and simply clone them en masse. I have done this countless times during "pen testing" where I simply sneak into the area, clone every computer of interest, and haul all of it off site. In other cases I simply grab the computer, and clean out everything that even remotely looked like a USB drive, external HD, CD, DVD, and ANYTHING that could even remotely contain confidential information. Sometimes the actual removal of the computer is desirable, but sometimes it is better to copy all the drives. Then consolidate all of the information onto a single drive farm, and index all of the files into a searchable data source. Yeah, I can get some of the same data by technically penetrating the computer, or owning their network, but it is much more reliable to enter the area, grab the computers, open the HDD bay and clone the drive. Extra points if you remove the HDD and leave your business card taped to the HD bay, or attached to LCD screen. I have also copied the drive (which I removed), and then hammered a steel dagger through the LCD screen or keyboard with a notice that I just cleaned them out. (I get a damage budget of maybe 50k for the gig so I can break stuff). After hours I go to the outside of every executives' offices (using a ladder if required) and try to read sensitive information which they may have left out on their desk, and use a camera to read documents they have left in view.

Hit the recycling bins in the executive area, harvest documents out of shedder or recycling boxes. Visit the server closet, remove or copy the hard drives from servers.

Visit alarm controller, remove it, or at least steal the computer connected to it. Ditto for the access control computers and video surveillance systems. Clean out all tapes, backups, off line storage, or other media. Locate breakers for computer room/server room and the executive areas, remove the circuit breaker for their specific areas, leave your card. Remove doors from executives' offices, unscrew from wall, and remove their chairs so that they have to stand up for a few hours. Remove all file cabinets… completely from the building…. Remove telephone headsets, leave the phone themselves. Extra points if your remove everything from the targeted offices, to include the doors, carpet, ceiling tiles, and install a milk crate and folding card table instead of their fancy desk. Leave their personal items on the desk, or place all personal items in a box in the center of the now stripped office. On top of the box leave an envelope, and in the enveloped leave them a letter that you just owned them, and that they need to get more serious about security.

I would (and have) provided the over 800 hard drives of extremely sensitive and classified information that they never knew they lost. I also try to weigh in with roughly 4,000 pounds of actual documents that I can pile up on a wall of the presentation room. I've actually rented semi-trucks to haul out the company, have grabbed entire mainframe computers, gutting complete server rooms, etc. Hit a defense contractor a couple of years ago, came across several huge caches inside the company (lots of classified documents), found that one of the executives/directors was stealing documents from one of their competitors, putting the CEO in a delicate position as he did the ethical thing and returned the stolen documents, and then offered up the head of the executive behind the thefts to the competition."

Nor is physical security merely a "Guards, Guns, and Gates" mentality that sees to the strength of the physical perimeter. In the 21st century, it should extend to concerns about your road warrior's mobile office, as well as conditions at the facilities of your contractors and outsourcers, and even the circumstances of any of your enterprise's storage media while in transit.

Are You Owned?

Two All-Too-Typical Tales of Woe

United Parcel Service Inc. (UPS) has confirmed that the financial data of nearly 4 million Citigroup Inc. customers has been lost…According to local media reports, Citigroup says UPS cannot account for computer tapes containing personal information—including names, Social Security numbers, account numbers and payment history—of 3.9 million of its CitiFinancial customers, including information from closed accounts.

Continued

UPS was transporting the tapes to a credit bureau when they were lost, according to the report…Citigroup says it will now encrypt financial data and send it electronically. (*Secure Destruction Business On-Line*, 6-7-05)

Users of the Bank of America Corp.'s Visa Buxx prepaid debit cards are being warned that they may have had sensitive information compromised following the theft of an unencrypted laptop computer. In a letter sent to Buxx users and dated September 23, the Charlotte, North Carolina, bank warned that customers may have had their bank account numbers, routing transit numbers, names and credit card numbers compromised by the theft. Visa Buxx is a prepaid credit card for teenagers that the Bank of America (BofA) stopped selling in January. The laptop, which belonged to an unnamed Bank of America "service provider" was stolen on August 29, said Diane Wagner, a BofA spokeswoman. The bank was notified of the theft on September 9, and began sending out the letters after a two-week investigation, she said. Though the information on the laptop would not have been easily accessible to thieves, it was not encrypted, Wagner said. She would not name the service provider, say how many BofA customers had been affected or even confirm that the theft had occurred within the U.S.… This is not the first time BofA has had to notify account holders of identity theft. In March, it confirmed that information on about 60,000 of its customers had been stolen by an identity-theft ring. The March disclosure came just a month after BofA revealed that it had lost digital tapes containing the credit card account records of 1.2 million U.S. federal employees. (IDG, 10-7-05)

Such 21st century physical security issues underscore the need for a holistic approach.

Mitigating the physical security vulnerabilities introduced by the road warrior's mobile office is dependent largely on awareness and education; e.g., you can supply your business travelers with laptop cable locks, but getting them to use them both consistently and cleverly is a very different challenge.

Seeing to the security posture of contractors and outsourcers demands that your enterprise has made a meaningful, organizational commitment to an intellectual property protection program and that no agreements will be signed without assurances that the security programs of contractors and outsourcers are adequate, and that processes for verification and review have been established.

The physical security of storage media, e.g., tapes and disks, in transit via third-party shipping companies, and so forth can only be adequately addressed by implementing a cyber security control, i.e., encryption. Table 9.1 is an IP protection program assessment for physical security.

Table 9.1 IP Protection Program Assessment—Physical Security

IP Protection Program Assessment Tool: Physical Security	Current Posture				
	100%	50%	0%	N/Z	Remarks
Does your enterprise conduct comprehensive threat assessments, on an annual basis, for all facilities in order to identify and prioritize risks?					
Do your enterprise's local security managers, or those otherwise responsible for security at the local level, regularly interface with embassy or consulate, local law enforcement, and your enterprise's own global security team on a regular basis to review vis-à-vis threats or other developments that would impact security?					
Does your global and/or local security team liaison with other security teams of other companies with interests or facilities in the area concerning risks that confront both of your organizations?					
If you rent the space for your facilities, do you engage in regular contact with building management as well as your fellow tenants concerning risks that confront all of you?					
Do your assessments factor in recent crimes and other security-related incidents, which have occurred either to your local facilities or their neighbors or surroundings?					
Have you conducted a security survey of all your enterprise's facilities to evaluate your overall security posture, including security physical and personnel security controls, information security controls, incident response, business continuity, and crisis management contingencies, etc.?					
Does your enterprise conduct such surveys annually?					
Does your enterprise maintain a record of all security incidents at all facilities, and review this record on an ongoing and regular basis both to monitor the progress of individual investigations and to look for emerging patterns, possible links, or developing trends?					
Have you identified which, if any, of your facilities are located in areas that are considered highly vulnerable to either natural risks (e.g., earthquakes or typhoons) or risks related to human activity (e.g., violent crime or terrorist attacks)?					

Continued

Table 9.1 Continued. IP Protection Program Assessment—Physical Security

IP Protection Program Assessment Tool: Physical Security	Current Posture				
	100%	50%	0%	N/Z	Remarks
Have additional security controls and contingency plans been implemented for any or all facilities located in such high-risk areas?					
If your enterprise has facilities located in such high-risk areas, has the executive team considered relocating them in less risky environments?					
Do all your enterprise's facilities have security plans that address their unique circumstances?					
Are the security plans for these facilities updated annually?					
Do your facilities have dedicated personnel (e.g., receptionists and/or telephone operators) who process all visitors and respond to calls coming into the enterprise's general telephone number?					
Have these receptionists and telephone operators been provided with training in regard to emergency situations (i.e., threatening or harassing telephone calls, political protest activity, bomb threats, visitors engaging in violent or otherwise inappropriate behavior, and so forth)?					
Do these receptionists and/or telephone operators have a discrete means to summon immediate assistance from security personnel (e.g., a "panic button" under their desks)?					
If there is such a means to summon immediate assistance from security personnel, are the device and the process it initiates tested on a regular basis?					
Do your enterprise's facilities have on-site security personnel?					
Are these on-site security people employees of your enterprise, or of the building management firm, or of third-party contractors?					
If these on-site security people are not enterprise employees, are their activities controlled directly by your enterprise or by the building management firm?					

Continued

Table 9.1 Continued. IP Protection Program Assessment—Physical Security

IP Protection Program Assessment Tool: Physical Security	Current Posture				
	100%	50%	0%	N/Z	Remarks
Do on-site security personnel undergo adequate background investigations, and can these background investigations be verified or reviewed to your satisfaction?					
Do on-site security personnel undergo adequate and appropriate security-related training before they are assigned, and can this training be verified and reviewed to your satisfaction?					
How many hours of such training do these on-site security people undergo, and what subject matters are addressed (e.g., criminal law, procedures for conducting searches, procedures for subduing and detaining suspects, how to handle emergency equipment, the basics of fire safety and first aid, and so forth)?					
Do on-site security personnel have a 24×7 presence in your facilities?					
Are the assigned contingents of on-site security people considered adequate to meet the needs of your facilities?					
Do the on-site security people assigned to your facilities rotate their posts regularly?					
Do the on-site security people assigned to your facilities respond to alarms?					
Do the on-site security people assigned to your facilities receive documented procedures that detail their personal duties and responsibility, and give them a clear understanding of your expectations?					
Do the on-site security personnel operate under direct, ongoing supervision?					
Do on-site security personnel conduct regular patrols both of the buildings in which your facilities are housed and their immediate areas?					
Do on-site security people have communication capabilities while they are on patrol (e.g., walkie-talkies, cell phones, and so forth)?					

Continued

Table 9.1 Continued. IP Protection Program Assessment—Physical Security

IP Protection Program Assessment Tool: Physical Security	Current Posture				
	100%	50%	0%	N/Z	Remarks
Is there an on-site logbook in which all security incidents are recorded, and is this logbook adequately maintained and regularly reviewed?					
If you utilize a third-party contractor for your on-site security guards, is there adequate, current, and verifiable proof that this third-party contractor upholds appropriate recruitment criteria?					
Have you installed CCTV systems, wherever they are deemed warranted, feasible, and cost-justifiable within your facilities?					
If so, do these CCTV systems provide coverage of the whole perimeter or all points of vulnerability?					
Has the CCTV coverage for your facilities been challenged in penetration tests to determine if it has blind spots in regard to physical attempts or technical vulnerabilities to technical tampering or manipulation?					
Does someone conduct live monitoring of your CCTV system, or is it recorded, or do you do both?					
Either way, or both ways, do you have documented procedures for monitoring the CCTV system?					
Does the CCTV system record the date and time? Are the CCTV systems' recordings reviewed adequately and on a regular basis?					
Is there a program of ongoing and adequate maintenance in place for your CCTV systems, and have you received sufficient and verifiable confirmation that maintenance personnel are subject to all appropriate background checks, recruitment criteria, etc.?					
Are your CCTV systems checked on a daily basis (at minimum) to make certain that all of the cameras are functioning properly?					
Have alarm systems been installed in each of your facilities, or the buildings in which they are housed?					

Continued

Table 9.1 Continued. IP Protection Program Assessment—Physical Security

IP Protection Program Assessment Tool: Physical Security	Current Posture				
	100%	50%	0%	N/Z	Remarks
Do the alarm systems only sound-off—or otherwise initiate notification—locally, or are the systems monitored at a central, off-site command center?					
Do your alarm systems link directly to appropriate law enforcement, notifying them of possible intrusions or other emergencies?					
If your alarm systems do link into appropriate law enforcement, has this law enforcement agency been provided the names and contact information of designated personnel to contact if the alarm is triggered outside of normal working hours (e.g., nights, weekends, or holidays)?					
Are the alarm systems in place throughout the whole of each building or facility, or are they only implemented in sensitive and/or vital areas?					
What intrusion detection methods or techniques are utilized in your alarm system (e.g., disrupting an infra-red light beam, or contact with a door or window)?					
Do your alarm systems cover all your facilities' exits and entrances?					
Is a password and/or other authentication/ authorization method (e.g., a key) required to activate and/or deactivate your alarm systems?					
Is the method for activating and/or deactivating the alarm systems itself adequately safeguarded? For example, if a password is required, is the password regularly changed?					
Does each person authorized to activate and/or deactivate the alarm systems have their own password or other authentication/authorization method, or is one password or device shared among numerous people?					
Do your on-site security people conduct appropriate searches of employees, visitors, contractors, etc., as they enter or leave your facilities or the buildings in which they are housed?					

Continued

Table 9.1 Continued. IP Protection Program Assessment—Physical Security

IP Protection Program Assessment Tool: Physical Security	Current Posture				
	100%	50%	0%	N/Z	Remarks
Does your enterprise have established policies and procedures that govern why, how, under what circumstances, and by whom such searches are carried out?					
Are your policies concerning searches clearly posted so that those entering and exiting the premises are made aware that your enterprise reserves the right to undertake such searches?					
Does the posted policy contain a list of those items that are not allowed into your facilities (e.g., guns, knives, illicit drugs, cameras, cell phones with cameras, audio, video recording equipment, etc.) without authorization?					
Are searches made of bags, packages, and other containers being brought into or taken out of the building?					
Have your on-site security personnel been provided with instructions and proper training, on what to do if someone refuses to comply with the search, or has been revealed to be transporting your enterprise's property (whether physical or digital) or any banned item?					
Have the security officers been adequately trained in appropriate and professional (e.g., legal, efficient, courteous, etc.) search techniques?					
Is there an established system (e.g., issuance and logging of property passes) for individuals who are taking your enterprise's property out of the building or off the premises?					
Are there established procedures to directly inform all visitors of your enterprise's prohibition against the use or possession of cameras, cell phone cameras, audio and video recording devices, etc. inside your facilities?					
Are signs notifying visitors of the prohibition against cameras, etc. (unless authorized) posted at all entrances, and as appropriate, within corridors and work areas to notify visitors of the prohibition of audio and video recording?					

Continued

Table 9.1 Continued. IP Protection Program Assessment—Physical Security

IP Protection Program Assessment Tool: Physical Security	Current Posture				
	100%	50%	0%	N/Z	Remarks
Are there established procedures to directly inform all those who enter (i.e., employees, contractors, visitors, and others) of your enterprise's prohibition against possession of guns, knives, illegal narcotics, etc. in your facilities?					
Are signs notifying visitors of your enterprise's prohibition against illegal narcotics, guns, knives, hazardous materials, etc. posted at all entrances, and as appropriate, within corridors and work areas to notify visitors of these prohibitions?					
Do all of your enterprise's employees have unrestricted access to facilities on a 24-hour basis, or do they have to request specific authorization and/or make special arrangements to access facilities after normal work hours or over weekend or holiday periods?					
Is there an established procedure and log book for employees to sign in if they are accessing facilities after normal working hours or over weekend or holiday periods?					
Is there a receptionist assigned to process all visitors and deal with other walk-in traffic at your facilities?					
Do you require all visitors to check in at an established reception area or security post?					
Do your facilities have clearly marked signage informing all visitors that they must report to the designated reception area or security post and showing them the way?					
Are policies and procedures in place for your employees to provide advanced notice reception and/or security to expect visitors on a designated day and time (including number of visitors in party and identities)?					
Are the employees notified that visitors have come to meet them by reception or security personnel?					
Do your facilities contract with an outside office cleaning service?					

Continued

Table 9.1 Continued. IP Protection Program Assessment—Physical Security

IP Protection Program Assessment Tool: Physical Security	Current Posture				
	100%	50%	0%	N/Z	Remarks
Have you received assurances that the outside cleaning service's staff has been properly vetted, and is there any way to verify this assurance?					
Are your facilities cleaned during or after normal business hours?					
Are cleaning service personnel supervised when working in executive boardrooms, executive offices, and other sensitive areas?					
Do cleaning service personnel have unfettered access to your facilities, or do you control their access?					
Does your enterprise utilize access card readers at all entrances to all facilities?					
Does your enterprise utilize access card readers at all entrances to areas in which confidential information or valuable assets are stored (e.g., computer rooms or research and development laboratories)?					
Are access control reports, which list both entry and exit times for all cardholders, generated and reviewed on a regular basis?					
Do all the office and closet doors in your enterprise's facilities have locks installed on them?					
Do your facilities' cabinets have locks installed on them, so that confidential information and other valuable assets can be securely stored?					
Does your enterprise physically secure vital equipment and other valuable assets to furniture, walls, or floors as appropriate?					
Does your enterprise issue cable locks or other security devices to personnel, contractors, etc. to secure computers and other portable equipment, and are these security devices used pervasively?					
Do the buildings that house your facilities have a master key system?					
Is a registry of all master keys maintained and kept up-to-date at all times?					

Continued

Table 9.1 Continued. IP Protection Program Assessment—Physical Security

IP Protection Program Assessment Tool: Physical Security	Current Posture				
	100%	50%	0%	N/Z	Remarks
Are master keys issued on a temporary or full time basis, or on one or the other depending upon the recipient?					
Are periodic inventories of the actual master keys conducted and in turn reconciled with what is listed in the registry, in order to determine whether or not all the keys are accounted for (i.e., that none are missing)?					
Does your enterprise or the building management assign a particular employee who is to bear personal responsibility for the giving out and retrieval of all master keys?					
Is there a list of those individuals who have been authorized to receive and use master keys, and is this list maintained adequately (e.g., complete and kept up-to-date)?					
Are master keys not in use kept secured (e.g., in a locked cabinet) for which, in turn, all keys (or combinations) are tightly held?					
Are there procedures in place for reporting the loss of keys, and is a list of such reports (with their resolutions) compiled and kept available for review when called for?					
When a master key is lost are all locks impacted by the loss changed expeditiously?					
Have all your enterprise's personnel been provided with photographic identification badges?					
Does your enterprise have procedures in place for the issuance of temporary badges for both visitors and employees who have misplaced or left behind their photo identification badges?					
Are your enterprise logos and company name intentionally kept off access control badges so that they are not easily identifiable if lost?					
Are all your enterprise's employees required to wear their identification badges in such a manner that they are easily referenced in all circumstances?					

Continued

Table 9.1 Continued. IP Protection Program Assessment—Physical Security

IP Protection Program Assessment Tool: Physical Security	Current Posture				
	100%	50%	0%	N/Z	Remarks
Does your enterprise issue photo identification badges to all contractors working on-site?					
Are the identification badges that your enterprise issues to contractors working on-site in extended engagements distinctly different from those issued to your enterprise's personnel?					
Do the identification badges your enterprise issues to on-site contractors working in limited engagements automatically expire at the time appointed for the conclusion of their engagement?					
Are all contractors required to wear their identification badges in such a manner that they are easily referenced in all circumstances?					
Does your enterprise have established procedures for ensuring that contractor badges are secured when not being used?					
Are all visitors required to wear their visitor identification badges in such a manner that they are easily referenced in all circumstances?					
Does your enterprise have established procedures for ensuring that contractor badges are secured when not being used?					
Are all visitors required to wear their visitor identification badges in such a manner that they are easily referenced in all circumstances?					
Do established policies and procedures require that all visitors be accompanied at all times during their stay at your enterprise's facilities?					
Does the employee responsible for escorting the visitor collect the visitor's identification badges before his or her guest leaves the facility?					
Are there established procedures to ensure that all visitor badges are adequately and appropriately secured when not signed out to visitors?					
Are all of the loading and shipping docks sufficiently separated from your facilities' internal areas?					

Continued

Table 9.1 Continued. IP Protection Program Assessment—Physical Security

IP Protection Program Assessment Tool: Physical Security	Current Posture				
	100%	50%	0%	N/Z	Remarks
Is all motor vehicle access to your facilities' parking areas adequately controlled and monitored?					
Is the display of some form of sticker, tag, or other form of identification required for all authorized vehicles?					
Are all your facilities' parking areas adequately secured and monitored?					
Are all your facilities' parking areas adequately illuminated during the hours of darkness?					
Is there an established procedure for maintaining a list of the license plates and owners of all motor vehicles authorized to park in your facilities' designated parking areas?					
Are all your facilities' parking areas adequately secured after normal working hours?					
Are your facilities' physical perimeters patrolled on a regular basis both during normal working hours and outside of normal working hours?					
Does the regular perimeter patrol include the inspection of doors and windows to make certain that they are adequately secured?					
Are trees, shrubs, or other growth around the facilities' perimeter trimmed on a regular basis? Are all areas surrounding your facilities properly maintained (e.g., are they kept clear of garbage to prevent an accumulation, which could create a hazard or provide cover)?					
Is all access to your facilities from building roofs safely secured?					
Is there an sufficient perimeter lighting for the buildings that house your facilities?					
Are your enterprise's mailroom personnel adequately trained in the proper methods for identifying and dealing with suspicious packages and envelopes?					

Continued

Table 9.1 Continued. IP Protection Program Assessment—Physical Security

IP Protection Program Assessment Tool: Physical Security	Current Posture				
	100%	50%	0%	N/Z	Remarks
Is a list of indicators for suspicious packages and envelopes posted prominently in the mailroom as a reminder to personnel handling incoming mail?					
Do all your enterprise's facilities have evacuation plans, which include the best routes out of the building and pre-determined gathering places?					
Are evacuation plans and procedures for your facilities tested annually at a minimum?					
Is there is an on-site manager (and at least one alternate) for each facility, who is responsible for making the determination that an evacuation should be initiated?					
Does your enterprise have established contingency plans for what to do in the event of a bomb threat at one of your facilities?					
Does your enterprise provide receptionists or telephone operators with training and documented procedures for dealing with bomb threats and collecting vital information concerning such threats when they are received?					
Does your enterprise provide receptionists and telephone operators with a checklist of emergency procedures, which is kept in a place immediately accessible to them at their workstations?					
Do your enterprise's emergency plans and procedures include instructions to notify appropriate law enforcement immediately?					
Does your enterprise have bomb search procedures, and are these procedures reviewed and tested as appropriate?					
Has your enterprise undertaken a threat assessment to identify areas in which most sensitive documents are produced and in which they are stored?					
Does your enterprise have established policies and procedures for the destruction of confidential information?					

Continued

Table 9.1 Continued. IP Protection Program Assessment—Physical Security

IP Protection Program Assessment Tool: Physical Security	Current Posture				
	100%	50%	0%	N/Z	Remarks
Does your enterprise utilize cross-cut shredders as appropriate?					
Does your enterprise utilize secure cabinets or lockers for information that is either confidential or sensitive?					
Does your enterprise have an established "clean desk" policy for all of its facilities?					
Is your enterprise's "clean desk" policy enforced?					
Are your facilities' conference rooms properly cleaned up after meetings (e.g., any notes containing sensitive information retrieved, all white boards erased)?					
Have all of your enterprise's sensitive equipment and assets been identified and properly secured?					
Have all areas that require additional security (e.g., boardrooms, executive conference rooms, and executive offices) been identified within your enterprise's facilities?					
Are all of your enterprise's boardrooms, executive conference rooms, and executive offices kept locked when not in use?					
Does one of your enterprise's employees supervise the cleaning of boardrooms, executive conference rooms, and executive offices?					
Is special attention given to boardrooms and executive conference rooms after important meetings, to make certain that they have been cleansed of all sensitive information and other proprietary materials?					
Does your enterprise utilize electronic countermeasures, as appropriate, to thwart eavesdropping in boardrooms, executive conferences rooms, and executive offices?					

Chapter 10

Protecting Intellectual Property in a Crisis Situation

Introduction

Business continuity, disaster recovery, and crisis management are vital aspects of your enterprise's overall security program. The primary concerns are, of course, the safety of your people and the rapid resumption of your operations either in the same locale or elsewhere.

But in regard to intellectual property and trade secret theft, another dimension often receives insufficient attention: protection of your data while in the midst of a crisis.

Your IT professionals should have an inventory of all your enterprise's information assets in any given area at any given time.

They should also have a replication of all those assets in a geographically separated area in the event the primary location is destroyed. In a perfect situation this replication would be accomplished via a real-time process configured for automatic switchover.

But it is not simply a question of not losing the information, or of how quickly you can get your information systems up and running again; it is also a question of the potential exposure or misappropriation of information assets that are abandoned or otherwise compromised in the chaos prior to or in the immediate aftermath of an emergency evacuation or the destruction of a building.

If the emergency is an earthquake, you get zero warning.

If the emergency is a hurricane, you get weather reports.

If the emergency is a military incursion, you will probably hear the rattling of sabers.

As your enterprise's champion of intellectual property (IP) and trade secret theft protection, you need to advocate a TEN-SEVEN-FIVE-THREE-ONE-NOW approach. If you had ten days' notice, what could you do to protect your information assets? Now make a list assuming you had only seven days.

Next, working with the seven days' list, you re-prioritize and develop a list of what you could do if you only have five days notice.

Likewise, make a list of what you can do with three days' notice.

With one day's notice, of course, you can do only the minimal. But the planning and prioritizing that goes into the process of working down from ten to one will ensure that you get the most out of that one desperate day.

And, of course, when disaster hits all of a sudden, right *now*, with no warning, it is a matter of self-preservation and assistance to those in your immediate environment.

IP Protection Designing & Planning...

The TEN-SEVEN-FIVE-THREE-ONE-NOW Approach

Here's how it works:

You are responsible for a branch office. You have your asset inventory in hand, including both human and technological assets.

You have 15 desktop computers, all possessing critical intellectual property and new developmental work, such as the designs for the newest widget and so on. You also have three storage servers, one mail server, and one server used to allow employees to create a virtual private network into the branch office when they are working in a mobile mode. You have 15 persons (14 regular staff and one visiting employee from your corporate headquarters).

You now must identify those items which require more than seven days to implement a protective regime (destruction, replication, relocation).

You should develop a list of protection measures you can take with 10 days' notice for the information assets at risk in any particular facility.

Then, working down from the 10-day list, you prioritize and draw up a list of what you can do if you only have seven days' notice.

In Table 10.1 a plan is laid out for the office itself, as well as for its vital IP elements, for example, desktop computers, the storage servers, the communications server, the corporate papers, and the personnel. Each inventoried element has a set of corresponding procedures to be enacted on the basis of amount of time remaining before the incident or disaster.

Table 10.1 Countdown Plan for Protecting Intellectual Property in Crisis Situations

Intellectual Property	Day 10	Day 7	Day 5	Day 3	Day 1	Crisis
Location of the IP (Server, Client, Safe, etc.)	Situation Normal	Items identified as taking 7 or Fewer man-days to address	Items identified as taking 5 or Fewer man-days to address	Items identified as taking 3 or Fewer man-days to address	Items identified as taking 1 day to address	Crisis – deal with crisis at hand and then address the IP at risk
Desktop Computer #1–15 – CAD diagrams, New Development Work, PII, etc.	Encrypt hard drive	N/A	Force Replication to HQ's server	Copy hard drive to DVD and encrypt	Secure or destroy hard drive	When safe, recover hard drive
Storage Server	Server encrypted Daily replication to HQ server	N/A	N/A	N/A	N/A	When safe, inspect server
Communications Server	Begin Alternate Routing protocol	100% data replication to Alt-Route location	Dual mode at Branch and at Alt-Route	Switch-over to Alt-Route	Activate Alt-Route	Activate Alt-Route
Corporate Papers	Scan crucial documents	Continue scanning	Secure or relocate all important docs according to importance	Secure or relocate all important docs according to importance	Secure all important docs	When safe, secure all important documents.
Personnel	Test phone tree and alternate forms of communication	Implement phone tree with situation report	Non-Essential personnel begin or enact alternate work environment plan	Non-Critical personnel begin or enact alternative work environment plan	Remaining personnel enact emergency procedures, if safe	Protect self – then property

On the flip side, you also have to develop a plan for re-constitution from day zero to day ten. How long is it going to take to put it all back together? Far too often, the disaster preparedness planning stops when the "crisis" appears to have concluded, and then the reassembly isn't conducted with the same level of planning. Once again, intellectual property is inadvertently put at risk.

You will also want to conduct a damage assessment that addresses, among other issues, whether there was or could have been exposure or compromise of IP or trade secrets.

If there is an earthquake, a zero notice event, and no one is in the office at the time, the lines go down and your servers are sitting there unprotected. You can mitigate the danger to your data using some technological fixes, such as encryption of the server.

If you have a facility in an environment where earthquakes are prevalent but there are no hurricanes, you are less likely to have ten-day scenarios; most of your scenarios will be zero or one-day notice, so maybe you should consider using technology such as encryption to mitigate the fact that you will not get the opportunity to off-load in your most likely emergencies.

Of course, in environments such as Seattle, where you have earthquakes, heavy rains, and flooding, as well as the threat of volcanoes and tsunamis, you have to anticipate and prepare for numerous scenarios.

When you chat with your colleagues about this issue, they will probably look at you as if you were a multi-horned beast. They will protest, "Who has the time to plan for all of that?" Our suggested response: "How can you afford not to?"

One reasonable compromise in such circumstances is to identify those locales most susceptible to day zero events in the disaster vectors—such as political hot spots, war zones, close proximity to fault lines, coastal areas vulnerable to hurricanes and tsunamis, inland areas prone to tornadoes—and address them as a priority.

But if you do not know what your inventory of information assets is, you do not know how long it will take to protect it.

You do not simply have to plan for protecting your data or destroying it; you also need to know how long it takes to do each of these tasks. You must realistically test your plan within the context of personnel and infrastructure limitations; you won't know if you can do what appears to be "impossible" unless you practice.

Answering these questions and putting a viable plan in place ensures that you are not a victim of haphazard processes, but rather are simply inconvenienced, since you planned ahead and created a solution to a potentially damaging situation.

There is more to it than being able to say, "Everyone is out alive, and we are up and running."

The best crisis management planning demands that you think outside the box, and when you factor in protecting intellectual property during a crisis situation, you must stretch your mind even more.

> **NOTE**
>
> A building housing a conglomerate's headquarters, in a developing country, burst into flames in the middle of the night.
>
> The fire brigade showed up and began to fight the flames. These were robust, physically imposing individuals, who fearlessly engaged the fire.
>
> As the fire began to come under control, but while it still was unsafe to re-enter the building, a second wave of "firefighters" arrived, looking similar to the first brigade. However, the attentive might have noticed that some of them were not as "fit." These individuals had trouble scaling the ladder into the building and didn't appear terribly happy to have been placed in this situation by their superiors.
>
> The second wave of responders turned out not to be firefighters after all. They had bribed their way into the building in an attempt to obtain items of value (presumably documents and other important papers not destroyed by the fire) under circumstances in which the rightful owners could not notice and would assume that they had been destroyed rather than stolen.

If someone is targeting your intellectual property, and is watching your company closely, it is quite possible that that person would take advantage of your misfortune, particularly if your protection program were otherwise robust. Table 10.2 is an example of an IP protection program assessment for business continuity and crisis management.

Table 10.2 IP Protection Program Assessment—Business Continuity and Crisis Management

IP Protection Program Assessment—Business Continuity and Crisis Management	Current Posture				
	100%	75%	50%	25%	Remarks
Does your enterprise have a formal Crisis Management Team (CMT), with a designated CMT Director, CMT Deputy Director, and CMT representative for all functions, facilities, regions, and/ or divisions, as appropriate?					
Does your enterprise have a documented crisis management plan, which is regularly reviewed and updated?					
Is your enterprise's crisis management plan tested regularly (for example, quarterly or annually), and does this testing include drills and exercises based on plausible scenarios?					

Continued

Table 10.2 Continued. IP Protection Program Assessment—Business Continuity and Crisis Management

IP Protection Program Assessment—Business Continuity and Crisis Management	Current Posture				
	100%	75%	50%	25%	Remarks
Does your enterprise's crisis management team maintain emergency contact numbers for all team members, delegated back-ups, and all other personnel who would be called to act in an emergency capacity?					
Does your enterprise have a designated crisis management command center?					
Is your enterprise's crisis management command center equipped with all necessary communications devices, TVs and radios, IT infrastructure, independent power supplies, and emergency supplies (water, rations, medical supplies, etc.)?					
Does your enterprise have an established Business Continuity Team?					
Does your enterprise have a formal Business Continuity Plan?					
Does your enterprise's business continuity plan identify alternate sites, as appropriate, for facilities in the event of an emergency or other natural disaster?					
Does your enterprise's business continuity plan factor in all information technology (i.e., systems and data) requirements should it be necessary to get up and running at an alternative site? COMP: Please format as a table (@TblColHd, TblTxt, etc.) The Table Col Hds "IP Protection Program … Current Posture … etc." needs to be repeated at the top of each page for continuity.					

Chapter 11

Top Ten Ways to Shut Down Hackers

Introduction

Presented in no particular order, here are the 10 best ways to shut down hackers.

Go Undercover

Keep it secret. Gandalf had it right when he said, "Keep it secret, keep it safe." Don't work on private stuff in public spaces, and don't make yourself a target. Be aware of the profile you present, and tone it down if necessary. If you've got to work on private stuff in public, consider a laptop privacy filter. Of course, bear in mind that an experienced shoulder surfer will see a privacy filter and rightly assume you're working on something sensitive. Because of this, the mere existence of a filter can make you or your machine a target. Did I mention leaving the private stuff out of public spaces? That's your best bet.

Play it smart. You might be proud of the company you work for, but sometimes flying the team colors is a bad idea. Depending on current events, the political climate or other factors anyone can become a target of public scrutiny or unwanted attention. Government agencies have requested for years that employees travel low profile, but those same agencies still produce signature items sporting the agency logo. The best advice I can offer you is to play it smart. Take a moment to consider your profile, and every now and then play it paranoid. A hacker may be the least of your worries.

Say no to stickers. If you're forced to have company stickers on your gear, consider putting a sticky note over them when you're traveling. This will at least keep the sticker (and the information that can be inferred from it) hidden from too-curious eyes.

Let's (not) go to lunch. It's all too easy to have private conversations in public spaces, especially when grabbing a bite with coworkers. Be aware that hackers love to hang out at the corporate watering hole or food trough. So, don't fill their all-too-eager ears with company jargon and secrets.

Shred Everything

The golden rule is to shred everything. But shredding is a subjective word. There are lots of varieties of shredders, each of which provides a different level of security. While a basic shredder that churns out 3/8" strip seems decent enough, it's trivial to reassemble the pieces. Obliterating your docs with a particle shredder is nice, but those things are pretty expensive, and unless you're truly evil (or paranoid), it's just overkill.

A decent "micro-cut" shredder from an office supply store will cost around $200, and can cut paper, CDs and even credit cards into 3/32 × 5/16 pieces, for better than average security. Generally speaking, you'll get what you pay for. But whatever you choose, anything's better that putting documents in the trash in one piece, or laying them in the parking lot.

It's also a great idea to get to know what's in your trash before the bad guys do. If you're in charge of security for your company, consider at least a weekly visit to your dumpster to get a feel for what's being tossed and what condition it's in when it lands in the big green box. If you're a consumer looking to protect your privacy, get a personal shredder and have a discussion with your family members about what should be shredded before being thrown away. If your family refuses to comply, you might consider relocating them.

Get Decent Locks

Forget everything you've seen on TV—all locks are not created equal. Our experts chime in on selecting a good lock. We've already seen that many locks can be shimmed. We can shutdown shimmers by selecting shim-proof locks. Here's advice for selecting a shim-proof lock:

- Select a lock that can only be shut by using the key or combination.

- Select a key *retaining padlock*, which hangs onto the key when the lock is open.

- Look for "double ball" mechanism locks.

- Select padlocks which feature a *collar* or *boot* on the shackle.

This is great advice, but I found myself asking the obvious question: "Which locks do the pros recommend?"

- EVVA MCS (www.evva.at/at/technology/mcs): Given the choice of one lock, experts agree: "Give me the MCS padlock."

- Schlage Everest Primus (http://everestprimus.schlage.com): Experts agree: the Primus is excellent. These guys were making a pick-resistant and bump-proof lock before the media even knew this was a problem.

- Abloy Protec (www.abloy.com.au): Experts say this company is great about refining their design to make many attacks ineffective."

- Sargent & Greenleaf 8088 and 8077 series locks (http://www.sargentandgreenleaf.com): These puppies are often found on Department of Defense filing cabinets.

The ABUS Diskus (http://www.acelock.com) is also worth mentioning.

Also, keep in mind that no matter how secure your locking systems may be, you should always keep your keys out of sight of the bad guys. Barry Wels of The Open Organization of Lockpickers (Toool) reminds us that professionals can "read" a key just by looking at it, giving him a head start on either duplicating the key or picking the lock it was made for. He even reports to have heard rumors that "surveillance teams try to make photographs of keys visibly worn by suspects to give the NDE (non-destructive operator) a head start …." He goes on to say in his blog at www.toool.nl/blackbag that some prison guards "carry keys in a way the inmates can not see them." One solution is to consider a customized key carrying device like a "key port" from www.key-port.com, which conceals the keys from view, but makes them simple to take out when they are needed.

Experts suggest some sound physical security advice:

- Check all locks at work and home, and report or fix any that are malfunctioning.

- Don't prop doors open, and report any that you do find propped open.

- Get all your locks re-keyed when you move into any home, and when you suspect that someone has been inside.

- Always consult a professional to evaluate the physical security of your home or workplace.

Put that Badge Away

Like Doris "Mama Soul" Troy used to sing, "Just one look, that's all it took, yeah just one look." This oldie's hook is like a hacker's anthem. One look is all a hacker needs to memorize, duplicate, laminate, infiltrate, and frustrate. Put that badge away. It really is that simple.

Check Your Surveillance Gear

If you can bypass your own security cameras and motion sensors, a bad guy can, too (and probably already has). Test out all your surveillance gear, and consider the following advice:

- Better quality cameras are less susceptible to bright light attacks.

- Domes and films can deter flaring attacks, but remember that any optic treatment can block light the camera relies on, like the infrared light used by low-light cameras.

- Use multiple cameras with fully overlapping views.

- Consider armored housing and protect the camera's video feed and power source from physical attack.

- Hidden cameras never hurt, especially when mixed with more obvious units.

Shut Down Shoulder Surfers

Watch your angles. Remain aware of the angles that shoulder surfers rely on. Don't put yourself in situations that invite shoulder surfers. Position your back to the wall when using your machine, and never leave it unattended. Don't wear company logos and remove extraneous markings and information from your mobile computing devices, especially if your company name might entice an adversary. The tech support folks in your shop can probably provide you a long list of tech things to avoid when traveling. Follow their advice.

Keep those digits to yourself. What's the point of any kind of pass code if you enter it in plain site of everyone? When entering sensitive data, create some sort of barrier between the keys and wandering eyes. This might require you to reposition your body, or create a shield with your spare hand. If you aren't willing to do this, why have a pass code at all?

Throw down! I'm not suggesting you body tackle every oddball that might be shoulder surfing you. What I would suggest is that you close your laptop (or turn off your monitor) if you think you're a target and become suddenly (and obviously) interested in something else, like sipping your coffee. Most hackers will know they've been busted and move along. If they do bail, keep a casual eye on them as they leave and try to get a good look at them and their car/bike/skateboard/Segway before they bail. When they've cleared out, take a look at what you were working on, consider all of it compromised, and act accordingly. If your surfer doesn't bail after you close your lid, keep an eye on him or her anyhow. If he or she continues acting suspiciously, do something about it. Inform a manager, security guard, or hall monitor. Do *something*. If that something involves physical violence, just don't tell the judge it was my idea.

Block Tailgaters

Don't let them in. If someone you don't recognize attempts to tailgate behind you, slam the door on their wanna-be hacker fingers. That will not only keep them out of your building, but will also put a serious cramp in their Google-hacking mojo. If they turn out not to be a hacker, apologize, and take them out for lunch. Be nice and make it a place with some one-handed fare—fast food joints offer a great selection. Strangers will come to fear you, but the security goons will love you, and that's important.

Err on the side of caution. Don't settle for taking the world at face value. Too many people see a logo or a uniform and make bad assumptions. Don't be that person. If your Spidey-sense tells you something's wrong, it probably is. If you don't have Spidey-sense, walk loudly and carry a big stick. Whatever you do, don't let the security of your home or workplace rest on poor assumptions.

Quit smoking. I love smoking entrances. They are my preferred method of entry to even the most secured facilities. So either quit smoking, buck the system and just smoke in the office, or remember that the stranger hanging outside with you might just be me.

Policy rhymes with "juicy," kind of. Policies are good. Tailgating is a difficult to stop without a corporate policy that requires all employees to challenge strangers following them into the building. If such a policy doesn't exist, employees should at least be encouraged to notify security if they think they may have let someone unauthorized inside.

Clean Your Car

Stickers are not your friends. Hackers can tell an *awful* lot by checking out your car's stickers. If you don't absolutely need them, take them off. The worst offenders are oil change stickers, parking permits, and membership stickers. Some required stickers don't need to be permanently attached. If you can get away with it, mount the sticker to an index card, and store it behind your visor when you aren't using it.

Get rid of that junk. Remember the old adage of the eight P's: "Printouts, paychecks, personal and private papers persuade peeping people." So it's not exactly wisdom of the ages, but I guess it works. That junk in your car might be much more than an eyesore—it might provide information that a bad guy could use to profile you. Prevent profiling by practicing proper pick-up. And avoid a pithy-saying battle when your opponent is armed with a thesaurus.

Play it smart, G-Man. Government parking permits on cars in the parking lot indicate a government facility is nearby. Be extra vigilant if you work in a building that contains a large number of these permits, and be on your guard as the building may be the target of an attack in the form of a tailgating, social engineering, dumpster diving exercise—or worse.

Watch Your Back Online

Avoid Instant Messaging profile pitfalls. We could do an entire book on the privacy implica-tions of using instant messenger (IM) programs. When you sign up for a new IM user account, most services create all sorts of personal data trails that a hacker or identity thief could uncover. Never enter personal information about yourself that you wouldn't give to a personal stranger. Also, make sure your client is set to confirm every action a remote user might take such as uploads, downloads, and requests for profile information. Poorly configured IM clients are bad news if you're concerned about your privacy.

Keep an eye on P2P software.   It's scary to think about a hacker targeting your personal information, but understand that P2P hacking is not about targeting specific individuals. P2P hacking is about finding interesting information based on specific keywords. If a hacker's after you, he or she is probably not going to log into a P2P client in search of your information because this makes the assumption that you're running a P2P client *and* that you have shared personal data there. Both of these are rather wild assumptions. So if you do run P2P software, make sure you know exactly what it is you are sharing, and then make sure your personal firewall, and virus/spyware/adware software is current and correctly configured.

Google yourself.   Even if it's not your fault, your personal information can end up landing on the Web. If it gets on the Web, Google will crawl it. If Google crawls it, your stuff's open to the low-tech hacking techniques of Google hackers. Googling yourself is never a bad idea, but remember that Googling an entire credit card number or all the digits of your social security number is a bad idea—the search term itself then becomes private data. Instead, search for your name and address, or a portion of your name along with a portion of a sensitive number. Better yet, use the *numrange* operator to search for your name along with a range of numbers *around* those sensitive digits. For more on advanced searching with Google, I've heard that *Google Hacking for Penetration Testers* from Syngress publishing is pretty decent.

Beware of Social Engineers

It's not about the giving.   For a social engineer, it's about getting something. You might not know when you're being conned, but whenever a stranger elicits sensitive information from you, it's a distinct possibility.

Stay constantly aware.   There are potential social engineers in every stranger who calls you.

Get into a program.   If you're in charge of security for your company, you should conduct social engineering awareness training explaining how to avoid becoming a victim. Security awareness training is the overall least expensive and most effective countermeasure that you can employ in your security plan. Role playing is an effective way of showing what social engineering looks like, as are social engineering "tiger team" attacks that focus on uncovering and revealing weaknesses and sharing lessons learned with employees.

Mutual Non-Disclosure Agreement

Introductory Note

This is a conventional form of mutual Non-Disclosure agreement.

Bracketed language is optional or provides alternatives.

Provisions that are optional include a clause prohibiting hiring of the other party's personnel and the somewhat controversial "residuals" clause. You should be careful in use of the residuals clause to be sure it fits your needs. (See discussion of this clause in Chapter 2.)

The optional "feedback" clause also carries some risk, because it allows the company that receives feedback to have a free license to information.

Mutual Non-Disclosure Agreement

This Mutual Non-Disclosure Agreement (the "Agreement") is entered into between SoftCo, Inc. ("SoftCo") and _____ ("Company") as of the date that both parties have signed this Agreement ("Effective Date").

Under this Agreement, it is contemplated that each party will disclose and discuss its Confidential Information (as defined below). The parties have entered into this Agreement to define the rights and duties of the parties concerning such disclosure. For the purposes of this Agreement, the term "Disclosing Party" will refer to either party in the case of each such party's disclosure of Confidential Information, and the term "Recipient" will refer to either party, as the case may be, in the case of each such party's receipt of Confidential Information.

1. **Definition of Confidential Information**

   1.1. "Confidential Information" means (subject to Sections 1.2 and 1.3) information that Disclosing Party provides to the Recipient, including, without limitation, information regarding Disclosing Party's technology, software, code, plans, specifications, marketing or promotion, customers, and practices and information received from others that Disclosing Party is obligated to treat as confidential.

   [Comment: Many companies do not want the risk of obtaining Confidential Information of another party that is not documented. Therefore they insist that oral or visual disclosures be confirmed in writing. However, some consider written confirmation to be too burdensome. The text at the end of section 1.2 provides a choice of either approach.]

   1.2. Information as described in paragraph 1.1 will be deemed Confidential Information only under the following circumstances: (a) if in written or tangible form, is stamped or marked as "proprietary" or "confidential" (or bears a similar legend denoting the Discloser's confidentiality interest therein), or (b) if in oral or visual form, is treated as confidential at the time of disclosure[, and is designated as confidential in a written memorandum to Recipient's primary representative within thirty (30) days of disclosure, summarizing the information disclosed] [, and is the type of information that the Recipient should reasonably have understood to be confidential].

   1.3. Confidential Information does not, however, include any information that: (i) is or subsequently becomes publicly available without Recipient's breach of any obligation owed

Disclosing Party; (ii) became known to Recipient prior to Disclosing Party's disclosure of such information to Recipient; (iii) became known to Recipient from a source other than Disclosing Party other than by the breach of an obligation of confidentiality owed to Disclosing Party; or (iv) is independently developed by Recipient.

2. **Non-Disclosure and Non-Use of Confidential Information**

   2.1. Confidential Information is provided to the Recipient for review and evaluation only. No other use is permitted.

   2.2. Recipient will not disclose Confidential Information to anyone other than its employees [and agents] who legitimately need access to it for permitted use. Recipient will notify its employees [and agents] who are given access to Confidential Information that they have an obligation not to disclose Confidential Information and will take such steps as are reasonably necessary to insure compliance with this obligation.

   2.3. Recipient will safeguard Confidential Information with reasonable security means at least equivalent to measures that it uses to safeguard its own confidential information. Recipient will store Confidential Information in a safe and secure location.

   2.4. Recipient may make copies of Confidential Information only as is necessary for its evaluation process. Recipient will duplicate on any copy of Confidential Information all copyright, trademark, trade secret, confidentiality, and patent notices found on Confidential Information. Recipient will not reverse engineer any Confidential Information in hardware or software form. Recipient will not use the Confidential Information for any product design or development unless otherwise expressly agreed in writing.

   2.5. The obligations regarding Confidential Information in this Agreement will apply [for ___ years after disclosure] [for so long as such information remains Confidential Information as provided in Section 1].

3. **Reservation of Rights**. No rights are granted by implication. In addition to the restrictions of this Agreement, Disclosing Party reserves its rights under any such patents, copyrights, trademarks, or trade secrets except as otherwise expressly provided in this Agreement.

4. [**Residuals**. The terms of confidentiality under this Agreement shall not be construed to limit either the Disclosing Party or the Recipient's right to independently develop or acquire products without use of the other party's Confidential Information. Further, the Recipient shall be free to use for any purpose the residuals resulting from access to or work with the Confidential Information of the Disclosing Party, provided that the Recipient shall not disclose the Confidential Information except as expressly permitted pursuant to the terms of this Agreement. The term "residuals" means information in intangible form, which is retained in memory by persons who have had access to the Confidential Information, including ideas, concepts, know-how or techniques contained therein. The Recipient shall not have any obligation to limit or restrict the assignment of such persons or to pay royalties for any work resulting from the use of residuals. However, this Section shall not be deemed to grant to the Recipient a license under the Disclosing Party's copyrights or patents.]

5. [**Feedback**. Either party may from time to time provide suggestions, comments or other feedback to the other party with respect to Confidential Information provided originally by the other party (hereinafter "Feedback"). Both parties agree that all Feedback is and shall be entirely voluntary and shall not, absent separate agreement, create any confidentiality obligation for the Recipient, provided that the Recipient will not disclose the source of any feedback without the providing party's consent. Except as otherwise provided herein, each party shall be free to disclose, receive, and use Feedback as it sees fit, entirely without obligation of any kind to the other party. The foregoing shall not, however, affect either party's obligations hereunder with respect to Confidential Information of the other party and this Section shall not be deemed to grant to the Recipient a license under the Disclosing Party's copyrights or patents].

6. **No Warranty**. ALL CONFIDENTIAL INFORMATION IS PROVIDED "AS IS," WITHOUT ANY EXPRESS OR IMPLIED WARRANTY OF ANY KIND.

7. **Return of Confidential Information**. Within ten business days of receipt of Disclosing Party's written request or when negotiations or business relations between Disclosing Party and Recipient cease (whichever is earlier), Recipient will return to Disclosing Party all documents containing Confidential Information. All copies of Confidential Information made by Recipient will be turned over to Disclosing Party or destroyed. For purposes of this Section, the term "documents" includes any medium, including paper, disks, optical media, magnetic memory, and any other means of recording information. The Recipient will, upon request, certify in writing that it has complied with this Section.

8. **Equitable Relief**. Recipient hereby acknowledges that unauthorized disclosure or use of Confidential Information will cause immediate and irreparable harm to Disclosing Party. Accordingly, Disclosing Party will have the right to seek and obtain preliminary and final injunctive relief to enforce this Agreement in case of any actual or threatened breach, in addition to other rights and remedies that may be available to Disclosing Party.

9. [**Hiring Restraint**. From the Effective Date of this Agreement and continuing for one year after business discussions contemplated by this Agreement terminate (which, for the purposes of this Section will be presumed to be the situation if no business discussions under this Agreement have taken place for 30 days), each party agrees not to hire or attempt to hire executive, marketing, sales, or technical employees of the Company whose identity or qualification were disclosed to the other during the negotiations.]

10. **General Provisions**

    10.1.   This Agreement constitutes the entire agreement of the parties concerning its subject matter and supersedes all prior or contemporaneous oral or written agreements concerning this subject.

    10.2.   This Agreement may not be assigned by either party and neither party's obligations under this Agreement may be delegated without the prior written consent of the other party. Subject to such restriction, this Agreement is binding and inures to the benefit of the permitted successors and assigns.

10.3.   This Agreement may be amended only by a writing signed by both parties.

10.4.   This Agreement will be governed by and construed in accordance with the substantive laws of _____. The state and federal courts located in _____ will have exclusive jurisdiction and venue over any dispute arising from this Agreement or its subject matter.

So Agreed by the parties:

SoftCo, Inc.   Company: _____

By:_____   By:_____

Name:_____   Name:_____

Title:_____   Title:_____

Date:_____   Date:_____

Appendix 2

Evaluation Agreement (Pro-Recipient)

161

Introductory Note

This simple evaluation agreement is drafted for the benefit of the recipient of software or other material for evaluation use. It is drafted as the form agreement of the fictitious software company SoftCo, Inc.

The company that uses this form promises very little—and that's the whole idea. The form expressly gives the recipient the right to develop products similar to those submitted for evaluation, and it gives no assurances of confidentiality. The person or company that submits information under this form has the protection of the copyright laws and (if applicable) patents, but nothing else.

Evaluation Agreement

IF YOU ACCEPT AND AGREE WITH ALL OF THE PROVISIONS OF THIS AGREEMENT, PLEASE SIGN THIS AGREEMENT AND RETURN IT (BY MAIL, FAX OR AS AN EMAIL PDF) TO SOFTCO, INC. ("SOFTCO") TOGETHER WITH A COPY OF YOUR MATERIAL FOR SUBMISSION. THIS AGREEMENT COVERS BOTH ELECTRONIC AND PHYSICAL SUBMISSION OF YOUR MATERIAL, INCLUDING ANY MATERIAL YOU SUBMIT BEFORE OR AFTER SIGNING AND RETURNING THIS AGREEMENT.

IF YOU DO NOT ACCEPT AND AGREE WITH ANY PROVISION OR PARAGRAPH OF THE AGREEMENT, DO NOT SUBMIT YOUR MATERIAL TO SOFTCO.

1. You represent that you are 18 years of age or older. If you are younger than 18, you should include with this Agreement a written consent from your parent or legal guardian for your entering into this Agreement.

2. You hereby authorize SoftCo to use and copy your program, content or other material ("Material") for evaluation. You agree that SoftCo owes you no compensation for submitting the Material to SoftCo. SoftCo may (but is not obligated to) decide to negotiate an agreement with you to exploit the Material for commercial purposes.

3. You represent and warrant (a) that you have all rights to provide the Material, (b) that your submission of the Material to SoftCo and SoftCo's copying and use for its review and evaluation of such Material will not violate or infringe any personal or property right of any person or entity and (c) that your Material does not constitute a defamation of any person or entity. You also represent that you are the sole owner of the Material and all rights therein and that it is your own original work. You agree to indemnify SoftCo and hold SoftCo harmless from any claim asserting actual or alleged infringement or violation of any third party rights that arises from the Material if used by SoftCo as permitted in this Agreement.

4. You represent that the Material you are submitting is not obscene, pornographic, defamatory, or illegal.

5. Your submission of the Material does not create any confidential or fiduciary relationship between you and SoftCo.

6. You represent that you have retained one or more copies of the Material in your possession. SoftCo is not obligated to return the Material. SoftCo will not be liable to you if any Materials are destroyed, damaged or misplaced.

7. SoftCo may, from time to time, receive submissions of material similar to yours, or we may be developing similar materials, content, ideas, or products. SoftCo does not agree to treat as confidential your Material, your ideas or any information which you may choose to disclose to us during the course of our evaluation whether or not marked as confidential or proprietary.

8. SoftCo's acceptance of your material for evaluation does not imply that SoftCo will market your material nor does it prevent us from marketing or developing other products which may be similar in idea or concept so long as we do not infringe your copyright or patent rights.

9. This Agreement will remain in effect indefinitely and covers all Materials that you may provide.

10. This Agreement is subject to the substantive laws of the state of _____. Any disputes or claims that you may have against SoftCo regarding this Agreement or the Material will be resolved exclusively by the state or federal courts located in the state of _____ USA in the city of _____, and you agree and submit to the exclusive jurisdiction of such courts.

11. This is a complete statement of the agreement of the parties and supersedes any other oral or written understanding or agreement.

By signing below, you accept and agree to the foregoing as a binding agreement between SoftCo and you.

[*Signature*]

If you are an individual, print your name and address:

Print Name: _____

Address: _____

_____

Date: _____

If the party entering into this Agreement is a corporation or other business entity, print the name of the entity and its address and the name and title of officer or agent signing this Agreement:

Print Company Name: _____

Print Signer's Name and Title: _____

Address: _____

Date: _____

Appendix 3

Employee Agreement

165

Introductory Note

This is a form of Employee Agreement. You should review Chapter 3 *before using it, and you may wish to seek advice of your own legal counsel because employment law has significant state-by-state variations.*

This form includes both non-competition provisions and restraints on solicitation of other employees or customers.

As noted in Chapter 3, *some states require, as a condition of enforcing such restraints, that the employer make a payment to the employee in cash (or something else of value) as "consideration" for the restraint, particularly if the agreement is signed after employment begins.*

If you are a California employer, you should know that California prohibits most non-competition restraints. California law on non-solicitation clauses is less clear, but it is possible that the non-solicitation restraints in the following form may need to be narrowed or modified to meet California requirements. Another California requirement is to give employees notice of California Labor Code Section 2870. There are analogous notice requirements in some other states. (These laws are discussed in Chapter 3.)

This form contains some optional and alternative provisions in brackets.

Employee Agreement

This Employee Agreement (the "Agreement") is entered into by and between *[name of employer corporation or entity]* ("Employer"), and the individual whose name appears on the signature page below (the "Employee"). This Agreement is effective as of the Effective Date (as defined below).

   Purpose of This Agreement. Employer desires to employ Employee, and Employee desires to be employed by Employer subject to the terms and conditions contained in this Agreement. Employee and Employer agree that the following provisions are fair and appropriate for protection of the Employer's interests.

   THEREFORE, in consideration of the mutual promises of this Agreement, and other good and valuable consideration, the receipt and sufficiency of which are acknowledged by the parties, Employer and Employee agree as follows:

1. **Definitions**. Capitalized terms used herein and not otherwise defined herein will have the meanings set forth below:

    1.1. "Affiliate" will mean, for a specified business entity, a business entity which directly or indirectly through one or more intermediaries, controls, is controlled by or is under common control with such entity.

    1.2. "Company" will mean Employer and all Affiliates of Employer.

    1.3. "Company Business" will mean the business and technical activities, products and services, and operations of the Company as presently conducted, included plans for expansion of the same, and such other additional activities, products and services, and operations as may be conducted or planned at any time during the Employment Period.

    1.4. "Confidential Information" means any information or data, whether in oral, graphic, written, optical, electronic, machine-readable, hard copy or any other form, possessed by, used by, or under the control of Company that is not generally available to the public. Confidential Information includes but is not limited to inventions, designs, data, source code, object code, programs, other works of authorship, know-how, trade secrets, techniques, ideas, discoveries, technical, marketing and business plans, customers, suppliers, pricing, profit margins, costs, products, and services.

1.5.   "Effective Date" is the earlier of (i) the beginning of Employee's employment with Company, (ii) the date and time at which any Confidential Information was, or is, first disclosed to Employee, or (iii) the date that both parties have signed this Agreement.

1.6.   "Intellectual Property Rights" will mean all copyrights, copyright registrations and copyright applications, trademarks, service marks, trade dress, trade names, trademark registrations and trademark applications, patentable inventions or discoveries, patents and patent applications, trade secret rights, and all other rights and interests existing, created or protectable under any intellectual property law of any nation.

1.7.   "Restriction Period" will mean during the period of Employee's employment with the Company and for a period of _____ [months] [years] following the date on which Employee's employment with Company is terminated regardless of cause.

1.8.   "Work Product" means any and all inventions, discoveries, original works of authorship, Intellectual Property Rights, developments, improvements, formulas, techniques, concepts, data and ideas (whether or not patentable or registrable under patent copyright, or similar statute) made, conceived, created, discovered, or reduced to practice by Employee, either alone or jointly with others, that (i) result from work performed by Employee for Company or are created in the course of his or her employment, (ii) are made by use of the equipment, supplies, facilities, or Confidential Information of Company or are made, conceived or completed, wholly or in part, during hours in which Employee is employed by Company, or (iii) are related to the Company Business or the actual or demonstrably anticipated business plan, research or development of Company.

2.   **Employment**

2.1.   Employee acknowledges that he or she is and will be employed by Company "at-will" and that either Company or Employee will have the right to terminate Employee's employment at any time for any reason or for no reason at all. The period of time during which Employee is employed by Company is sometimes referred to herein as the "Employment Period."

2.2.   Employee acknowledges that his or her employment with the Company constitutes adequate consideration for this Agreement. [In addition, Employee acknowledges actual receipt of the sum of $_____ in connection with and as consideration for this Agreement.]

3.   **Confidential Information**

3.1.   Employee acknowledges and agrees that Confidential Information constitutes a valuable asset of Company and is and will be the sole property of Company. Where Employee has any doubt whether information is Confidential Information, Employee will request a determination from his or her supervisor.

3.2. Employee agrees to preserve and protect the confidentiality and security of Confidential Information. At all times during and after Employee's employment with Company, Employee will hold in trust, keep confidential and not disclose to any third party or make any use of, the Confidential Information, except as may be authorized by the Company in the course of Employee's employment.

3.3. Employee agrees to abide by policies established by Company for the protection of Confidential Information, and to take reasonable security precautions to safeguard Confidential Information, including without limitation, the protection of documents from theft, unauthorized duplication and discovery of contents, and restrictions on access by other persons.

3.4. Employee acknowledges that unauthorized use or disclosure of Confidential Information will be prejudicial to the interests of Company or the entities with which Company has business relationships and may be an invasion of privacy or a misappropriation or improper disclosure of trade secrets.

3.5. Employee agrees that all documents containing Confidential Information, whether produced by Employee or others, are at all times the property of Company.

4. **Third Party Information**

4.1. Employee acknowledges that Company has received and in the future may receive confidential or proprietary information from third parties, subject to a duty on Company's part to maintain the confidentiality of the information and to use it only for certain limited purposes. Employee agrees to hold all such confidential or proprietary information in the strictest confidence in compliance with the terms of any agreement or other obligation Company may have with such third parties, and not to disclose it to any person, firm or corporation or to use it except as necessary in carrying out Employee's duties for Company, consistent with the terms of any agreement Company may have with such third parties.

5. **Return of Company Property**. Upon termination of employment with Company for any reason, Employee will promptly deliver to Company all Company documents and materials pertaining to (i) Employee's employment, (ii) the Confidential Information of Company or the other entities with which Company has relationships, or (iii) Work Product (as defined above), whether prepared by Employee or otherwise coming into Employee's possession or control. Employee also agrees to return to Company all equipment, files, software programs and other personal property belonging to Company on separation from employment. Employee will not retain any written or other tangible materials (in hard copy or electronic form) that evidence, contain or reflect Confidential Information or Work Product of Company. Employee agrees, on or before the date of termination of employment, to execute and deliver to Employer a Termination Certification in the form set forth as Exhibit A to this Agreement.

6. **Work Product**

6.1. *Assignment*. All Work Product is and will be the sole property of Company. Employee hereby assigns to Company, without royalty or further consideration to Employee, all rights, title, and interest Employee may have, or may acquire, in and to all Work Product including but not limited to all Intellectual Property Rights. Employee agrees that Company or its designee will be the sole owner of all domestic and foreign patents, patent rights, copyrights, and other Intellectual Property Rights included in or pertaining to all Work Product.

6.2. *Disclosure.* Employee will promptly disclose all Work Product that consists of inventions, discoveries, developments, improvements, formulas, techniques, concepts, data or ideas to Company in writing. Employee agrees to keep adequate and current written records of all such Work Product, in the form of notes, sketches, drawings, electronic records and/or other reports, which records are, and will remain, the property of Company and will be available to Company at all times.

6.3. *Copyrights.* Employee further agrees that all copyrightable materials that Employee authors, creates, modifies, or prepares, wholly or in part, will be, to the maximum extent permitted by law, work-made-for-hire for the Company under copyright law, and to the extent not work-made-for-hire are hereby assigned to the Company.

6.4. *Execution of Documents.* Whenever requested by Company, Employee will promptly sign and deliver to Company, both during and after employment, any and all applications, assignments and other documents that Company considers necessary or desirable in order to: (a) assign, apply for, obtain, and maintain letters patent or other forms of Intellectual Property protection or registration in the United States and for other countries with regard to Work Product, (b) assign and convey to Company or its designee the sole and exclusive right, title, and interest in and to Work Product, (c) provide evidence regarding Work Product that Company considers necessary or desirable, and (d) confirm or perfect Company's ownership of the Work Product, all without royalty or any other further consideration to Employee.

6.5. *Assistance to Company.* Whenever requested by Company, both during and after employment, Employee will assist Company, at Company's expense, in assigning, obtaining, maintaining, defending, registering and from time to time enforcing, in any and all countries, Company's right to the Work Product including but not limited to Intellectual Property Rights. This assistance may include, without limitation, testifying in a suit or other proceeding and executing all documents deemed by Company to be necessary or convenient for such purposes. If Company requires assistance from Employee after termination of Employee's employment, Employee will be compensated for time actually spent in providing assistance at an hourly rate equivalent to Employee's salary or wages at the time of termination of employment together with Employee's reasonable expenses of providing such assistance.

6.6. *Power of Attorney.* For use in the case that Company cannot obtain Employee's signature on any document that Company considers necessary or desirable in order to assign, apply for, prosecute, obtain, or enforce any patent, copyright or other right or protection relating to any Work Product, whether due to Employee's mental or physical incapacity, non-cooperation, unavailability, or any other reason, Employee hereby irrevocably designates and appoints Company and each of its duly authorized officers and agents as Employee's agent and attorney-in-fact to act for, and on Employee's behalf, to execute and file any such document and to do all other lawfully permitted acts to further the assignment, transfer to Company, application, registration, prosecution, issuance, and enforcement of patents, trademarks, trade secrets, copyrights, or other rights or protections, with the same force and effect as if executed and delivered by Employee.

6.7.   *Excluded Work Product.* Employee represents that any inventions, original works of authorship, discoveries, concepts or ideas, if any ("Excluded Work Product") to which Employee presently has any right, title or interest, and which were previously conceived either wholly or in part by Employee, and that Employee desires to exclude from the operation of this Agreement are identified on Exhibit B of this Agreement. Employee represents that the list contained in Exhibit B is complete to the best of Employee's knowledge.

6.8.   [*California Labor Code Section 2870.* This Section 6 does not apply to any Work Product to the extent that it is subject to the provisions of Section 2870 of the California Labor Code as described in Exhibit C to this Agreement.]

7.   Non-Competition; Non-Solicitation

7.1.   [*Non-Competition.* During the Restriction Period, Employee will not engage or become interested, directly or indirectly, as an owner, employee, director, partner, consultant, through stock ownership, investment of capital, lending of money or property, rendering of services, or otherwise, either alone or in association with others, in the operation, management or supervision of any type of business or enterprise that at any time during the Restriction Period is in competition with the Company Business, except that this provision will not be breached by Employee's ownership of shares in a publicly-traded corporation or publicly-traded mutual fund or publicly-traded limited partnership in which Employee's ownership interest is five percent (5%) or less. [Employee acknowledges that the scope of the markets in which Company competes is global and therefore agrees that no geographic limitations on this non-competition provision of this Section will apply.] [The geographic scope of the limitations set forth in this Section will extend to every geographic market, state, province or country in which Company or any Affiliate does business during the term of this Agreement or in which the Company or any Affiliate was, during the term of this Agreement, actively planning or preparing to do business.]

7.2.   *Non-Solicitation.* During the Restriction Period, Employee will not, directly or indirectly, whether on behalf of himself or anyone else: (i) solicit or accept orders from any present or past customer of the Company for a product or service offered or sold by, or competitive with a product or service offered or sold by, the Company; (ii) induce or attempt to induce any such customer to reduce such customer's purchases from the Company; (iii) use for his or her benefit or disclose the name and/or requirements of any such customer to any third party; or (iv) solicit any of the Company's employees to leave the employ of the Company or hire anyone who is an employee of the Company.

7.3.   *Judicial Modifications.* If any restriction set forth in this Section is found by a court of competent jurisdiction to be unenforceable because it extends for too long a period of time or over too great a range of activities or in too broad a geographic area, it will be enforced only over the maximum period of time, range of activities or geographic area for which it may be enforceable.

8. **Remedies of Company**

   8.1. *Injunction*. Employee acknowledges that immediate and irreparable damage will result to the Company and its business and properties if Employee breaches the obligations of this Agreement regarding Confidential Information or the provisions set forth in Section 6 or Section 7 of this Agreement and that the remedy at law for any such breach will be inadequate. Accordingly, in addition to any other remedies and damages available, the Company shall be entitled to injunctive relief without the necessity of posting a bond, and Employee may be specifically compelled to comply with such obligations under this Agreement.

   8.2. *Expenses*. Company shall be entitled to reimbursement by Employee for all costs and expenses, including reasonable attorneys' fees, which Company may incur in connection with the enforcement of its rights regarding Confidential Information or under Sections 6 and 7 of this Agreement.

9. **Notices and Other Communications**. All notices and other communications will be in writing and will be deemed effectively given upon personal delivery, and in the case where delivery is made by an established courier delivery service, delivery will be deemed to occur on the day after delivery to such delivery service, upon confirmed completion of transmission in the case where such notice is transmitted by telecopy, or on the fifth (5th) day following mailing by registered or certified mail, return receipt requested, postage prepaid, addressed (a) if to Employee, at his or her address set forth below his or her signature, and (b) if to Company at the following address: *[indicate address for notice]* or addresses as the parties may specify by a written notice to the other from time to time.

10. **Entire Agreement; Amendment; Survival**. This Agreement constitutes the entire agreement between the parties and supersedes all prior agreements and understandings, whether written or oral, relating to the subject matter of this Agreement. This Agreement may be amended or modified only by a written instrument executed by both Company and Employee. The provisions of this Agreement (except for Section 2.1) will survive the termination of Employee's employment and the assignment of this Agreement by Company to any successor-in-interest or other assignee.

11. **Governing Law**. This Agreement will be construed, interpreted and enforced in accordance with the laws of the state of _____, not including its choice of law provisions. Both parties agree to jurisdiction and venue in the state and federal courts located in _____ with regard to this Agreement and its subject matter.

12. **Successors and Assigns**. This Agreement will be binding upon and inure to the benefits of both parties and their respective successors and assigns; provided, however, that the obligations of Employee are personal and will not be assigned by Employee.

13. **Miscellaneous**. No delay or omission by Company in exercising any right under this Agreement will operate as a waiver of that or any other right. A waiver or consent given by Company on any one occasion will be effective only in that instance and will not be

construed as a bar or waiver of any right on any other occasion. In case any provision of this Agreement will be invalid, illegal or otherwise unenforceable, the validity, legality and enforceability of the remaining provisions will in no way be affected or impaired.

EMPLOYEE ACKNOWLEDGES AND UNDERSTANDS THAT THIS AGREEMENT AFFECTS HIS OR HER RIGHTS TO INVENTIONS HE OR SHE MAKES DURING HIS OR HER EMPLOYMENT BY THE COMPANY, [CONTAINS NON-COMPETITION AND] NON-SOLICITATION PROVISIONS, AND RESTRICTS HIS OR HER RIGHTS TO DISCLOSE OR USE THE COMPANY'S CONFIDENTIAL INFORMATION DURING SUCH EMPLOYMENT AND THEREAFTER.

This Agreement is executed as a binding agreement of the parties as of the Effective Date.

Employee

Name: _____

Address: _____

Signature: _____ Date: _____
[**Employer Name**] by its authorized agent:

Name: _____

Address: _____

Signature: _____ Date: _____

Exhibit A

Termination Certification

This is to certify that I do not have in my possession, nor have I failed to return, any devices, records, data, notes, reports, proposals, lists, correspondence, specifications, drawings, sketches, materials, equipment, other documents or property or any reproductions of any of these items belonging to Company, its subsidiaries, Affiliates, successors or assigns (collectively "the Company").

I further certify that I have complied with, and will continue to comply with, all the terms of Employee Agreement that I signed with the Company, including, without limitation, those that relate to Work Product, Confidential Information, [Non-Competition], and Non-Solicitation of customers and Company employees.

Upon the termination of my employment with Company, I will be employed by _____ _____ and will be working in connection with the following technologies and business areas: _____.

Employee Name: _____

Date: _____

Signature: _____

Address for Notifications: _____

_____

_____

Exhibit B

Employee Statement
Regarding Employee's Prior Work Product

Except as set forth below, I acknowledge that at this time I have not made or reduced to practice (alone or jointly with others) any Work Product relevant to the subject matter of my employment with Company except those (if any) listed below:

[Employee to list any applicable Work Product or write "None."]

Employee certifies that the foregoing is true, accurate and complete.

Employee Name: _____

Date: _____

Signature: _____

Exhibit C

Notification to Employee of California Labor Code Section 2870

The provisions of this Agreement regarding ownership of Work Product do not apply to Employee's inventions which qualify for protection under California Labor Code ("Section 2870"). As currently in effect, Section 2870 covers Employee's inventions for which no equipment, supplies, facility or trade secret information of Company was used and which were developed entirely in Employee's own time, and (i) which do not relate, at the time of conception or reduction to practice of the invention, to the business of Company, or to Company's actual or demonstrably anticipated research or development, or (ii) which do not result from any work performed by Employee for Company. Employee agrees to disclose to Company during the term of his or her employment in confidence each such invention in order to permit the Company to make a determination as to compliance by Employee with this Agreement. Employee acknowledges that it is his or her burden to prove to Employer that Section 2870 applies.

Employee acknowledges receipt of this notice.

Employee Name: _____

Date: _____

Signature: _____

Software Development Agreement

Introductory Note

This is a sample software development agreement. This is a "long form" that is designed for substantial custom software development. It could also be used for major customization of the Developer's pre-existing application. This is a relatively balanced form, but some variations favor one party or the other.

This draft includes many provisions that commonly occur in these agreements, including some common variants and alternatives (but certainly does not have all possible variants). There are further variations discussed in Chapter 4 of this book. Text in brackets within sections is also optional. There are some combinations and permutations that work together and some that will not make sense when combined, so you need to be sure you think through how sections work with one another.

We left the Schedule letters (or numbers) to be filled in because there are many choices in this text.

Software Development Agreement

This Software Development Agreement ("Agreement") is effective as of *[insert date]* (the "Effective Date") between _____ ("Customer") with an office at _____ and _____ ("Developer") with an office at _____.

Purpose of This Agreement

This is an Agreement for Developer to develop software for Customer in accordance with the terms set forth below.

Wherefore, intending to bound, the parties agree as follows:

1. **Definitions**

*[**Comment:** Definitions in any agreement need careful attention because they often depart from the "plain meaning" of a word or phrase or resolve ambiguities in ways that favor one side or the other. Additional definitions can appear in the text and in schedules. Depending on choices that you make in the remainder of the Agreement, you may need to add to these definitions or delete some of them.]*

As used in this Agreement, the following definitions will apply:

1.1. "Affiliate" means any corporate entity that controls, is controlled by or is under the common control of a party to this Agreement.

1.2. "Defect" means, with respect to any Deliverable, any material deviation from the Specification [or any defect in quality or operation].

1.3. "Deliverables" are the items that are specified in the Specification and the Milestone Schedule as items to be delivered to Customer.

1.4. "Intellectual Property" means all inventions, discoveries, patents, trademarks, domain names, design rights, copyrights, database rights, know-how, trade or business names, and other similar rights (in each case whether or not registered or registerable and including all applications for any registerable rights) throughout the world, for the full duration of such rights.

1.5. "Milestone" means each stage of development of the Program as set out alongside a Milestone Date in the Milestone Schedule.

1.6. "Milestone Date" means each of the dates for achieving a Milestone in the Milestone Schedule.

1.7.   "Milestone Payment" means each of the Milestone-based payments set forth in the Milestone Schedule.

1.8.   "Milestone Schedule" means the delivery and payment schedule for the Program [as described in Schedule __] [as developed under this Agreement], as it may be amended from time to time by written agreement of the parties hereto.

1.9.   "Program" will mean the computer program entitled [*name of program*] to be developed by Developer, which will consist of all Deliverables [including the User Manual], as stated in the Specification and the Milestone Schedule.

1.10.   "Services" means Developer's services to be provided under this Agreement.

1.11.   "Specification" means the specifications for the Program as set forth in Schedule __, with any modifications that may be agreed upon by the parties in writing. [After the parties' agreement on the Detailed Specification prepared under this Agreement, the term "Specification" will refer to the Detailed Specification.]

1.12.   "User Manual" means a manual containing instructions for end users that enables them to operate the Program.

[Optional Provision:]

2.   **Preparation of Detailed Specification**

2.1.   Developer will prepare a detailed specification ("Detailed Specification") for the Program on or before [date]. The Detailed Specification will include, at a minimum:

2.1.1.   A detailed statement of the Program's functionality.

2.1.2.   A specification of third party products and technologies to be included in the Program.

2.1.3.   A Milestone Schedule for development.

2.1.4.   The total development cost and expected expenses.

2.1.5.   A detailed schedule of Milestones and Milestone Payments.

2.2.   After submission of the Detailed Specification documents mentioned in the previous Section, the Customer may accept or reject the same in writing. [Failure of Customer to reject the Detailed Specification in ___ days will constitute acceptance.]

2.3.   In the case of rejection of the Detailed Specification, the parties will confer in good faith regarding changes to the Detailed Specification. If there is no written agreement on a Detailed Specification in a further __ days, either party may terminate this Agreement without fault. In case of such a termination, each party will be discharged of further obligations except as follows:

2.3.1.   The parties will remain obligated under provisions regarding Confidential Information (as stated below).

2.3.2.   Developer will be paid for the Detailed Specification on the following basis: [*describe compensation; it may be a fixed fee or hourly with a cap*].

2.3.3. [Customer will be free to use the versions of the Detailed Specification supplied by Developer for any purpose, provided that Developer makes no warranty as to results that may be obtained from such versions of the Detailed Specification, and Developer will be deemed to supply the Detailed Specification "AS IS."]

3. **Development of Program**

*[**Comment:** In this section, the Developer undertakes a duty to create the Program in accordance with the Specification.]*

3.1. [On the Effective Date or within [*number*] of days thereafter] [upon acceptance of the Detailed Specification], Developer will begin work [and will use reasonable efforts] to develop the Program.

4. **Change Orders**

*[**Comment:** Disputes arise from changes to the Specification that are not documented. Often customers will ask for additional features without expecting to pay more. Developers will do extra work as a result and expect extra pay. This draft requires the parties to negotiate changes in specifications, payment, and delivery schedules.]*

4.1. Either Customer or Developer may propose a "Change Order." Change Orders are effective when signed by both parties. The parties agree to include in each Change Order as many of the following as are relevant:

4.1.1. Description of the change.

4.1.2. Description of the additional or changed services to be performed by Developer.

4.1.3. Effects of the change on the Specification.

4.1.4. New or changed Customer obligations.

4.1.5. Effects on the Milestone Schedule, including dates and pricing of services.

4.1.6. Changes in acceptance criteria.

4.2. Customer may not require work or features not set forth in the Specification unless agreed to in writing in a Change Order. Developer will not be compensated, other than as stated in the Agreement, unless such additional payments are agreed to in a Change Order in advance in writing or unless otherwise agreed in writing.

[Optional Provision:]

5. **Resources to Be Provided to Developer**

*[**Comment:** Sometimes the Developer needs technical or business information from the Customer to do its work. Sometimes the Developer needs access to the Customer's computer system or to a code base in the Customer's possession. The following clause deals with these and other such requirements. Where the Customer's cooperation is substantial or it has to supply software, data, or content for the Developer to use, these requirements could be put in a separate schedule.]*

5.1. Customer will supply to Developer all information and resources that Developer will reasonably require to carry out the work required by this Agreement, including: *[include list or refer to a schedule of Customer tasks].*

5.2. [Customer grants to the Developer a non-exclusive, non-transferable, and limited license to use the Customer's software and other materials solely as necessary to perform its obligations under this Agreement.]

6. **Responsibility for Employees**

6.1. Developer is solely responsible for paying the salaries and wages of its employees, for ensuring that all required tax withholdings are made, and for ensuring that each employee has the legal right to work in the United States. Developer further agrees that it is solely responsible for workers' compensation insurance. Developer will defend, indemnify and hold harmless Customer, its affiliates, and their respective officers, directors, employees, servants and agents from any cost, including attorneys' fees, and any liability that arises from Developer's breach of these obligations.

7. **Subcontractors**

[Option 1. Subcontractors Restricted.]

7.1. [Unless otherwise authorized in writing by Customer, Developer will provide all Services by use of its own employees. Developer will use subcontractors under this Agreement only with Customer's express prior written permission.]

[Option 2. Subcontractors Permitted.]

7.2. Developer may retain qualified subcontractors to work under this Agreement. Developer warrants the performance and full compliance with this Agreement by each subcontractor. Developer will be responsible for all acts and omissions of each subcontractor and each subcontractor's staff, as if they were Developer's own acts and omissions.

8. **Assigned Personnel**

8.1. "Personnel" means those individuals engaged by the Developer, whether as employees or (if permitted) as subcontractors or the subcontractors' employees.

8.2. [The Personnel assigned to work under this Agreement will be those listed on Schedule __. The Developer will not reassign such Personnel to any other work without Customer's prior written consent. If any such Personnel are no longer available to Developer, Developer will supply equally qualified replacements, which will be assigned to work under this Agreement only with Customer's prior written consent.]

8.3. Developer will ensure that its employees and permitted subcontractors will, whenever on Customer's premises (or on any Customer's client's premises or other location), obey all applicable work and safety rules.

8.4.   Developer has obtained and will at all times obtain and maintain in effect non-disclosure, assignment of rights and other appropriate agreements with its employees and (if use of subcontractors is permitted) subcontractors sufficient to protect Customer's Confidential Information and sufficient to allow it to provide Customer with the assignments and licenses provided for herein. Such agreements must contain terms and conditions no less restrictive than the terms and conditions set forth in this Agreement. [Upon Customer's request, Developer will cause all employees and subcontractor staff members engaged under this Agreement to sign Customer's form of Intellectual Property Transfer and Confidentiality Agreement, as issued by Customer from time to time.]

*[**Comment:** The final text (in brackets) is designed to obtain from each member of the Developer's team an obligation to assign intellectual property. This is prudent if the development work is likely to result in patentable inventions, because a company that wants to patent an invention must get the individual inventor(s) to assign the patent rights.]*

9.   **Delivery and Acceptance of Deliverables**

*[**Comment:** The following provision mandates delivery within dates specified in the Milestone Schedule. Optional language allows the Developer some flexibility in meeting deadlines. There are many ways to write provisions under which the Customer may accept or reject the Milestones. The version that follows provides a time frame for Customer's acceptance and allows a cure period if the Program is rejected. As an option, this version also allows the Customer to accept a defective Program and to have Defects fixed at the Developer's expense.*

There is an optional provision stating that Customer's "productive use" of a Program is deemed acceptance. This clause is used by Developers to avoid the Customer using the Program in its business while claiming it is defective and refusing to make the final payments.]

9.1.   Developer will deliver various Deliverables at the times and in the manner specified in the Milestone Schedule. [At its option, Developer may extend the due dates of the Milestone Schedule by giving written notice to the Customer provided that the total of all such extensions will not exceed *[specify number]* days.]

9.2.   Each Deliverable that consists of software [will be delivered in binary form only][will be delivered in binary form together with source code, programming documentation sufficient to permit replication of the binary Deliverables, and any relevant Developer proprietary programming tools].

9.3.   [If Developer fails to make timely delivery of any Deliverable as specified in the Milestone Schedule, Customer may give Developer notice of the failure. After such notice, Developer will have *[specify number]* days to make the specified delivery. Failure to submit the Deliverables within such period will be a material breach that will entitle Customer to terminate this Agreement in accordance with the provisions on termination.]

9.4.   Customer may inspect and test each of the Deliverables when received to determine if it [substantially] conforms to the requirements of the Specification. [Testing will be in accordance with the testing procedures specified in *[Name of Testing Procedure Document or Schedule]*]. [Customer will not unreasonably withhold acceptance.]

9.5.   [Any Deliverable not rejected in *[specify number]* days will be deemed accepted.] If any Deliverable is rejected, Customer will give Developer reasonably detailed written notice of the rejection and the reasons for rejection. Developer will then have *[specify number]* days to cure deficiencies. After resubmission within such *[specify number]* day period, Customer may again inspect the Deliverable to confirm that it [substantially] conforms to requirements of the Specification. [If the resubmitted Deliverable is not rejected in the *[specify number]* days after resubmission, the Deliverable will be deemed accepted.] [Appropriate adjustments in the dates that Milestones are due will be made for delays caused by Customer's delays in carrying out its obligations.]

9.6.   If the resubmitted Deliverable does not [substantially] conform to the requirements of this Agreement, the failure will be a material breach that will entitle Customer to terminate this Agreement in accordance with the provisions of this Agreement regarding termination. If the resubmitted Deliverable is rejected, Customer will give notice to Developer stating the reasons for rejection.

9.7.   [Notwithstanding the foregoing, acceptance will be deemed to have occurred if Customer makes Productive Use of the Program for a period of more than *[specify number]* days (not including acceptance test use in accordance with any written acceptance plan agreed to by the parties in writing). "Productive Use" means use in Customer's business.]

[Optional Provision:]

9.8.   In case of termination by Customer for Developer's failure to provide Deliverables as required by this Agreement or for Developer's providing Deliverables that are properly and finally rejected by Customer, Customer will pay for completed Milestones only. Developer will deliver to Customer all work in process, including binary code, source code and any relevant proprietary Developer tools, all of which will be deemed provided "AS IS" and "WITHOUT WARRANTY" but with all rights granted to Customer regarding ownership and/or exploitation otherwise provided for in this Agreement. [Remedies expressly provided in this Agreement for termination under such circumstances will be Customer's sole and exclusive remedies for such breach.]

[Optional Provision:]

9.9.   In case of termination by Customer for Developer's failure to provide Deliverables as required by this Agreement or for Developer's providing Deliverables that are properly and finally rejected by Customer, Developer will refund to Customer [all] *[specify percentage or other refund formula]* of amounts paid by Customer under this Agreement as liquidated damages for such breach. [Remedies expressly provided in this Agreement for termination under such circumstances will be Customer's sole and exclusive remedies for such breach.]

[Optional Provision:]

9.10.   As an alternative to termination of this Agreement, if Developer has failed to complete development and/or to cure Defects as required in this Agreement, Customer, at its option, may accept the Program as non-conforming. If it does so, it will give prompt notice to Developer stating the known Defects, and may withhold and deduct, from amounts otherwise due and payable to Developer for development of the Program, the amount of reasonable out-of-pocket costs to correct, modify, and/or complete the Program in accordance with the Specification. From time to time, and as soon as is practicable, Customer will provide Developer with notice of all sums withheld and expended and will turn over to Developer all funds withheld that are not so applied when such remedial work is completed. Such remedy [will be Customer's sole and exclusive remedy for failure to deliver the Program in accordance with this Agreement] [will be in addition to any other remedies that may apply].

10. **Payment**

[*Comment:* *The following text sets a time limit for payments and a remedy if prompt payment is not made.*]

10.1. Customer will pay Developer the amount due upon the execution of this Agreement as specified in the Milestone Schedule. Upon acceptance of each Deliverable, Customer will pay Developer the amounts as specified in the Milestone Schedule. Payment will be due within _____ (__) days of acceptance of each Deliverable. Payment by mail will be deemed made [when mailed] [when received].

10.2. Payments for any fee or amount other than Milestone Payments under this Agreement will be due _____ (__) days after invoice or other written request for payment.

10.3. If any payment is not made as required, Developer may give notice of the failure to pay. The failure to pay, if not cured within _____ (__) days after notice, will entitle Developer, at its option, to suspend work and/or terminate this Agreement in accordance with the provisions upon termination of this Agreement.

10.4. Payments not received within _____ (__) days of their due date will be subject to late charges of one percent (1%) per month, or if lower, at the highest legal rate.

[Optional Provision:]

11. **Early and Late Performance**

11.1. *Early Delivery*. If Developer provides Final Deliverables (as defined in the Milestone Schedule) suitable for acceptance on or before [*specify earlier than otherwise scheduled date*], then the final Milestone Payment will be increased by _____.

11.2. *Late Delivery*. In the event that Final Deliverables suitable for acceptance are Deliverables not provided to Customer until [date] or thereafter, then (in addition to other remedies that may apply) the final Milestone Payment will be decreased by [*specify amount*] for each day's delay, provided that maximum cumulative decrease in such Milestone Payment cannot be more than [*specify percentage*]. Developer will not incur any reduced payment to the extent that delays are caused by Customer, by a third party vendor, or a Force Majeure event.

12. **Intellectual Property; Grant of License**

*[**Comment:** Option 1 provides that the Customer obtains all Intellectual Property that the Developer creates in the engagement and all interests that the Developer has to provide in the Deliverables. The only exception in this version is the Developer retains ownership of Developer Background Technology—which is limited to technology that the Developer has from before or outside of this Agreement. If there is no relevant Developer Background Technology, that exception can be omitted.*

Option 2 provides that the application will be owned by the Developer and licensed to the Customer. This is a provision that a Developer will be most likely to obtain when (a) the Program is largely based on Developer's pre-existing code base or (b) the Customer does not have any business reason to obtain sole control of the Program. If the Developer provides binary code only, it will want to include a "no reverse engineering" and "no service bureau use" provision as provided below.]

[Option 1. Transfer of Ownership, Except for Developer Background Technology]

12.1. "Customer Technology" means software, materials, software development tools, supplies, proprietary information, work product, files, technology, related scripting and any related Intellectual Property owned or provided by Customer.

12.2. "Developer Background Technology" means Developer's software, materials, software development tools, supplies, proprietary information, work product, files, technology, related scripting and programming and any related Intellectual Property that Developer owned on the Effective Date of this Agreement or that Developer creates or acquires independently of Developer's services under this Agreement.

12.3. [Conditioned upon Customer's payment of all amounts due to Developer,] Customer will be the sole owner of all Intellectual Property created by or for Developer under this Agreement. Subject to the paragraph below with regard to Copyrighted Works, Developer will assign, and does hereby assign, to Customer all of Developer's present and future rights, title, and interest in all such Intellectual Property.

12.4. With regard to any works subject to copyright ("Copyrighted Works") created under this Agreement or included in any Deliverable (other than Developer Background Technology), [conditioned upon Customer's payment of amounts due to Developer,] Developer agrees that, to the maximum extent permitted by law, Copyrighted Works are and will be "works made for hire" for the benefit of Customer, and to the extent not "works made for hire," Developer hereby assigns such rights exclusively to Customer.

12.5. Customer (and Customer's suppliers, if applicable) owns and will continue to own the Customer Technology (including all Intellectual Property in them), and this Agreement will not transfer any ownership of such Customer Technology to the Developer. Except for Developer Background Technology, Customer will own all the Deliverables (including all Intellectual Property in them).

12.6.   The Developer owns and will continue to own the Developer Background Technology (including all of Developer's Intellectual Property in them). Developer will grant and does hereby grant Customer a perpetual paid-up sublicensable license under Developer Background Technology to use, alter, distribute, make, have made, copy or otherwise exploit any Deliverables and Services or any derivatives of the Deliverables.

12.7.   [Conditioned upon Customer's payment of amounts due to Developer,] Developer will, upon request of Customer, execute, acknowledge, deliver and file any and all documents necessary or useful to vest in Customer all rights allocated under this Section or to transfer, perfect, obtain, confirm and enforce any such rights and will cause its Personnel to do the same. [Developer hereby irrevocably designates and appoints Customer and its duly authorized officers and agents as its agent and attorney-in-fact, to act for and in its behalf, in the event Customer is unable, after reasonable efforts, to secure its signature on any application for patents, copyright or trademark registration or other documents regarding any legal protection, to execute and file any such application or applications or other documents and to do all other lawfully permitted acts to register, transfer, perfect, obtain, confirm and enforce patents, copyrights or trademarks or any other legal protection with the same legal force and effect as if executed by it.]

12.8.   Upon transfer of such rights, Customer may register the copyright to the Program [and any derivative work] in any and all countries and jurisdictions, and take such further steps as it deems fit to provide legal protection to intellectual property relating to the Program.

[Option 2. Developer Grants a License Only]

12.9.   Developer and its suppliers will own all rights to the Program. This Agreement grants Customer license rights only. [Conditioned upon Customer's payment of amounts due to Developer,] Developer grants Customer the worldwide, non-exclusive, perpetual right, solely for its own internal business operations:

12.9.1.   To install and use the Programs on one [or more] computer[s] [and on testing and backup computers].

12.9.2.   To use the User Manual and any training materials solely for purposes of supporting Customer's use of the Program.

12.9.3.   To permit third parties (such as consultants, contractors and system integrators), so long as they are subject to a reasonable written confidentiality agreement, to install, integrate, and implement the Program.

12.9.4.   To copy the Program for the purpose of installation and licensed use and to make a reasonable number of backup copies.

12.9.5.   To copy the User Manual for internal use.

12.10.   [Customer will not: (a) copy the Program except as expressly authorized in this Agreement; (b) create derivative works of or otherwise modify the Program,

(c) decompile, disassemble or reverse engineer (except as and to the extent permitted by applicable local law) the Program, or (d) use the Program to provide remote access, software-as-a-service, service bureau or similar services to third parties.]

[Optional Provision:]

13.   **Exclusivity**

*[**Comment:** If the Program is licensed only, the Customer may want assurances that, for a period of time, it will not be licensed to others.]*

13.1.   For a period of _____ years from the Effective Date of this Agreement, Developer will not grant to any competitor of Customer any right to use the Program developed by Developer for Customer hereunder, or any portion or derivative of the Program, without the prior written consent of Customer.

*[**Comment:**   Regardless if the Program is transferred to the Customer or only licensed, the Customer may want assurances that the Developer will not supply similar software to competitors.]*

13.2.   For a period of _____ years from the Effective Date of this Agreement, Developer will not supply or agree to supply to any party other than Customer computer software with functionality similar to the Program or software that will or is likely to be competitive with the Program.

14.   **Confidentiality**

14.1.   "Confidential Information" means non-public information, technical data or know-how of a party and/or its Affiliates, which is furnished directly or indirectly to the other party in written or tangible form in connection with this Agreement. Oral disclosure will also be deemed Confidential Information if it would reasonably be considered to be of a confidential nature or if it is confirmed at the time of disclosure to be confidential. [Conditioned upon Customer's payments of amounts due to Developer,] Confidential Information created by Developer under this Agreement will be deemed to be the Confidential Information of Customer and may be used only for the purposes of this Agreement.]

14.2.   Notwithstanding the foregoing, Confidential Information does not include information which is: (i) already in the possession of the receiving party and not subject to a confidentiality obligation to the providing party; (ii) independently developed by the receiving party; (iii) publicly disclosed through no fault of the receiving party; (iv) rightfully received by the receiving party from a third party that is not under any obligation to keep such information confidential; (v) approved for release by written agreement with the disclosing party; or (vi) disclosed pursuant to the requirements of law, regulation, or court order, provided that the receiving party will promptly inform the providing party of any such requirement and cooperate with any attempt to procure a protective order or similar treatment.

14.3.   Neither party will use the other party's Confidential Information except as reasonably required for the performance of this Agreement. Each party will hold in confidence the other party's Confidential Information by means that are no less restrictive than those used for its own confidential materials. Each party agrees not to disclose the other party's Confidential Information to anyone other than its employees or permitted subcontractors who are bound by confidentiality obligations and who need to know the same to perform such party's obligations hereunder. [The confidentiality obligations set forth in this Section will survive [for _____ (_) years after the termination or expiration of this Agreement.]

14.4.   Upon termination or expiration of this Agreement, except as otherwise agreed in writing or otherwise stated in this Agreement, each party will, upon the request of the disclosing party, either: (i) return all of such Confidential Information of the disclosing party and all copies thereof in the receiving party's possession or control to the disclosing party; or (ii) destroy all Confidential Information and all copies thereof in the receiving party's possession or control. The receiving party will then, at the request of the disclosing party, certify in writing that no copies have been retained by the receiving party, its employees or agents.

14.5.   In case a party receives legal process that demands or requires disclosure of the disclosing party's Confidential Information, such party will give prompt notice to the disclosing party, if legally permissible, to enable the disclosing party to challenge such demand.

15.   **Warranty**

15.1.   Subject to Customer's payment of applicable amounts under this Agreement, Developer represents and warrants that the Program will conform in all material respects to the Specification for _____ (_) days after the date of acceptance of the Program ("Warranty Period"). In the event that Customer provides written notice of a material Defect during the Warranty Period, Developer's sole obligation under this warranty is to respond promptly and [to use all reasonable efforts] to promptly remedy such Defect within a reasonable time[; provided that if the Defect cannot be reproduced with reasonable efforts, Developer's warranty will not apply and Developer will have no obligation to remedy the cited Defect].

15.2.   This warranty does not apply to corrections or remedies for any issues arising from any Program modification, system change, or improper configuration or use of the Program, any third party software, or other causes external to the Program. If Customer requests Developer assistance with any non-warranty issue or problem, Developer will provide assistance, subject to Developer Personnel's availability, on its then standard time and material terms.

16.   **No Harmful Code**

16.1.   Developer warrants and represents that the Program will contain no routine, program, "virus" or code which [functions so as to] [has been intentionally designed or created by Developer to]: (a) allow unauthorized access to, or use of, the Program by any agent or employee of Developer or by any third party; or (b) cause the Program or other program or programs to malfunction; or (c) allow unauthorized access to, or use of, Customer's network computing environment, individual client computers or any other computing resource, by any agent or employee of Developer or any third party.

17.   **Program Maintenance and Support**

*[**Comment:** Most software development agreements have a provision for maintenance, that is, ongoing error correction and some kind of technical support. In some cases, there would be a schedule that states the maintenance and support offering. In Option 1, we provide a provision that refers to such a schedule that could be added. Option 2 is the provision of such services on an as-agreed basis.]*

[Option 1. Maintenance and Support Schedule]

17.1.   Developer agrees to provide Customer with ongoing maintenance and support for the Program and other software supplied under this Agreement as set forth in Schedule ___. Developer agrees to provide qualified personnel as necessary to provide such maintenance and support service. Annual minimum support fees are stated in Schedule ___.

17.2.   Provided that Customer continuously purchases annual maintenance, Developer agrees to maintain and support the Program distributed by Customer for at least ___ years after acceptance.

[Option 2. Maintenance and Support to Be Agreed Upon]

17.3.   Upon request by Customer, Developer agrees to negotiate in good faith with Customer with respect to providing maintenance, support or other ongoing services with respect to the Program after acceptance.

[Optional Provision:]

18.   **Program Improvements**

18.1.   Customer may from time to time request additional functionalities to be made to the Program. Upon request by Customer, Developer agrees to make such adaptations, or develop such enhancements, subject to agreement on terms and conditions to be mutually agreed upon in writing, which will provide for additional payments to Developer. The fee for any such adaptations or enhancements [will be at the Developer's then current rates] [will be negotiated].

[Optional Provision:]

19.   **Technical Assistance and Training**

19.1.   Developer agrees to provide to Customer training [and training materials] for Customer personnel on use of the Program as further set forth in Schedule ___. Payment for such training shall be as set forth in Schedule ___.

20.   **Warranty Disclaimer and Limitations of Liability**

The language about warranties being "DISCLAIMED" is keyed to statutory provisions of the Uniform Commercial Code (UCC).]

20.1.   EXCEPT FOR WARRANTIES EXPRESSLY STATED HEREIN, DEVELOPER DISCLAIMS AND EXCLUDES ALL WARRANTIES, EXPRESS AND IMPLIED, INCLUDING WARRANTIES OF MERCHANTABILITY, FITNESS FOR A PARTICULAR PURPOSE, AND OF NON-INFRINGEMENT.

20.2. The procedures for repair and replacement of the Program during the Warranty Period [and purchase of maintenance and support services] are Customer's sole and exclusive remedy for any Defect or other issue or problem in the Program or any Deliverable.

20.3. [Except for breach of the confidentiality provisions of this Agreement] [or under the provisions on indemnification,] Developer shall not be liable for any special, incidental, indirect or consequential damages, even if warned of the possibility of such damages. Developer does not warrant that use of the Program will be uninterrupted or error free.

20.4. [Except for breach of the confidentiality provisions of this Agreement] [or under the provisions on indemnification,] Developer's aggregate liability to the Customer for any and all claims in any way arising from or related to the Program or this Agreement will not exceed *[specified amount]* [the total of the Milestone Payments made to or owed to Developer under this Agreement].

21. **Third Party Software**

21.1. Developer may use and incorporate third party software products or components ("Third Party Software") as indicated in the Specification. Developer will not incorporate into the Deliverables any Third Party Software without the prior written authorization of Customer. [Developer will be solely responsible for obtaining licenses to any such Third Party Software.] [Customer will be solely responsible for obtaining licenses to any such Third Party Software.]

21.2. DEVELOPER MAKES NO WARRANTIES OR REPRESENTATIONS, EXPRESS OR IMPLIED, AS TO THE QUALITY, CAPABILITIES, OPERATIONS, PERFORMANCE OR SUITABILITY OF THIRD PARTY SOFTWARE, INCLUDING THE ABILITY OF NEW RELEASES TO INTEGRATE WITH THE PROGRAM. [Responsibility for the quality, performance, support, and maintenance of such Third Party Software lies solely with the vendor or supplier of such Third Party Software.]

[Optional Provision:]

22. **No Open Source**

22.1. Except as is expressly stated in the Specification, Developer will not include any software or code that is under the GNU General Public license or any open source license.

[Optional Provision:]

23. **Software Escrow**

*[**Comment:** This provision would only be appropriate if (a) Developer delivers the Program solely in binary form and (b) the Customer is insisting on a software escrow.*

This version requires a "mutually acceptable" escrow agent and escrow form. An alternative is to designate an escrow agent in the Agreement and to include as a Schedule the form of escrow agreement.]

23.1.   Within _____ days after acceptance of the Program, Developer will deposit a copy of all materials relating to the Program, including the binary and source code for the Program, and all tools used by Developer to generate such software that are not generally commercially available, such as Developer-authored development tools, etc., such that a reasonably skilled programmer could understand and modify such Program (collectively, the "Source Materials") in escrow with a mutually acceptable escrow agent and the parties will enter into a mutually acceptable source code escrow agreement on customary terms consistent with the provisions of this Section. Developer will deposit all Source Materials with the escrow agent in accordance with the escrow agreement, but in no event shall such deposits be required more frequently than once in each six month period. Customer shall have the right to inspect any deposited Source Materials after delivery to the escrow agent, but only on the premises of the escrow agent and only as is necessary to verify the completeness of such Source Materials. Customer shall pay all fees of the escrow agent.

23.2.   In the event that Developer ceases to carry on business for thirty (30) consecutive days or ceases to provide maintenance and support for the Program to which Customer is entitled under this Agreement, which inability continues for thirty (30) days after Customer notifies Developer in writing of the alleged failure in maintenance and support, the deposited Source Materials shall be delivered to Customer by the escrow agent.

23.3.   Delivery of the deposited materials will be made to Customer after written request by Customer to the escrow agent, with written notice also to Developer, stating the grounds upon which the request is made. On receipt of the request from Customer, the escrow agent will mail a copy of the request to Developer and will then deliver the deposited Source Materials to Customer forthwith thirty (30) days after the copy of the request is mailed to Developer. If Developer disputes the occurrence of any release event specified in Customer's request, the escrow agent will not deliver the requested Source Materials to either party until directed to do so by Customer and Developer jointly, or until ordered to do so by final order of a court of competent jurisdiction or pursuant to an arbitration proceeding initiated by either of the parties, in accordance with the then-current rules of the American Arbitration Association. The arbitration shall take place in _____. The decision of the arbitrator will be binding and either party will have the right to enter such order in a court of competent jurisdiction.

23.4.   On the occurrence of the escrow agent's release of the Source Materials to Customer under the terms of the escrow agreement, Customer may use the Source Materials, either directly or indirectly, through a third party programmer or analyst engaged by Customer only as follows: to complete or continue Developer's work, to maintain [and enhance] and support the Program, and to make a reasonable number of copies of the Source Materials to assist in the performance of such tasks.

23.5.   Customer acknowledges that the Source Materials constitute Confidential Information of Developer. Customer may disclose the Source Materials only to those employees of Customer (or Affiliates) required to have knowledge of such information to perform their duties. Customer shall protect the Source Materials with the same degree of care as it protects its own confidential information, and in no event less than a reasonable degree of care and shall ensure that any third party that is permitted to access or use the Source Materials is under equivalent contractual restrictions.

24.   **Intellectual Property Warranty**

*[**Comment:** Many software development agreements contain an intellectual property warranty—a guarantee that the code provided is original and does not infringe the intellectual property rights of third parties. There are potential variants to this provision.*

The following text makes warranties only as to rights under United States law. Some developers will resist warranties concerning foreign intellectual property laws, because it is more difficult to determine what foreign intellectual property rights the program might infringe. However, when the Customer plans to use the program in one or more foreign states, it way wish to negotiate an indemnification provision that includes the law of some or all foreign countries.]

[Option 1. Warrants No Knowledge of Infringement:]

24.1.   Developer represents and warrants that it knows of no fact or circumstance indicating that the Program, used and copied as permitted in this Agreement, will infringe any Intellectual Property rights existing under the laws of the United States or any state thereof of any other person or entity.

[Option 2. Broadly Warrants Non-Infringement:]

24.2.   Developer represents and warrants that Developer has full and absolute right to [transfer] [license] the Program as required in this Agreement and that the permitted use and copying of the Program will not infringe any rights existing under the laws of the United States or any state thereof. [Customer's sole and exclusive remedy for breach of this warranty will be indemnification as provided in this Agreement.]

25.   **Indemnification**

*[**Comment:** In the following Section, the Developer indemnifies the Customer against infringement claims. Sometimes there is broad indemnification: the Developer must pay all costs and liability for any intellectual property suit against the Customer (even if it turns out that the suit is without merit). Sometimes there is a narrow indemnification: the Developer must pay only if it turns out that there was infringement and the Developer was aware of it. Obviously, the Customer, if it is sophisticated, will seek the broad one. The scope of indemnification is a matter for negotiation. The rather quaint terminology of "holding harmless" the other party is a promise to pay any and all costs arising from a third party infringement claim.]*

[Option 1. Broad Indemnification:]

25.1.   Developer agrees to defend, indemnify and hold harmless Customer, its officers, directors, employees, agents and representatives, at its own expense, from and against any and all costs, demands, losses, damages, liabilities, costs and expenses (including reasonable attorney's fees) and any award of damages or costs made against Customer that is based on any claim that the Program or its permitted use infringes any Intellectual Property rights of a third party (collectively, "Claim"). Developer's obligations under this Section do apply to or cover any claim or liability arising from the combination of the Program and any technology or content not provided by Developer.

[Option 2. Indemnifies for Knowing Infringement Only:]

25.2.   Developer agrees to defend, indemnify and hold harmless Customer, its officers, directors, employees, agents and representatives, at its own expense, from and against any and all fees, costs and expenses (including reasonable attorney's fees) and any award of damages or costs made against Customer that arises from Developer's intentionally creating and supplying the Program and Deliverables while knowing that such Program or Deliverables infringe the Intellectual Property rights of a third party (collectively, "Claim"). Developer's obligations under this Section do apply to or cover any claim or liability arising from the combination of the Program and any technology or content not provided by Developer.

25.3.   If Developer deems that the Program or any Deliverable furnished under this Agreement is subject to a substantial threat of a Claim or is held to constitute an infringement and its use enjoined, Developer [may] [must], at its own expense, use commercially reasonable efforts to: (1) procure for Customer the right to continue using the Program; or (2) replace or modify the Program with a functional, non-infringing equivalent.

25.4.   Customer will defend, indemnify, and hold Developer harmless from and against any and all third party claims arising or alleged to arise from (i) any unlicensed use of the Program or (ii) any claim or liability arising from the combination of the Program and any technology or content not provided by Developer, to the extent that the Program alone is non-infringing.

25.5.   The party requesting indemnity under this Section shall provide the indemnifying party with prompt and reasonable notice of the Claim, and shall allow the indemnifying party to conduct the defense or settlement in its sole discretion, and provide reasonable cooperation with the indemnifying party in such defense or settlement.

25.6.   [The foregoing is the parties' sole and exclusive remedies for infringement or claimed infringement of third party Intellectual Property rights.][Developer's maximum aggregate liability under this Section will not exceed the sum of $_____.]

25.7.   [Notwithstanding the foregoing, Developer's obligation under this Section will be effective only if Customer has made all or substantially all of the payments required by this Agreement.]

26.   **Term and Termination**

*[**Comment:** The term and termination clause of some development contracts grants the Customer an absolute right to cancel at will on no notice, or on short notice. This would allow the Customer to get out of further obligations if it decides that there no longer is any market for the Product that is being developed. Often the Developer will resist the inclusion of such an "escape" clause unless there is a termination fee to compensate the Developer for loss of expected revenues.]*

26.1.   The term of this Agreement will commence on the Effective Date, and will continue until this Agreement is terminated in accordance with the provisions set forth in this Agreement.

26.2. Either party may terminate this Agreement:

26.2.1. In accordance with the provisions stated in this Agreement that provide for termination.

26.2.2. In the event that the other party ceases business operations or is in any bankruptcy, state law insolvency or receivership proceeding, or other equivalent proceeding that is not dismissed in ___ (__) days or assigns its assets for the benefit of creditors, or

26.2.3. In the event of any material breach by the other party which is not cured within _____ (__) days after notice.

[Optional Provision:]

26.3. Customer may terminate this Agreement for convenience on _____ days written notice. If Customer terminates for convenience, Customer will pay Developer for completed Milestones and on a percentage-of-completion basis for uncompleted Milestones. On receipt of such payment, Developer will deliver to Customer all work in process, including binary code, source code and any relevant proprietary Developer tools, all of which will be deemed provided "AS IS" and "WITHOUT WARRANTY" but with all rights granted to Customer regarding licenses, ownership and/or exploitation otherwise provided for in this Agreement. [In case of Customer's termination for convenience, an additional termination fee of *[state amount or formula for a termination fee]* will also be due and payable to Developer.]

27. **Effect of Termination**

27.1. Upon any termination of this Agreement by any party, the following Sections will survive termination: 12 (Intellectual Property), [13 (Exclusivity)], 14 (Confidentiality), 15 (Warranty) (if applicable), 16 (No Harmful Code), 20 (Warranty Disclaimer and Limitations of Liability), 24 (Intellectual Property Warranty), 25 (Indemnification), 27 (Effect of Termination), [28 (Non-Solicitation of Staff),] and 29 (General Provisions) together with accrued obligations and any provisions that recite that they survive or by their terms apply after termination.

[Optional Provision:]

28. **Non-Solicitation of Staff**

28.1. Customer agrees not to solicit to hire, hire, or otherwise obtain the services of, or to assist any third party to solicit to hire, hire, or obtain the services of any Developer employee or other person assigned by Developer to work under this Agreement while engaged in Services or for one year thereafter.

28.2. The parties agree that it is impossible to fix with certainty the damage to Developer for breach of this Section, and the parties therefore agree that Customer will pay, for each breach of this Section, as liquidated damages, an amount equal to one hundred percent (100%) of the affected employee's average monthly compensation over the most recent six full months multiplied by twelve. Such amount will be due and payable by the Customer within ten (10) days of receipt of an invoice from Developer.

29.   **General Provisions**

[*Comment:* *The following are some general (or "boilerplate") provisions. Similar provisions are found in many commercial contracts.*]

29.1.   *Relationship of Parties.* Developer will be deemed to have the status of an independent contractor, and nothing in this Agreement will be deemed to place the parties in the relationship of employer-employee, principal-agent, partners or joint venturers. Developer is responsible for all payments to its subcontractors [, and guarantees their observance of their confidentiality requirements referred to herein.]

29.2.   *Payment of Taxes.* Developer will be responsible for any withholding taxes, payroll taxes, disability insurance payments, unemployment taxes, and other taxes or charges incurred in the performance of the Agreement for its Personnel.

29.3.   *Force Majeure.* Neither party will be deemed in default of this Agreement to the extent that performance of their obligations or attempts to cure any breach [other than with regard to payment] are delayed or prevented by reason of any act of God, fire, natural disaster, accident, act of government, shortages of materials or supplies, or any other cause beyond the control of such party ("Force Majeure") provided that such party gives the other party written notice thereof promptly and, in any event, within fifteen (15) days of discovery thereof and uses its best efforts to cure the delay. In the event of such a Force Majeure, the time for performance or cure will be extended for a period equal to the duration of the Force Majeure but not in excess of sixty (60) days. If a Force Majeure delay exceeds sixty (60) days, the other party may terminate this Agreement without fault.

[*Comment:* *The following provisions relate to assignment of the Agreement by the Developer or the Customer. There are a number of options presented in the following text. If there is an assignment, the Developer may want the Customer to remain responsible for payment if the assignee fails to pay. Owners of businesses may want the freedom to sell or assign all the assets of a business, including all its contracts. Normally the Customer, who contracted for the skills of a particular developer, may resist granting the Developer any right to assign the agreement.*]

29.4.   *Assignments.* This Agreement may not be assigned by Customer in whole or in part without consent of Developer [which consent will not be unreasonably withheld]. [Customer may assign this Agreement, without Developer's consent, to any third party which succeeds by operation of law to, purchases, or otherwise acquires substantially all of the assets of Customer and assumes Customer's obligations hereunder.] [Notwithstanding the above, Customer will retain the obligation to pay if the assignee fails to pay as required by the payment obligations of this Agreement.] [Developer may not assign its obligations under this Agreement without Customer's written consent, which Customer may withhold in its complete discretion.]

29.5.   *Partial Invalidity.* Should any provision of this Agreement be held to be void, invalid, or inoperative, the remaining provisions of this Agreement will not be affected and will continue in effect as though such provisions were deleted.

29.6.   *No Waiver.* The failure of either party to exercise any right or the waiver by either party of any breach will not prevent a subsequent exercise of such right or be deemed a waiver of any subsequent breach of the same or any other term of the Agreement.

29.7. *Notice.* Any notice required or permitted to be sent hereunder will be in writing and will be sent in a manner requiring a signed receipt, such as courier delivery, or if mailed, registered or certified mail, return receipt requested. Notice is effective upon receipt. Notice to Customer will be addressed to [*specify name, title and address*] or such other person or address as Customer may designate. Notice to Developer will be addressed to [*specify name, title and address*] or such other person or address as Developer may designate.

29.8. *Modifications.* No modification of this Agreement will be effective unless in writing and signed by both parties.

29.9. *Injunction.* The parties acknowledge that damages may not be an adequate remedy for breach of the Sections of this Agreement on confidentiality [and exclusivity] [and non-solicitation]. Without limiting other rights or remedies, the parties will have the right in the event of breach or anticipated breach of such provisions to seek injunctive or other equitable relief to remedy or prevent the breach or anticipated breach.

29.10. *Governing Law.* This Agreement will be governed and interpreted in accordance with the substantive law of the State of _____.

29.11. *Venue and Jurisdiction of Legal Actions.* Any legal action brought concerning this Agreement or its subject matter will be brought only in the state and federal courts located in *[indicate state and county]*, and both parties agree to the exclusive jurisdiction and venue of these courts.

*[**Comment:** The following "entire agreement clause" (also known as an "integration clause") is designed to eliminate any claim that oral promises not in the Agreement are effective. This clause, a standard feature of many types of agreements, will usually be enforced. If there are promises made or "side agreements" outside the text of the Agreement, it is important to get them into the text before the Agreement is signed.]*

29.12. *Entire Agreement.* This Agreement, including the Schedules thereto, states the entire agreement between the parties on this subject and supersedes all prior negotiations, understandings, and agreements between the parties concerning the subject matter.

29.13. *Counterparts.* This Agreement may be executed in multiple counterparts, each being deemed an original and this being one of the counterparts. Execution by fax is permitted.

IN WITNESS WHEREOF, the parties have executed this Agreement.

Developer: _____   Customer: _____

By: _____   By: _____

Name: _____   Name: _____

Title: _____   Title: _____

Date: _____   Date:_____

Schedule ___ Specifications

[To be added]

Schedule ___ Milestone and Payment Schedule

*[**Comment:** Every development agreement will have its own Milestone and Milestone Payment schedule. The following are some terms that might fit a Milestone Schedule.]*

The following Schedule will govern milestones and payments for the development of the Program.

1. **Definitions.** The following definitions and provisions apply to this Schedule:

    1.1. "Working Model Code" will mean Program code written by Developer that has Critical Features (as defined in the Specification). This version of the Program demonstrates the technical feasibility of the Program.

    1.2. "Alpha Code" will mean Program code written by Developer that includes all operations, functions, capabilities, and performance in the Specification implemented, integrated and fully functional. It is code that is not necessarily "bug free" and may be in need of adjustment and tuning of functions, operations, and graphics.

    1.3. "Beta Code" will mean Program code written by Developer that includes all operations, functions, capabilities, and performance implemented, integrated and functional substantially in accordance with the Specification. This version will have all known serious bugs and errors corrected.

    1.4. "Final Deliverables" will mean the version of the Program written by Developer that has passed through user tests and which [fully] [substantially] complies with the Specification. [This version is the Beta Code version that has been corrected to address the bugs and errors that have been documented during testing.]

[Optional Provision:]

    1.5. "Technical Documentation" will mean commented source code and other documentation sufficient to permit the Program to be modified by a reasonably skilled technician with knowledge of the languages in which the Program is written but no prior knowledge of the Program. Technical Documentation is further defined as follows: *[specify]*.

2. **Delivery and Payment Schedule**

    The delivery and payment schedule will be as follows:
    [Specify Dates, Milestones and Payment Amounts]
    [Add Other Schedules as Required]

Appendix 5

Software Consulting Agreement (Favors Consultant)

Introductory Note

This is a software consulting agreement with a variety of clauses that "lean" toward Consultant rather than Customer. These include the provisions on the performance obligations of Consultant, acceptance, correction of defects, warranties, intellectual property ownership, and indemnification.

You can contrast these provisions with those of Appendix 6, which is a pro-Customer version of a consulting agreement.

This form is for use when Consultant is a corporation or other legal entity. It will require some modification if Consultant is an individual.

Bracketed language is optional.

Software Consulting Agreement

This Software Consulting Agreement ("Agreement") is entered into this day of 20__, by and between _____, having its principal place of business at _____ ("Customer"), and _____, having its principal place of business at _____ _____ ("Consultant").

In consideration of the mutual covenants and promises set forth below, the parties agree as follows:

1. **Services**

   1.1. *Statement of Work.* All services to be performed by Consultant under this Agreement ("Services") will be set forth in a written statement of work ("Statement of Work") signed by authorized representatives of both parties. Each Statement of Work will set forth the description of the Services to be done and the hourly, daily or other fees for the Services to be performed, and other matters as the parties may agree upon. The initial Statement of Work(s) is (are) attached as <u>Schedule 1</u>.

   1.2. *Provisions of Services.* Consultant agrees to use commercially reasonable efforts to provide the Services to Customer in accordance with the terms and conditions of this Agreement and the applicable Statements of Work.

   1.3. *Support Not Included.* Unless expressly included in a particular Statement of Work or otherwise agreed in writing, Consultant is not obligated to provide any support or maintenance services for any deliverables provided pursuant to this Agreement.

   1.4. *Estimated Times.* The parties agree that, unless otherwise expressly stated in a particular Statement of Work or otherwise agreed in writing, where a time or amount of Services required for a particular task or deliverable is described in a Statement of Work, it is an estimate only. [Consultant will use reasonable efforts to advise Customer as soon as is practicable if the time or amount of Services required is likely to exceed the estimate by more than ___ percent.]

2. **Third Party Products and Services**

   2.1. Unless otherwise stated in a particular Statement of Work, Customer will arrange for third party products and services required for implementation of the Statement of

Work, including third party software and tools. CONSULTANT MAKES NO WARRANTY REGARDING THIRD PARTY PRODUCTS AND SERVICES.

3. **Performance of Services; Changes**

   3.1. Consultant will determine the details and means of performing the Services to be performed for Customer under Customer's general guidance and direction. Services will be performed at such times and at such places set out in the Statements of Work or as the parties may otherwise agree in writing.

   3.2. Changes to any Statement of Work can be made only by written change order signed by both parties or by an additional Statement of Work. Any change to a Statement of Work which is agreed to by the parties will specify the changes ordered, any increase or decrease in the estimated charges for performance, timing issues, and any changes to other matters as may be affected.

4. **Payment**

   4.1. Customer will pay Consultant at the fee rates specified in the Statements of Work. If rates are not specified in the relevant Statement of Work, Services performed by Consultant on behalf of Customer will be undertaken on a time and materials basis at Consultant's applicable standard rates.

   4.2. Customer will reimburse Consultant for reasonable out-of-pocket expenses incurred in the provision of Services, including, without limitation, all travel, accommodation, and meal expenses for Services performed at Customer site or Customer's client's site.

   4.3. Consultant will render invoices to Customer on a monthly basis, indicating the Services for which the invoice is rendered, the period of time it covers, the fees due, and any other additions, expenses or taxes (evidenced by receipts), and any other detail reasonably required for Customer to verify the amount invoiced. All invoices submitted under this Agreement and the Statements of Work will refer to this Agreement and the applicable Statement of Work.

   4.4. Customer will pay all invoices within thirty (30) days of receipt. In the event that Customer wishes to dispute an item or items on an invoice, Customer will notify Consultant in writing within fourteen days of receipt of that invoice, setting out its reasons in reasonable detail. If no notice of dispute is received by Consultant fourteen days after receipt of an invoice by Customer, the invoice will be deemed accepted, and Customer will be obliged to pay the invoice in accordance with its terms. In case of a dispute regarding billing, Customer must pay all undisputed charges and items.

   4.5. Customer is responsible for all taxes resulting from the Services, including any sales taxes, but excluding taxes on Consultant's net income. Consultant may bill for such taxes and pay them to the relevant tax authorities.

   4.6. If Customer fails to pay any amount payable by it under this Agreement within 30 days of receipt of an invoice, Consultant will be entitled to charge and Customer will pay 1.50% interest per month (or if less the highest legal rate), compounded daily, on the overdue amount.

5.   **Personnel**

   5.1.   Consultant will perform the Services by means of the services of suitably experienced staff and/or may delegate its obligations hereunder by commercially reasonable use of one or more subcontractor individuals or firms, provided that, in any case, Consultant will remain responsible for provision of Services as required by this Agreement. The individuals who provide Services under this Agreement are the "Personnel." [Consultant will use reasonable efforts to provide Customer with a list of the Personnel assigned to Services under each Statement of Work.]

   5.2.   Consultant will seek to ensure continuity of staffing for Services under each Work Statement. Consultant, from time to time, may replace Personnel with suitably experienced alternative Personnel or subcontractors. [In this event, Consultant will use reasonable efforts to provide to Customer reasonable notice of each replacement.]

   5.3.   Consultant will determine matters such as Personnel's working hours and holidays taking into account Customer's business requirements. Personnel may take state and local holidays.

6.   **Cooperation; Facilities to Be Provided by Client**

   6.1.   Customer agrees to provide reasonable cooperation to Consultant and access to information that Consultant reasonably requires to perform its obligations under this Agreement.

   6.2.   Customer will make available to Consultant (including its subcontractors and any third parties contemplated within this Agreement) free of charge any premises, facilities, assistance, information, and services reasonably required to enable them to perform the Services. Such facilities will include, but not be limited to, desks, PCs, office facilities and telephones.

   6.3.   Where the Services are to be provided at the premises of a client of Customer, it is the responsibility of Customer to ensure that the foregoing are provided at such location.

7.   **Independent Contractor**

   7.1.   The parties agree that Consultant is acting, in performance of this Agreement, as an independent contractor. The parties agree that the Personnel supplied by Consultant hereunder are not Customer's employees or agents.

   7.2.   Consultant will be solely responsible for the payment of compensation and any benefits to the Personnel, and the Personnel will not be entitled to the provision of any Customer employee benefits.

   7.3.   This Agreement is mutually non-exclusive. Customer will retain the right to have services of the same or a different kind performed by its own personnel or other consultants, and Consultant will retain the right to provide similar services to others.

8.   **Confidentiality**

   8.1.   "Confidential Information" means non-public information, data or know-how of a party and/or its affiliates, which is furnished directly or indirectly to the other party in written or tangible form in connection with this Agreement. Each oral disclosure of a party will also be deemed Confidential Information if the recipient should reasonably understand it to be non–public information.

8.2.   Notwithstanding the foregoing, Confidential Information does not include information which is: (i) already in the possession of the receiving party and not subject to a confidentiality obligation to the providing party; (ii) independently developed by the receiving party; (iii) publicly disclosed through no fault of the receiving party; (iv) rightfully received by the receiving party from a third party that is not under any obligation to keep such information confidential; (v) approved for release by written agreement with the disclosing party; or (vi) disclosed pursuant to the requirements of law, regulation, court order or other applicable requirement, provided that the receiving party shall promptly inform the providing party of any such requirement and cooperate with any attempt to procure a protective order or similar treatment.

8.3.   Neither party will use the other party's Confidential Information except as reasonably required for the performance of this Agreement. The confidentiality obligations set forth in this Section shall survive for five (5) years after the termination or expiration of this Agreement. Each party will hold in confidence the other party's Confidential Information by means that are no less restrictive than those used for its own confidential materials but in any case by commercially reasonable means. Each party agrees not to disclose the other party's Confidential Information to anyone other than its employees or subcontractors who are bound by confidentiality obligations consistent with this Agreement and who need to know the same to perform such party's obligations hereunder.

8.4.   Upon termination or expiration of this Agreement, except as otherwise agreed in writing or otherwise stated in this Agreement, each party shall, upon the request of the disclosing party, either: (i) return all of such Confidential Information of the disclosing party and all copies thereof in the receiving party's possession or control to the disclosing party or (ii) destroy all Confidential Information and all copies thereof in the receiving party's possession or control. The receiving party shall then, at the request of the disclosing party, certify in writing that the requirements of this Section have been carried out and that no copies have been retained by the receiving party, its employees or agents.

8.5.   In case a party receives legal process that demands or requires disclosure of the disclosing party's Confidential Information, such party shall give prompt notice to the disclosing party, if legally permissible, to enable the disclosing party to challenge such demand.

8.6.   The parties acknowledge that damages may not be an adequate remedy for breach of this Section. Therefore, without prejudice to any other rights or remedies, the parties will have the right in the event of such breach or anticipated breach to seek injunctive or other equitable relief to remedy or prevent the breach or anticipated breach.

9. **Ownership of Software**

9.1.   From time to time, Consultant has created software tools and code and/or will during the course of the Agreement create, and/or improve, software tools and software code that are reusable or are useful for one or more other products, tasks and projects. Such tools and code provided to Customer under this Agreement are termed

"Reusable Software." Software created and delivered under this Agreement other than Reusable Software is "Customer Specific Software."

9.2.   Upon payment of amounts due to Consultant with regard to each Statement of Work, Customer Specific Software under such Statement of Work will belong to Customer and will be, to the fullest extent permitted under the US copyright act, a work-made-for-hire for Customer. To the extent that it is not work-made-for-hire, Customer Specific Software (including, as applicable, ownership of the binary code and source code) is hereby assigned to Customer.

9.3.   Customer agrees that the Consultant Reusable Software will be the property of and will belong to Consultant. Upon payment of amounts due to Consultant with regard to each Statement of Work, Consultant will be deemed to grant to Customer a non-exclusive, worldwide, perpetual, irrevocable and fully paid up license to use, modify, adapt, sublicense, and otherwise exploit the Consultant Reusable Software solely for use with the deliverables under such Statement of Work and derivatives of such deliverables.

9.4.   Each party agrees to provide, at the other party's expense, the documents necessary or useful to vest in each party its respective Intellectual Property under this Agreement.

9.5.   Except as expressly stated in this Agreement, each party retains its own rights. No rights are created or transferred by implication.

9.6.   Customer hereby grants to Consultant a non-exclusive and non-transferable license to access and use Customer's computer and network systems and proprietary software and to use Customer Specific Software as reasonably required for Consultant to carry out its obligations under this Agreement.

10.   **Warranty and Indemnity**

10.1.   Each party warrants that it has all required corporate authority to execute and perform this Agreement.

10.2.   Consultant warrants that to the best of its actual knowledge that all deliverables provided or to be provided under this Agreement do not and will not infringe or violate any valid third party patent right, copyright or trade secret right in the United States.

10.3.   Customer warrants that it has all required ownership, rights and/or permissions for any materials, software or other items that it provides for Consultant's use under this Agreement.

10.4.   Consultant agrees to defend, indemnify and hold harmless Customer from any litigation or proceeding arising from Consultant's breach of the warranty in Section 10.2. Customer agrees to defend, indemnify and hold harmless Consultant from any litigation or proceeding arising from Consultant's breach of the warranty in Section 10.3.

10.5.   In case of any claim that is subject to indemnification under this Agreement, the Party entitled to indemnification ("Indemnitee") shall provide the indemnifying party ("Indemnitor") prompt notice of the relevant claim. Indemnitor shall defend and/or settle, at its own expense, any demand, action, or suit on any claim subject to indemnification under this Agreement. The Indemnitee shall cooperate in good faith with the Indemnitor to facilitate the defense of any such claim. Claims may be settled without the consent of any Indemnitee unless the settlement includes an admission of wrongdoing, fault or liability on behalf of the Indemnitee.

11. **Limitations of Liability**

   11.1. *Warranty Exclusion.* EXCEPT AS EXPRESSLY STATED IN THIS AGREEMENT, CONSULTANT DISCLAIMS ALL EXPRESS AND IMPLIED WARRANTIES, INCLUDING IMPLIED WARRANTIES OF NON-INFRINGEMENT, MERCHANTABILITY AND FITNESS FOR A PARTICULAR PURPOSE.

   11.2. *Damage Disclaimer.* Consultant will not be liable to Customer for any special, indirect, consequential, incidental or exemplary damages including without limitation, damages for loss of Customer's business profits, cost of procurement of substitute goods, technology or services, business interruptions or loss of information, even if Consultant has been advised of the possibility of such damages.

   11.3. *Limitation of Liability.* In no event will Consultant be liable to Customer for any amounts in excess in the aggregate of the fees paid by Customer to Consultant during the six (6) month period prior to the date the cause of action arose or, if less, the amount paid to Consultant with regard to the Statement of Work that is relevant to the liability.

12. **Non-Solicitation**

   12.1. Customer agrees not to solicit to hire, hire, or otherwise obtain the services of, or to assist any third party to solicit to hire, hire, or obtain the services of any Consultant employee or other person assigned by Consultant to work under any Statement for Work for the duration of Services under such Statement of Work or for one year thereafter.

   12.2. Because it is impossible to fix with certainty the damage to Consultant for breach of this Section, the parties agree that Customer will pay, for each breach of this Section, as liquidated damages, an amount equal to one hundred percent (100%) of the affected employee's average monthly compensation over the most recent six full months multiplied by twelve. Such amount will be due and payable by Customer within ten (10) days of receipt of an invoice from Consultant.

13. **Term and Termination**

   13.1. Unless otherwise agreed in writing by the parties, either Customer or Consultant may terminate this Agreement, or any Statement of Work, at any time by giving the other _____ (__) days written notice of termination, whereupon this Agreement or (as appropriate) the Statement of Work will terminate on the effective date specified in such notice. Termination of a Statement of Work will not operate to terminate this Agreement, unless this Agreement is also terminated in accordance with its terms.

   13.2. Either Party may terminate his Agreement for cause in the event of: (a) a material breach or default by the other party of an obligation under this Agreement which is not remedied within thirty (30) days after written notice; (b) the other party's filing for bankruptcy or becoming an involuntary participant in a bankruptcy proceeding, if such involuntary proceedings are not dismissed within sixty (60) days after commencement; or, (c) notice of the inability of the other party to perform due to the existence of a force majeure event for more than thirty (30) days.

13.3.   Where this Agreement is terminated, each Statement of Work will also be terminated and any Services being provided under that Statement of Work will cease. Consultant will issue, and Customer will pay, an invoice for Services provided up to the date of termination. In case of Customer's termination without cause, an additional termination fee of *[amount]* will also be due to Consultant.

13.4.   On receipt of payment of all amounts due, Consultant will deliver to Customer all work in progress. Uncompleted work in progress will be provided "AS IS" and "WITHOUT WARRANTY," but otherwise subject to the terms and conditions of this Agreement.

13.5.   The Sections of this Agreement regarding Confidentiality, Intellectual Property, Warranties, Limitation of Liability, Term and Termination, Non-Solicitation and General provisions will survive termination, as will accrued rights to payment.

14.   **Notices**

Any notice required to be given by either party hereunder will be in writing and will be hand delivered or sent by courier or pre-paid first class post or by confirmed fax transmission to the party receiving such communication at the address and fax numbers specified below or such other address or fax numbers as either party may in the future specify to the other party. Notice is effective upon receipt.

If to Consultant: [*add address, contact person and/or title, and fax number*]

If to Customer: [*add address, contact person and/or title, and fax number*]

15.   **General**

15.1.   *Compliance with Laws.* Each party hereby represents and warrants that it will comply with all applicable, local, state, provincial, and national laws and regulations, including, without limitation, US export control laws.

15.2.   *Assignment.* Customer may not assign this Agreement. Consultant reserves the right to transfer this Agreement to any affiliate. Consultant may also, without Customer's consent, transfer this Agreement in connection with the sale or disposition of its business or a line of business relevant to this Agreement, by asset transfer, merger, stock sale or otherwise.

15.3.   *No Third Party Beneficiary.* This Agreement is not intended to confer a benefit on, or to be enforceable by, any person who is not a party to this Agreement.

15.4.   *Status as Independent Contractor.* Each party is an independent contractor and neither party's employees will be considered employees of the other party for any purpose.

This Agreement does not create a joint venture or partnership, and neither party has the authority to bind the other to any third party.

15.5. *Applicable Law and Jurisdiction.* This Agreement will be governed and construed in accordance with the laws of the State of _____ without regard to the conflicts of laws or principles thereof. Exclusive jurisdiction and venue for any disputes, claims or litigation arising from or related in any way to this Agreement or its subject matter will lie exclusively in the state and federal courts located in _____ _____, USA. Each party expressly agrees to submit to the personal jurisdiction of such courts.

15.6. *Waiver.* No waiver of a breach of any of the provisions of this Agreement will be deemed a waiver of any preceding or succeeding breach of the same or any other provisions hereof. No such waiver will be effective unless in writing and then only to the extent expressly set forth in writing.

15.7. *Partial Invalidity.* If any provision of this Agreement is invalid or unenforceable under any statute or rule of law, the provision is to the extent to be deemed omitted, and the remaining provisions will not be affected in any way.

15.8. *Force Majeure.* Neither party will be responsible for any delay or failure in performance resulting from acts beyond such party's control ("Force Majeure"). Force Majeure will include but not be limited to: acts of God, government or war; riots or strikes; epidemics, fires, floods, or disasters.

15.9. *Modifications.* No modification of this Agreement will be effective unless in writing and signed by both parties.

15.10. *Counterparts.* This Agreement may be executed in multiple counterparts, each being deemed an original and this being one of the counterparts. Execution by fax is permitted.

15.11. *Entire Agreement.* This Agreement, including the attached Statement of Work and any supplements, constitutes the entire agreement between Consultant and Customer.

SIGNED: By, or on behalf of the parties on the date which first appears on this Agreement.

Consultant: _____   Customer: _____

By: _____   By: _____

Name: _____   Name: _____

Title: _____   Title: _____

Date: _____   Date:_____

Schedule 1

Schedule of Work

This is a Statement of Work referred to in the Software Consulting Agreement dated [_____ _____] ("the Agreement") by and between [_____] ("Consultant") and _____ _____ Inc. ("Customer"). This Statement of Work will be effective immediately after it has been signed by both Customer and Consultant.

[_____] Statement of Work Reference:

Personnel	Role	Start Date	End Date	Fee Rate

Consultant's time and materials fee billing rates are reset annually on no less than thirty (30) days' notice.

Description of Services

Location(s) where Services are to be performed

Normal working hours

Customer Relationship Manager

Consultant Relationship Manager

Agreed upon by the parties:

Consultant: _____

By: _____

Authorized Signatory

Name: _____

Title: _____

Date: _____

Customer: _____

By: _____

Authorized Signatory

Name: _____

Title: _____

Date: _____

Software Consulting Agreement (Favors Customer)

Introductory Note

This is a software consulting agreement with a variety of clauses that favor the Customer rather than Consultant. In essence, this form provides protection for the Customer and places most risks on Consultant. You may see forms of this kind used by large corporations for the purposes of procurement of consulting services.

The provisions of note include the performance obligations of Consultant, acceptance, correction of defects, warranties, intellectual property ownership, third party software, and indemnification. All of these points could be the subject of negotiation, and most Consultants would seek to "soften" many of the following provisions if they have the leverage to do so.

You can compare and contrast these provisions with those of Form Appendix 5, which is a pro-Consultant version of a consulting agreement.

Bracketed language is optional.

Software Consulting Agreement

This Software Consulting Agreement ("Agreement") is entered into this _____ day of 20__, by and between _____, having its principal place of business at _____ ("Customer"), and _____, having its principal place of business at _____ _____ ("Consultant").

    In consideration of the mutual covenants and promises set forth below, the parties agree as follows:

1. **Legal Status of Consultant**

    Consultant represents and warrants that it is a corporation or other legal entity that is capable of contracting. (This form of agreement is not intended for use with a consultant who is an individual person.)

2. **Duties of Consultant**

    2.1.   Consultant agrees to provide the professional services ("Services") described on statements of work (each, a "Statement of Work"). Each Statement of Work will describe the Services to be performed, the schedule or term of Services, specifications and requirements ("Specifications"), means of delivery, applicable rates and charges, and other appropriate terms.

    2.2.   Each item prepared, provided, delivered or required to be prepared, provided, or delivered under any Statement of Work is a "Deliverable."

    2.3.   No Services are authorized and no payment is due except as expressly stated in writing in a Statement of Work signed by the parties.

    2.4.   A Statement of Work cannot be varied or amended unless agreed in writing by the parties. Any change to a Statement of Work which is agreed to by the parties will specify the changes required, any increase or decrease in the charges for performance, any change in the times for performance, and other applicable changes.

3. **Standard of Performance. Acceptance of Deliverables**

    3.1.   Consultant agrees to provide all Services and Deliverables in conformity with the applicable Specifications, the Statement of Work, this Agreement and applicable industry standards and laws. Consultant agrees to: (a) perform the Services in a professional manner, (b) keep Customer advised of the progress of the Services, (c) permit any representative of Customer to obtain and review from time to time the results of the Services, (d) provide Customer with such Deliverables, including any work in process, upon request, (e) keep records of work performed which such records Customer may review from time to time upon reasonable notice to Consultant, and (f) ensure that Consultant and its employees comply with Customer's safety, security and code of conduct regulations. Consultant will comply with all reasonable instructions given by Customer in connection with the Services. Consultant will supply all tools and equipment necessary to perform the Services unless otherwise agreed to in the applicable Statement of Work.

3.2. Unless otherwise stated in an applicable Statement of Work, Deliverables are subject to acceptance ("Acceptance") under the following procedure: Customer will make reasonable efforts to carry out inspection and accept or reject each Deliverable within thirty (30) days from receipt. Acceptance of each Deliverable will occur only upon written notice of Acceptance by Customer; no other act or failure to act by Customer will constitute Acceptance. [Customer will not unreasonably withhold Acceptance.]

3.3. Unless otherwise expressly stated in the applicable Statement of Work, Deliverables consisting of software will include Consultant's delivery of source code and binary code, together with all relevant technical documentation. Customer reserves the option to require daily or other periodic deliveries of source code and binary code.

3.4. In case Customer discovers one or more deficiencies in a Deliverable, Customer will notify Consultant in writing (which may be by email) within a commercially reasonable time. Upon receiving such a notice, Consultant will promptly correct any such deficiency or make such changes within fifteen (15) days after receiving such notice and resubmit the Deliverable. If Consultant fails to provide a conforming Deliverable, Customer in its discretion may (but is not obligated to) terminate this Agreement and/or the applicable Statement of Work, or, at its option, may, by written notice, require Consultant to continue work and provide conforming deliverables within a further fifteen (15) days under the same procedure.

4. **Fees for Services Performed**

4.1. Consultant will be paid the fees set forth in each Statement of Work for Consultant's performance of Services under this Agreement as follows: Consultant will submit to Customer invoices setting forth the Services rendered in reasonable detail. Any relevant backup documentation regarding the Services that Customer may require will be included. Conditioned on performance satisfactory to Customer of the Services under a Statement of Work, Customer will pay proper invoices within forty-five (45) days of receipt of invoice. Such fees will be Consultant's sole compensation for rendering Services to Customer. In no event will Customer be obligated to pay Consultant any more than the maximum fee amount stated in the Statement of Work.

4.2.   If the Statement of Work provides for reimbursement of expenses, Customer will reimburse the reasonable pre-approved costs or expenses incurred by Consultant in performing the Services. Each invoice will cite the applicable agreement number and purchase order number. Consultant will submit invoices to: *[Insert billing address].*

4.3.   [Consultant represents and warrants that pricing and terms for the Services performed hereunder are and at all times will be at least as favorable as that charged to any other customer for the same or similar services.]

5.   **Confidentiality**

5.1.   Consultant acknowledges that in connection with the Services, Customer may deliver to Consultant non-public information. For purposes of this Agreement, "Confidential Information" is information provided by Customer, or created or discovered by, for or on behalf of Customer (including, without limitation, Deliverables and information created under this Agreement). Confidential Information includes, but is not limited to, information relating to products, processes, techniques, formulas, ideas, know-how, works of authorship, copyrightable works, inventions (whether patentable or not), technical information, trade secrets, computer programs, computer code, designs, technology, compositions, data, drawings, schematics, customers, product development plans, and other business, technical and financial information.

5.2.   At all times, both during this Agreement and after its termination, Consultant will protect Confidential Information from unauthorized dissemination and use with the same degree of care that Consultant uses to protect its own confidential information, but with not less than reasonable care and diligence, and will not disclose any Confidential Information without the prior written consent of Customer. Consultant may use such Confidential Information solely for the purpose of performing the Services under this Agreement and for no other purpose.

5.3.   Consultant agrees that immediately upon Customer's request and in any event upon completion of the Services, Consultant will deliver to Customer all Confidential Information including all copies, derivatives, and extracts thereof.

5.4.   Consultant will not be obligated under this Section with respect to information that Consultant can document: (a) is or has become publicly known through no fault of Consultant or its employees or agents; or (b) is received without restriction from a third party lawfully in possession of such information and lawfully empowered to disclose such information; (c) was rightfully in the possession of Consultant without restriction prior to its disclosure by Customer; or (d) is independently developed by or on behalf of Consultant.

5.5.   Consultant will treat the terms and conditions and the existence of this Agreement as Confidential Information of Customer. Consultant will obtain Customer's written consent prior to any publication, presentation, public announcement or press release concerning the existence or terms and conditions of this Agreement.

5.6.   Consultant acknowledges that any disclosure or unauthorized use of Confidential Information will constitute a material breach of this Agreement and cause substantial and irreparable harm to Customer for which damages would not be a fully adequate remedy, and, therefore, in the event of any such breach, in addition to other available remedies, Customer will have the right to obtain appropriate injunctive relief.

6. **Intellectual Property Ownership**

   6.1. "Intellectual Property" means all rights pertaining to developments, inventions and discoveries, whether or not patentable, copyrights, trademarks, trade secrets, mask works or other proprietary rights, or any applications for the above including, without limitation, those owned, conceived, improved, created, developed, discovered, reduced to practice, or written by Consultant, alone or in collaboration with others, in connection with any Services.

   6.2. Customer will be the sole owner of all Intellectual Property that is: (a) created by or for Consultant under this Agreement or (b) included in any Deliverable. Subject to the paragraph below with regard to Copyrighted Works (as defined below), Consultant will assign, and does hereby assign, to Customer all of Consultant's present and future rights, title, and interest in all such Intellectual Property.

   6.3. With regard to any works or content subject to copyright created under this Agreement or included in any Deliverable ("Copyrighted Works"), Consultant agrees that, to the maximum extent permitted by law, Copyrighted Works are and will be "works made for hire" for the benefit of Customer, and to the extent not "works made for hire," Customer hereby assigns such rights exclusively to Customer. Consultant hereby waives all "moral rights" under the law of any nation and under any treaty with regard to all Deliverables and the results of any Services.

   6.4. Consultant will, upon request of Customer, execute, acknowledge, deliver and file any and all documents necessary or useful to vest in Customer all of Consultant's rights, under this Section or to transfer, perfect, obtain, confirm and enforce any such rights. Consultant hereby irrevocably designates and appoints Customer and its duly authorized officers and agents as its agent and attorney-in-fact to act for and in its behalf, in the event Customer is unable, after reasonable efforts, to secure its signature on any documents regarding any legal protection. Customer's rights under this Section include the right to execute and file any such application or applications or other documents and to do all other lawfully permitted acts to register, transfer, perfect, obtain, confirm and enforce patents, copyright or trademarks or any other legal protection with the same legal force and effect as if executed by Consultant.

   6.5. Consultant will not incorporate into the Deliverables any software, code or other work product of any third party without the prior written authorization of Customer. Consultant will not disclose to Customer, and will not induce Customer to use any Intellectual Property, confidential information, or trade secrets of any third party.

7. **License Grants**

   7.1. Consultant will give, and hereby grants, to Customer a perpetual paid-up sublicensable license under Consultant's patents, trade secrets, trademarks, copyrights, and other proprietary rights which are reasonably required for Customer, its licensees, transferees, successors, and assigns to use, alter, distribute, copy or otherwise exploit any Intellectual Property created or supplied under this Agreement, Deliverables and any derivatives of Deliverables, Services, or any other subject matter or result of this Agreement.

7.2.   Consultant is licensed to use any Intellectual Property created under this Agreement solely as is necessary to carry out its obligations under the applicable Statement of Work. Consultant may keep original materials that it creates under this Agreement in its possession as reasonably required for follow-up Services, but must turn over all originals and copies of such materials to Customer upon Customer's request.

8.   **Consultant's Personnel**

8.1.   Unless otherwise authorized in writing by Customer, Consultant will provide all Services by use of its own employees. Consultant will use subcontractors under this Agreement only with Customer's express prior written permission. Any subcontract made by Consultant with the written consent of Customer will incorporate by reference the terms of this Agreement. Consultant warrants the performance and full compliance with this Agreement by any subcontractor used in performance of the Services.

8.2.   Consultant is solely responsible for paying the salaries, wages and benefits of its employees, for ensuring that all required tax withholdings are made, and for ensuring that each employee has the legal right to work in the United States. Consultant is solely responsible for its permitted subcontractors' compensation. Consultant will defend, indemnify and hold harmless Customer, its Affiliates (as defined below), and their respective officers, directors, employees, servants and agents from any cost, including attorneys' fees, and any liability that arises from Consultant's breach of these obligations. "Affiliate" means a person or entity that directly, or indirectly through one or more intermediaries, controls, or is controlled by, or is under common control with a Customer (with "control" meaning ownership of more than 50 percent of the voting stock of the entity or, in the case of a non-corporate entity, an equivalent interest).

8.3.   Consultant will ensure that its employees and permitted subcontractors will, whenever on Customer's premises (or on any Customer's client's premises or other location) obey all applicable work and safety rules.

8.4.   Consultant has obtained and will at all times obtain and maintain in effect non-disclosure, assignment of Intellectual Property, and other appropriate agreements with its employees and (if permitted) subcontractors sufficient to protect Customer's Confidential Information and sufficient to allow it to provide Customer with the assignments and licenses provided for herein. Consultant will provide Customer with copies of such agreements upon request. Upon Customer's request, Consultant will cause all employees and (if permitted) subcontractors engaged under this Agreement to sign Customer's form of Intellectual Property Transfer and Confidentiality Agreement in its most current form as issued from time to time.

9. **Warranties of Quality.** Consultant represents and warrants the following with respect to Services performed:

    9.1. *Compliance with Specifications.* Upon delivery, the Deliverables will comply with the requirements, descriptions and representations as to the Services and Deliverables (including performance capabilities, completeness, Specifications, configurations, and function) that appear or are referred to in the Statement of Work.

    9.2. *Compliance with Specifications after Acceptance.* For a period of 180 days after Acceptance under this Agreement, any computer programs, materials, or other Deliverables developed under this Agreement will operate in conformance with the Specifications for such computer programs unless such computer programs are modified by Customer, without Consultant's written permission, within the 180-day time period. Any non-conformity found during that period will be fixed by Consultant promptly without additional charge.

    9.3. *Non-Infringement of Third Party Rights.* The Services and the Deliverables will not violate or in any way infringe upon the rights of third parties, including any trademark, copyright, patent or other Intellectual Property rights.

    9.4. *No Open Source.* No open source software code or any derivative of any open source software code will be included in any Deliverable, except as may be expressly permitted in the applicable Statement of Work.

10. **Remedies**

    10.1. In the event that Consultant breaches any representations or warranties hereunder or fails to comply with any term or requirement of this Agreement, including but not limited to timely delivery of Services and/or Deliverables or if Consultant fails to cure deficiencies in Deliverables as permitted in this Agreement, Customer will be entitled to, in addition to any other remedies, at its sole option and without any liability to Customer:

        10.1.1. Terminate or cancel this Agreement in its entirety or as it relates to any specific Services and/or Deliverables;

        10.1.2. Reject non-conforming Services and/or Deliverables, in whole or in part;

        10.1.3. Withhold any payments relating to non-conforming Services and/or Deliverables;

        10.1.4. Recover any and all actual, incidental and consequential damages to Customer, including but not limited to actual or estimated loss of profits or sales and costs to cover, attorney's fees and costs;

        10.1.5. Require that Consultant either re-perform the Services, at no additional charge to Customer, or alternatively, refund to Customer the fees paid for such non-conforming Services and/or goods; and/or

        10.1.6. Offset any amounts due Consultant by any actual or estimated loss incurred by Customer.

10.2.   Remedies of Customer under this Agreement will not be exclusive but will be accumulative of any other remedy of Customer under this Agreement or under any statute or law.

11.   **Exclusivity and Non-Competition**

In order to safeguard Customer's Confidential Information and secure to Customer the full value of this Agreement, Consultant will not directly or indirectly work for any other company with respect to technology or Services substantially similar to those under or used in any Statement of Work and/or Deliverable during the term of this Agreement and for one (1) year after the termination or expiration of the relevant Statement of Work or Acceptance of the Deliverable.

12.   **Limits on Access to Introduced Clients**

12.1.   For purposes of this Agreement, an "Introduced Client" is a legal entity or individual that has purchased the software or services from Customer where (1) Customer introduced Consultant to such entity or individual and (2) the introduction led to Consultant performing services for the use or benefit of such entity or individual.

12.2.   Consultant agrees that Consultant will maintain its primary business and technical dealings with Customer with regard to each Introduced Client and will not deal with the Introduced Client on business or payment matters.

12.3.   Consultant further agrees that it will refrain from promoting or soliciting to provide or arrange to provide similar or competing services to any Introduced Client for a period during and for six (6) months after the completion of all Statements of Work ("Restriction Period") that relate to such Introduced Client.

12.4.   Should an Introduced Client contact Consultant directly for similar or competing services at any time during any Restriction Period, Consultant agrees to notify Customer and allow Customer to contact the Introduced Client and to cooperate in permitting such services to be contracted and arranged solely through Customer.

13.   **Insurance**

13.1.   Consultant will, at its own expense, at all times during the term of this Agreement and for one year thereafter, provide and maintain in effect those insurance policies and minimum limits of coverage as designated below. Coverage will be for the benefit of Customer, its Affiliates and their respective officers, directors, employees, servants, and agents. These requirements do not limit liability of Consultant assumed elsewhere in this Agreement:

13.1.1.   *Workers' Compensation.* Workers' Compensation insurance will be provided as required by any applicable law or regulation and, in accordance with the provisions of the laws of the nation, state, territory or province having jurisdiction over Consultant's employees.

13.1.2.   *General Liability.* Consultant will carry Commercial General Liability insurance covering all operations for bodily injury, property damage, personal injury and advertising injury, as those terms are defined by

Commercial General Liability insurance policies, with limits of not less than $_____ for each occurrence and an aggregate of $_____.

13.1.3. *Automobile Liability Insurance.* Consultant will carry Business Automobile Liability insurance, including bodily injury and property damage for all vehicles used in the performance of Consultant's Services under this Agreement. The limits of liability will not be less than $_____ combined single limit for each accident.

13.1.4. *Errors and Omissions.* Consultant will carry insurance for Errors and Omissions/Professional Liability with limits of not less than $_____ per occurrence or per claim and $_____ in the annual aggregate.

13.2. Consultant will supply Certificates of Insurance for the foregoing to Customer before work on any Services or Deliverables are commenced hereunder by Consultant and 30 days prior to policy renewal. The policy(ies) will be endorsed to stipulate that Consultant's insurance will be primary to and non-contributory with any and all other insurance maintained or otherwise afforded to Customer, its Affiliates and their respective officers, directors, employees, servants, and agents. Consultant and its respective insurers waive all rights of recovery or subrogation against Customer, its Affiliates and their respective officers, directors, employees, agents, and insurers except as prohibited by law.

13.3. Consultant will obtain insurance or will reimburse Customer and its Affiliates for loss or damage to any property of Customer or its Affiliates in the care, custody, or control of Consultant, for all losses including, but not limited to theft, loss, misap-propriation or destruction caused by Consultant, its employees, agents, or other representative.

13.4. In the event Consultant utilizes the services of subcontractors to perform any Services contemplated hereunder, Consultant will require from or provide for all subcontractors the same minimum insurance requirements detailed above. Customer reserves the right to require and obtain copies of Subcontractor's certificates and/or certified copies of insurance policies from Consultant upon request.

14. Indemnification

14.1. Consultant will defend, hold harmless and indemnify Customer, its Affiliates, and their respective officers, directors, employees, servants and agents (collectively the "Indemnitees") from and against any and all losses, claims, liabilities, damages, costs and expenses (including taxes, fees, fines, penalties, interest, reasonable expenses of investigation and attorneys' fees and disbursements) as each Indemnitee may incur arising out of or relating to:

14.1.1. Acts or omissions of Consultant that breach any term or condition of this Agreement;

14.1.2. Any claim or allegation by any third party of damage to or destruction of property or death or injury of persons, including but not limited to employees or invitees of such party, which damage, destruction, death or injury results from or is alleged to result from any Deliverable or Services or any negligent act or omission of Consultant, its employees, agents or subcontractors; or

14.1.3.   Any claim or allegation by any third party that any Deliverable or Services, or use, copying, distribution or exploitation thereof infringes (whether directly, contributorily, by inducement or otherwise), misappropriates or violates such third party's Intellectual Property or proprietary interest.

15.   Limitation of Liability

15.1.   *Consequential Damages.* Customer will not be liable to Consultant with respect to any subject matter of this Agreement under any contract, negligence, strict liability or other legal or equitable theory for any special, indirect, consequential, incidental or exemplary damages including without limitation, damages for loss of Consultant's business profits, cost of procurement of substitute goods, technology or services, business interruptions or loss of information, even if Customer has been advised of the possibility of such damages.

15.2.   *Limitation of Liability.* In no event will Customer be liable to Consultant for any amounts in excess of the aggregate of the fees paid by Customer to Consultant hereunder during the six (6) month period prior to the date the cause of action arose.

16.   Term

16.1.   This Agreement will commence on the Effective Date and will continue until the later of (i) [DATE], or (ii) so long as a Statement of Work is in effect and has not been completed to the satisfaction of Customer, unless this Agreement is terminated earlier as provided in this Agreement.

16.2.   Immediately upon the expiration or termination of this Agreement, Consultant will turn over all Confidential Information (including all copies, extracts, modifications and derivatives thereof) to Customer and will deliver to Customer all Deliverables, Intellectual Property, and work product (whether completed or not) developed or created under this Agreement in the performance of the Services.

17.   Termination

17.1.   Customer may terminate this Agreement or any Statement of Work, in whole or in part:

17.1.1.   For convenience upon thirty (30) days' written notice to Consultant; or

17.1.2.   If at any time after the commencement of the Services, Customer, determines that such Services are inadequate, unsatisfactory, or substantially non-conforming to the Specifications, descriptions, warranties, or representations contained herein and the problem is not remedied within thirty (30) days of Consultant's receipt of written notice describing the issue or problem.

17.2.   Either Party may terminate his Agreement for cause in the event of: (a) a material breach or default by the other party of an obligation under this Agreement which is not remedied within thirty (30) days after written notice; or (b) the other party's filing for bankruptcy or becoming an involuntary participant in a bankruptcy proceeding, if such involuntary proceedings are not dismissed within sixty (60) days after commencement.

17.3.   The Sections of this Agreement regarding Confidentiality, Intellectual Property Ownership, Warranties, Remedies, Exclusivity and Non-Competition, Limits on Access to Introduced Clients, Insurance, Indemnification, Limitation of Liability, Termination, and General provisions will survive termination, as will accrued rights to payment.

18.   **Assignment**

Consultant may not assign this Agreement without Customer's express prior written consent. Customer reserves the right to transfer this Agreement to any Affiliate. Customer may also, without Consultant's consent, transfer this Agreement in connection with the sale or disposition of its business or a line of business relevant to this Agreement, by asset transfer, merger, stock sale or otherwise.

19.   **General**

19.1.   *Notice.* Any notice to be given hereunder will be in writing and addressed to the party and address stated below, or such other address as the party may designate from time to time by written notice in accordance with this Section. Except as otherwise expressly provided in this Agreement, notices hereunder will be deemed given and effective: (i) if personally delivered, upon delivery, (ii) if sent by overnight rapid-delivery service with tracking capabilities, upon receipt; (iii) if sent by fax or electronic mail, at such time as the party that sent the notice receives confirmation of receipt by the applicable method of transmittal, or (iv) if sent by certified or registered United States mail, upon receipt.

If to Consultant: *[add address, contact person and/or title, and fax number]*

If to Customer: *[add address, contact person and/or title, and fax number]*

19.2.   *Compliance with Laws.* Consultant hereby represents and warrants that it will comply with all applicable, local, state, provincial, and national laws and regulations. Consultant will comply, to the extent applicable, with US export control laws.

19.3.   *No Third Party Beneficiary.* This Agreement is not intended to confer a benefit on, or to be enforceable by, any person who is not a party to this Agreement.

19.4.   *Status as Independent Contractor.* Consultant is an independent contractor, and neither party's employees will be considered employees of the other party for any purpose. This Agreement does not create a joint venture or partnership, and neither party has the authority to bind the other to any third party.

19.5.   *Applicable Law and Jurisdiction.* This Agreement will be governed and construed in accordance with the laws of the State of _____ without regard to the conflicts of laws or principles thereof and applicable US federal law. It is further agreed that any and all disputes, claims or litigation arising from or related in any way to this Agreement or any provisions herein will be resolved exclusively in the state and federal courts located in _____. The parties hereby waive any objections against and expressly agree to submit to the personal jurisdiction and venue of such state or federal courts.

19.6.   *Waiver.* No waiver by Customer of any breach by Consultant of any of the provisions of this Agreement will be deemed a waiver of any preceding or succeeding breach of the same or any other provisions hereof. No such waiver will be effective unless in writing and then only to the extent expressly set forth in writing.

19.7.   *Customer Affiliates.* Customer may cause or permit all rights and permissions granted in this Agreement to be exercised by or through any Affiliate.

19.8.   *No Delegation.* Consultant's performance and obligations under this Agreement may not be delegated without the prior written consent of Customer.

19.9.   *Severability.* If any provision of this Agreement is invalid or unenforceable under any statute or rule of law, the provision is to the extent to be deemed omitted, and the remaining provisions will not be affected in any way.

19.10. *Force Majeure.* Neither party will be responsible for any delay or failure in performance resulting from acts beyond such party's control ("Force Majeure"). Force Majeure will include but not be limited to: acts of God, government or war; riots or strikes; epidemics, fires, floods, or disasters. At its option, Customer may terminate any Statement of Work that is delayed more than 30 days by Force Majeure event(s).

19.11. *Entire Agreement.* This Agreement, including the attached Statement of Work and any supplements, constitutes the entire agreement between Consultant and Customer with regard to this subject matter.

19.12. *Modifications.* No modification of this Agreement will be effective unless in writing and signed by both parties.

19.13. *Counterparts.* This Agreement may be executed in multiple counterparts, each being deemed an original and this being one of the counterparts. Execution by fax is permitted.

IN WITNESS WHEREOF, the parties hereto have executed this Agreement as of the Effective Date set forth above.

CONSULTANT: _____   CUSTOMER: _____

By: _____   By: _____

Print Name: _____   Print Name: _____

Title: _____   Title: _____

Date: _____   Date: _____

Appendix 7

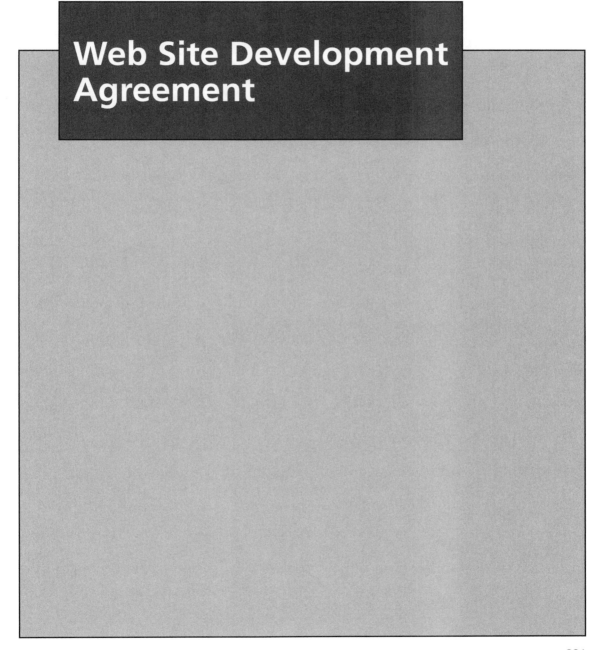

Web Site Development Agreement

Introductory Note

This is a straightforward web site design and development agreement. It could also be used, with minor changes, for adding functions or content to an existing web site.

Web development ranges from quite simple and low cost to complex and expensive. The more functionality, the more integration with back end data systems, the more complicated the graphics, and the higher the traffic that the web site must handle, then the more prolonged and expensive web development will be. This form is more suited to web site development that is more toward the lower end of the scale. If you want to contract for a more complex web site development, your agreement would look more like Appendix 4, which is a "long form" milestone-driven software development agreement.

Web development can be charged for on an hourly or daily rate basis, on a fixed fee basis, or on a milestone-based billing and payment scheme. This form uses a simple hourly time-and-expense pricing model.

This form is written to be generally favorable to the Developer. It has liability risk limiters that protect the Developer, and it provides the Customer with only a limited intellectual property warranty and indemnity.

Some of the important provisions to pay particular attention to (in addition to the payment provisions) when negotiating web development deals are:

- *The task description.*
- *Acceptance.*
- *Limitations on liabilities and damages.*
- *Indemnification.*
- *Ownership of intellectual property.*

This draft includes a few common variants and alternatives. The bracketed text provides optional or alternative language.

The next form in this book (Appendix 8) is for web hosting. Sometimes the provider of web services will offer a combined web development and web hosting agreement, which would be a combination of these forms.

Web Site Development Agreement

This Web Site Development Agreement ("Agreement") is effective as of the ___ day of _____ 20___ ("Effective Date") between *[Insert Developer company name]* (hereinafter "Developer"), with its principal office at _____, and *[Insert Customer company name]* ("Customer") with its principal office at _____ (each a "Party"; together the "Parties").

Purpose of This Agreement

A. Developer is in the business of providing web site design and development services.

B. Customer wishes to have a web site created in accordance with the specifications in this Agreement (the "Site").

In consideration of the mutual agreements set forth herein, Developer and Customer agree as follows:

1. **Design and Development**

   1.1. *Development.* Customer hereby engages the services of Developer to provide web development services. Developer will carry out the development of the Site in substantial compliance with the statement of work (the "Statement of Work") attached as Schedule A. The Parties may, by mutual agreement, execute additional Statements of Work under this Agreement.

   1.2. *Development Timetable.* Developer will use commercially reasonable efforts to complete development of the Site in accordance with the development timetable set forth in the Statement of Work. Developer will promptly notify Customer of any circumstances that may reasonably be anticipated to lead to a material delay.

   1.3. *Change Orders.* Customer may request additional services or modifications to the Site by delivering a written change order request to Developer. In the event that Developer receives a change order request, Developer will determine the cost and/or schedule impact, if any, of the requested change, and provide to Customer a proposal for a change order ("Change Order"). Each Change Order will be effective when signed by both Parties. Customer will not be liable for any charges under the Change Order, and Developer will not be obliged to perform the requested changes unless the applicable Change Order has been executed by the Parties.

   1.4. *Use of Third-Party Consultants.* Developer may retain qualified third parties to furnish services to it in connection with its work on the Site, provided that Developer will be responsible for the activities of such third parties as they relate to this Agreement.

2. **Customer Materials**

   2.1. Customer will supply content and materials, including any graphics, pictures, audio, video, logos and text for the Site ("Customer Materials"). Customer will retain ownership of Customer Materials. Customer grants Developer a license to use Customer Materials solely for the purpose of performance of its obligations under this Agreement. Customer represents and warrants that it has or will obtain all necessary ownership, licenses and/or permissions to grant such license and will defend, indemnify and hold Developer harmless with regard to any third party claim or allegation that the Customer Materials or Developer's licensed use of the Customer Materials infringes or violates any third party rights or violates any law.

3. **Acceptance Testing and Access**

   *[**Comment:** With web site development, the Developer will typically give the Customer initial access to a web site on a test server for acceptance testing purposes. The following text is based on a testing of the entire Site that is provided as a single "Deliverable." For a large-scale project, it would be common to break down the work into a series of deliverables and milestones that are subject to a corresponding series of acceptance tests. For examples of such deliverable-driven acceptance language see Appendix 4 and Appendix 6. In some cases, the Customer's initial acceptance of the web site may be subject to final acceptance after the web site "goes live." In that case, review on the test server would be a pre-final milestone, and acceptable performance during an agreed period of live deployment would be the last and final milestone.]*

3.1.   *Access to Site for Review.* Developer will make the Site accessible to Customer on a non-public test server ("Test Server") for review and acceptance testing. Developer will notify Customer by mail, email or fax when the Site is available for testing on the Test Server.

3.2.   *Acceptance Tests.* Customer will access the Site on the Test Server and perform all tests necessary to determine whether the Site conforms to the specifications set forth in the Statement of Work. Customer will have *[specify number]* days from the date upon which Developer provides notice that the Site is available for such testing (the "Initial Test Period"). In the event that the Site does not conform to the specifications set forth in the Statement of Work, Customer will deliver a written notice specifying each non-conformity in reasonable detail (a "Non-Conformity Notice") to Developer on or before the expiration of the Initial Test Period.

*[**Comment:** There are a number of choices on how to deal with errors and non-conformities on the Site. The most common provision simply requires that the Developer fix any errors. If the web site development tasks are relatively simple, there is a high probability that any errors and bugs can be readily fixed. An alternative approach includes language to allow the Customer to terminate the Agreement if non-conformities are not fixed after one or two opportunities to cure. In such a termination, the Developer might receive only partial payment, or in some deals (where the Customer has substantial leverage), the disappointed Customer is given a refund of some or all development fees. This form takes the first approach and simply requires that errors be fixed.]*

3.3.   *Corrective Action.* Developer will correct [at no additional cost to Customer] [on a time and materials basis] the non-conformities stated in the Non-Conformity Notice within a reasonable period of time. After Developer makes such corrections to the Site and makes the Site available to Customer for access on the Test Server, then Customer will have *[specify number]* days to re-test the Site ("Additional Test Period"). If any non-conformities remain, the process stated above will be repeated.

3.4.   *Deemed Acceptance.* Customer's failure to deliver a Non-Compliance Notice prior to the expiration of the applicable Initial Test Period or Additional Test Period will be deemed Customer's acceptance of the Site.

3.5.   *Delivery.* Upon the completion and acceptance of the Site, Developer will deliver a copy of the Site's computer code to Customer and will also [host the Site pursuant to the separate Web Hosting Agreement between the Parties] [deliver a copy of the Site's computer code to Customer's designated hosting provider].

4.   **Compensation**

4.1.   *Fees.* Unless otherwise provided by the Statement of Work, all services hereunder will be performed on a time and materials basis billed at the rates set forth on the Statement of Work.

4.2.   *Expenses.* Developer will be entitled to reimbursement of its reasonable [pre-approved] expenses incurred in connection with the Statement of Work for travel-related expenses and for such other items as the Parties may agree upon in writing. Expenses will be documented with receipts or other reasonable written evidence.

4.3. *Payment.* Developer will submit a [monthly] [weekly] statement and invoice to Customer for services rendered hereunder and its reimbursable expenses. Such invoices will be due and payable within ____ (__) days of the invoice date.

4.4. *Taxes.* The fees set forth herein are exclusive of taxes. Customer will be responsible for all taxes, levies, and assessments, excepting taxes based on the income of Developer.

4.5. *Records and Audit.* Developer will maintain books and records in connection with its services, billings, and expenses. Customer, by its independent certified public accountant, may audit Developer's records to determine whether Developer's billings charges and fees comply with the terms of this Agreement. Any such audits will be conducted during Developer's regular business hours at Developer's facilities subject to a reasonable confidentiality agreement, will not unreasonably interfere with Developer's business activities, and will take place not more than once in every calendar year. In the event of any overpayment or over-billing or underpayment, appropriate adjustments will be made within thirty (30) days of receipt of the audit report. In case the Developer has over-billed in an amount in excess of ten percent (10%) of the aggregate billings, accrued fees, and charges for the audited period (but in any case in excess of $_____), then Developer will pay Customer's reasonable accounting costs for conducting the audit.

5. **Ownership**

*[**Comment:** The following provisions allow the Developer to retain ownership in "Background Technology" which consists of Developer's existing code and technologies and any derivatives. The Background Technology is licensed to Customer for use in the Site. All other code or content created under this Agreement and included in the Site will be the Customer's property under the "work made for hire" clause. This formulation allows the Developer to keep what it already owns and improve it, but any wholly new code would belong to the Customer. A possible alternative, even more favorable to the Developer, is to give the Developer ownership of all code that is "reusable." For an example of such a formulation, see the "Intellectual Property" section of Appendix 5.]*

5.1. *Ownership of Work Product.* Except as provided in Section 5.2 with regard to Background Technology (as defined below), upon Customer's payment of fees due for the Site, Developer hereby assigns and agrees to assign to Customer all rights, title and interest in and to all source code, object code, data, and works of authorship, including those that constitute the Site (collectively, the "Work Product"). Except as provided in Section 5.2 with regard to Background Technology, upon Customer's payment of fees due for the Site, the Work Product will be deemed a "work-made-for-hire" to the extent provided by law, and to the extent not a work-for-hire, is hereby assigned to Customer. Developer agrees to cooperate with Customer in confirming Customer's ownership rights in the Work Product.

5.2. *License to Background Technology.* Developer will retain all rights, title and interest in all of (i) its pre-existing programs, materials, software development tools, supplies, proprietary information, files, technology, scripting, and programming, including, without limitation, those items which are utilized by Developer in providing the Site or the services under this Agreement, (ii) all improvements and derivatives of the foregoing and (iii) all intellectual property rights in the foregoing (the "Background Technology"). Upon payment in full of all development fees set forth herein, Developer hereby grants to Customer, a perpetual, non-exclusive, non-transferable (except as specifically provided in Section 11.1), world-wide right and license (the "License") to use, modify, copy or otherwise exploit the Background Technology as used in the Site (but not for resale or for the purpose of creating additional web sites, products, applications or other programs separable from the Site as it may be modified, used, copied or exploited).

6. **Warranty and Disclaimers**

*[**Comment:** When a Site is provided on a time-and-materials basis, it is most common that error correction also is charged for in the same way. Developers do sometimes provide error correction for a period at no extra cost. This form allows a choice of how error correction will be handled.]*

6.1. *Limited Warranty.* Developer warrants that for a period of ninety (90) days following the acceptance date, the Site will perform in accordance with the specifications set forth in the Statement of Work. Should the Site, during such warranty period, not perform as warranted herein, Developer will resolve the problem [on a time and materials basis] [free of additional charge] within a commercially reasonable period of time. The foregoing are Customer's sole and exclusive remedies.

6.2. *Exclusions from Warranty.* Developer will not be obligated under Section 6.1 to correct, cure, or otherwise remedy any nonconformity if (1) Customer has made any alteration to the Site without Developer's authorization; (2) the Site has been misused or damaged other than by personnel of Developer; or (3) Developer has not been notified of the existence and nature of such nonconformity or defect within the warranty period.

6.3. *Disclaimer.* EXCEPT AS EXPRESSLY STATED IN THIS AGREEMENT, DEVELOPER DISCLAIMS ALL WARRANTIES, EXPRESS OR IMPLIED, INCLUDING, WITHOUT LIMITATION, IMPLIED WARRANTIES OF TITLE, NON-INFRINGEMENT, AND MERCHANTABILITY OR FITNESS FOR ANY PARTICULAR PURPOSE.

6.4. *Limitation of Liability.* The cumulative liability of Developer to Customer for all claims whatsoever related to the Site, the services provided hereunder or this Agreement, including any cause of action sounding in contract, tort, or strict liability, will not exceed the total amount of all fees paid to Developer by Customer under this Agreement.

*[**Comment:** The foregoing is a unilateral damage cap clause. Sometimes, a Customer will insist that the damage cap be "bilateral" (i.e., that Customer also has the benefit of a cap on claims made by Developer). If a bilateral clause is used, Developer should consider excluding unlicensed use or copying of any Developer-licensed software or Background Technology from the mutual liability cap and from the consequential damages clause. The Developer should also make sure that its unpaid fees are not limited by the cap.]*

6.5. *Consequential Damages.* In no event will Developer be liable for any lost profits, incidental, exemplary, or consequential damages, even if Developer has been advised of the possibility of such damages.

6.6. *Third Party Materials.* Developer may, pursuant to the terms of the Statement of Work, incorporate third party software, code, content or materials (collectively, "Third Party Materials") in the Site; Developer makes no warranty with regard to Third Party Materials. Customer's sole and exclusive rights and remedies with respect to the Third Party Materials, including remedies in the event the presence of such a Third Party Material gives rise to an intellectual-property infringement claim, will be against the third party vendor of such materials and not against Developer.

6.7. *Authority.* Each Party warrants that it has all required authority to enter into this Agreement.

7. **Intellectual Property Warranty and Indemnification**

*[**Comment:** It is not unusual for a Customer to argue that the Developer should provide broad non-infringement warranties and indemnification with respect to the software code embodied in the Site. Developer will want to provide non-infringement provisions subject to various "carve-outs" and "a knowledge qualifier" like those in the following Section. There is probably not a lot of infringement risk in "plain vanilla" web development, but generally speaking Developers should try to avoid assuming material infringement risk.]*

7.1. *Developer's Intellectual Property Warranty.* To the best of its knowledge (but without an obligation to make any investigation), Developer's Contribution (as defined below) does not and will not infringe or violate any third party patents, copyrights, trademarks, trade secrets or other intellectual property rights. "Developer's Contribution" means the Site except for Customer Materials and Third Party Materials.

7.2. *Developer's Indemnification of Customer.* Developer will defend, indemnify, and hold harmless Customer with respect to any third party lawsuit or proceeding arising from Developer's breach of the warranty in Section 7.1 (each, a "Claim"). Indemnification under this Section is Customer's sole and exclusive remedy for the Claim and for breach of the warranty in Section 7.1.

8. **Procedure for Indemnification**. For any Claim that is subject to indemnification under this Agreement, the obligation to indemnify is subject to the Party entitled to indemnification (the "Indemnitee") providing the indemnifying Party (the "Indemnitor") reasonably prompt notice of the relevant Claim. Indemnitor shall defend and/or settle, at its own expense, any Claim subject to indemnification under this Agreement. The Indemnitee shall cooperate in good faith with the Indemnitor to facilitate the defense of any such Claim and shall tender the defense and settlement of the Claim to the Indemnitor. Claims may be settled without the consent of the Indemnitee, unless the settlement includes an admission of wrongdoing, fault or liability of the Indemnitee.

9. **Term and Termination**

*[**Comment:** This Agreement is written to terminate when the development tasks and any warranty period is completed. If a web development agreement includes provisions for the Developer to provide hosting or ongoing support services, it would need provisions under which the Agreement continues in effect.]*

9.1. *Term.* This Agreement will commence on the date first written above and will continue in effect until such time as all obligations (including services and the warranty period) hereunder are completed, unless terminated earlier in accordance with this Agreement.

9.2. *Material Breach.* Either Party may terminate this Agreement for a material breach which remains uncured for thirty (30) days after the breaching Party receives notice of such breach from the non-breaching Party.

*[**Comment:** Permitting a Customer to terminate for convenience fits a time and materials agreement. For a fixed fee agreement, there is commonly some compensation to the Developer (sometimes informally called a "kill fee") that will apply if the Customer terminates for convenience before the Site is done.]*

9.3. *Termination for Convenience.* Customer may terminate this Agreement for convenience upon ten (10) days' prior written notice to Developer. Upon the receipt of payment in full for all services performed through the effective date of termination, Developer will promptly deliver to Customer all work in-progress within ten (10) days of such payment. If Customer terminates before completion of the Site as described in the Statement of Work, all Deliverables will be deemed provided "AS IS," and the warranty in Section 6.1 will not apply.

9.4. *Survival.* The following Sections will survive the termination of this Agreement as applicable: 4.5 (Audit), 5 (Ownership), 6 (Warranties and Disclaimers), 7 (Intellectual Property Warranty and Indemnification), 8 (Procedure for Indemnification), 9.4 (Survival), 10 (Confidentiality) and 11 (General), together with accrued payment obligations.

10. **Confidentiality**

10.1. *Use of Confidential Information.* The Parties, from time to time, may disclose Confidential Information (as defined below) to one another. Accordingly, each Party agrees as the recipient (the "Receiving Party") to keep strictly confidential all Confidential Information provided by the other Party (the "Disclosing Party"). The Receiving Party further agrees to use the Confidential Information of the Disclosing Party solely for the purpose of exercising its rights and fulfilling its obligations under this Agreement. The Receiving Party may not use for its own benefit or otherwise disclose any of the Confidential Information of the Disclosing Party for any other purpose.

10.2. *Definition of Confidential Information.* "Confidential Information" means, subject to Section 10.3, information in any form, oral, graphic, written, electronic, machine-readable or hard copy consisting of (i) any non-public information provided by the Disclosing Party, including but not limited to, all of its inventions, designs, data, source and object code, programs, program interfaces, know-how, trade secrets, techniques, ideas, discoveries, marketing and business plans, pricing, profit margins, and/or similar information or (ii) any information which the Disclosing Party identifies as confidential information or the Receiving Party should understand from the context of the disclosure, to be confidential information.

10.3. *Exclusions.* The term "Confidential Information" will not include information that (a) is publicly available at the time of disclosure by the Disclosing Party; (b) becomes publicly available by publication or otherwise after disclosure by the Disclosing Party, other than by breach of this Section by the Receiving Party; (c) was lawfully in the Receiving Party's possession, without restriction as to confidentiality or use, at the time of disclosure by the Disclosing Party; (d) is provided to the Receiving Party without restriction as to confidentiality or use by a third party without violation of any obligation to the Disclosing Party, or (e) is independently developed by employees or agents of the Receiving Party who did not access or use the Confidential Information.

10.4. *Protection of Confidential Information.* The Receiving Party will inform those employees and consultants who have access to the Confidential Information of the Disclosing Party that such information is confidential and proprietary information of a third party. The Receiving Party agrees to disclose the Confidential Information of the Disclosing Party solely to its employees and consultants who need to know such information for the purpose of exercising the Receiving Party's rights and fulfilling the Receiving Party's obligations hereunder and who agree in writing to keep such information confidential. The Receiving Party will ensure compliance by its employees and consultants having access to the Confidential Information of the Disclosing Party and will be responsible for any breach by any such parties. The Receiving Party will notify the Disclosing Party without delay if it has reason to believe that any Confidential Information of the Disclosing Party has been used or disclosed in violation of this Section.

10.5. *Return of Confidential Information.* Promptly upon the written request of the Disclosing Party or upon termination of this Agreement, the Receiving Party will return to the Disclosing Party or destroy all copies of the Disclosing Party's Confidential Information.

10.6. *Legal Proceedings.* In the event that the Receiving Party becomes legally compelled to disclose any of the Confidential Information of the Disclosing Party, the Receiving Party will provide the Disclosing Party with prompt notice so that the Disclosing Party may seek a protective order or other appropriate remedy.

10.7. *Remedy.* Each Party acknowledges that the other Party will not have an adequate remedy in the event that it breaches the provisions of this Agreement regarding Confidential Information and that such Party may suffer irreparable damage and injury in such event. The breaching Party agrees that the non-breaching Party, in addition to seeking any other available rights and remedies as may apply, will be entitled to seek an injunction restraining the breaching Party from committing or continuing such violation.

11. **General Provisions**

*[**Comment:** The following clause, allowing assignment of the Agreement (and the included license to the Background Technology) under specified conditions is common. Some Customers may want broader rights to transfer the Site, including, for example, making the Site available to related companies or spin-off companies.]*

11.1. *Transfer or Assignment.* A Party will not have the right to transfer or assign this Agreement or rights granted under it except in connection with (a) the sale of all or substantially all of the Party's assets or a line of business sale; (b) the sale of a majority of the capital stock of the Party or (c) the merger of the Party with another entity. In each such instance, the Party may transfer the Agreement to the acquirer or surviving company (in the case of a merger). Any such transfer or assignment will become effective only if and when the transferee or assignee agrees in writing to be bound by the terms of this Agreement.

11.2. *Force Majeure*. Neither Party will be responsible for any delay or failure in performance resulting from acts beyond such Party's control ("Force Majeure"). Force Majeure will include but not be limited to: acts of God, government or war, riots or strikes, epidemics, fires, floods, or disasters. At its option, Customer may terminate any Statement of Work that is delayed more than sixty (60) days by Force Majeure event(s). Force Majeure may not extend any payment obligation by more than fifteen (15) days.

11.3. *Publicity*. All public announcements of the relationship of Developer and Customer under this Agreement shall be subject to the prior written approval of both Parties; provided, however, that Developer may list Customer as a customer of Developer on its web site and in marketing materials, press releases, and other promotional documents [subject to Customer's approval which is not to be unreasonably withheld].

11.4. *Non-Solicitation*. During the term of this Agreement and for a period of one (1) year thereafter, each Party agrees not to directly or indirectly solicit for employment any employee of the other Party who is or was materially involved in providing services pursuant to this Agreement unless the other Party consents in writing. This provision does not prevent general job solicitations, such as web and newspaper postings.

11.5. *No Agency*. Developer is an independent contractor and neither Party's employees will be considered employees of the other Party for any purpose. This Agreement does not create a joint venture or partnership, and neither Party has the authority to bind the other to any third Party.

11.6. *Notices*. Any notice to be given hereunder will be in writing and addressed to the Party and address stated below or such other address as the Party may designate from time to time by written notice. Except as otherwise expressly provided in this Agreement, notices hereunder will be deemed given and effective: (i) if personally delivered, upon delivery, (ii) if sent by overnight rapid–delivery service with tracking capabilities, upon receipt; (iii) if sent by fax or electronic mail, at such time as the Party that sent the notice receives confirmation of receipt by the applicable method of transmittal, or (iv) if sent by certified or registered United States mail, upon receipt.

For notice to Customer: *[Insert address information and officer to whom notice should be addressed]*

For notice to Developer: *[Insert address information and officer to whom notice should be addressed]*

11.7.   *Governing Law.* This Agreement will be governed and construed in accordance with the laws of the State of _____ without regard to the conflicts of laws or principles thereof and applicable U.S. federal law. Any and all disputes, claims or litigation arising from or related in any way to this Agreement or any provisions herein will be resolved exclusively in the state and federal courts located in _____. The Parties hereby waive any objections against and expressly agree to submit to the personal jurisdiction and venue of such state or federal courts.

11.8.   *Entire Agreement; Amendment.* This Agreement constitutes the entire agreement between the Parties and supersedes all prior agreements and understandings, whether written or oral, relating to the subject matter of this Agreement. This Agreement may be amended or modified only by a written instrument executed by both Parties.

11.9.   *Miscellaneous.* No delay or omission by either Party in exercising any right under this Agreement will operate as a waiver of that or any other right. A waiver or consent given by either Party on any one occasion will be effective only in that instance and will not be construed as a bar or waiver of any right on any other occasion. This Agreement may be executed in one or more counterparts, each of which will be deemed to be an original (a facsimile will be deemed an original), but all of which taken together will constitute one and the same instrument. If any provision of this Agreement is found to be invalid by any court or arbitrator having competent jurisdiction, the invalidity of such provision will not affect the validity of the remaining provisions.

IN WITNESS WHEREOF, the Parties have executed this Web Site Development Agreement on the date first above written.

Developer: _____   Customer: _____

By: _____   By: _____

Name: _____   Name: _____

Title: _____   Title: _____

Date: _____   Date: _____

Statement of Work

[Insert provisions of the Statement of Work, which may include:

Description of Project/Specifications.

Schedule of Work.

Milestone Deliverables (if any).

Fees and Payment Schedule/Standard Rates.

Third Party Software.

Hosting, Support and Maintenance Services.]

Appendix 8

Web Hosting Agreement

233

Introductory Note

THIS IS A FORM OF WEB HOSTING AGREEMENT FOR A COMMERCIAL WEB SITE. THIS FORM IS WRITTEN TO PROTECT AND FAVOR THE HOSTING PROVIDER, BUT PROVIDES A SIGNIFICANT AMOUNT OF SERVICES TO THE CUSTOMER.

BRACKETED LANGUAGE INDICATES OPTIONS OR ALTERNATIVE LANGUAGE. AS YOU WILL SEE, SOME OF THE OPTIONAL LANGUAGE ADAPTS THE FORM FOR USE IN HOSTING OF ONLINE RETAIL E-COMMERCE SITES THAT REQUIRE CREDIT CARD CLEARANCE. THIS FORM INCLUDES A SAMPLE SERVICE LEVEL AGREEMENT (OR "SLA"). THERE ARE MANY VARIATIONS IN THE CONTENT OF SLAS.

THE FORM IS INTENDED TO BE USED AS A SIGNED AGREEMENT. A SIMPLER (BUT SIMILARLY PRO-HOSTING-PROVIDER) VERSION WOULD BE USED FOR A "CLICKWRAP" HOSTING AGREEMENT.

Web Site Hosting Agreement

This Web Site Hosting Agreement (this "Agreement") is made and entered into as of the _____ day of ____ 20__ (the "Effective Date"), by and between _____, a _____ corporation with offices at _____ ("Provider"), and _____ a _____ corporation with offices at _____ ("Customer") (each being referred to individually as a "Party" and collectively, the "Parties").

Purpose of This Agreement

A. Provider is in the business of providing Internet services for hosting of Internet sites on the World Wide Web (known as the "Web"); and

B. Customer desires to engage Provider to provide such Web services on the terms and subject to the conditions set forth below.

Intending to be bound, the Parties agree as follows:

1. **Services**

    1.1. *Hosting Services.* Provider agrees to provide Customer with services for hosting of a site on the Web (the "Web Site") as described on <u>Schedule A</u> hereto (the "Hosting Services"). The Hosting Services are expected to make the Web Site accessible to third parties via the Internet.

    1.2. *Additional Services.* If Customer wishes to receive from Provider services other than the Hosting Services, for example, setup, configuration, software updating, FTP, or email (collectively, the "Additional Services"), arrangements for such services may be set forth in a separate addendum to this Agreement (the "Additional Services Addendum"). An Additional Services Addendum will be effective when executed by both Parties. Unless otherwise agreed in writing, each Additional Services Addendum will be incorporated into and be subject to this Agreement. (The Hosting Services and any Additional Services are referred to as the "Services.")

    1.3. *Liaison.* Each Party will designate a person who will act as the primary liaison for all communications regarding the Hosting Services and any Additional Services.

*[**Comment**: The term "PCI" in the following section refers to the Payment Card Industry Security Standards Council. This organization, formed by American Express, Discover Financial Services, JCB, MasterCard Worldwide and Visa International, sets security standards for credit card and debit card transactions and data storage. In an optional schedule to this Agreement are provisions relating to Provider's compliance with PCI standards. In essence, they say that Provider will try to comply with PCI security rules but will not be liable to either the Customer or the banks if there is a data breach that results in identity theft or financial loss.]*

    1.4. [*PCI Compliance*. Provider agrees to use commercially reasonable efforts to provide services compliant with the transaction security standards of the Payment Card Industry Security Standards Council ("PCI") as further stated in and subject to <u>Schedule D</u> to this Agreement.]

2. **Supply of Customer Content**

   Except to the extent that Provider has been separately engaged to develop and/or update the Web Site for Customer, Customer will provide to Provider all materials comprising the Web Site, including, but not limited to, any software, code, images, photographs, illustrations, graphics, audio, video or text (the "Customer Content"), which will be in Provider's acceptable format (as specified by Provider in consultation with Customer). Unless otherwise agreed in writing, Customer is solely responsible for Customer Content and its functionality.

3. **Availability of the Web Site**

   3.1. Unless otherwise indicated on <u>Schedule A</u> hereto, the Web Site will be accessible to third parties via the Internet twenty-four (24) hours a day, seven (7) days a week after installation and configuration, except for scheduled maintenance and required repairs, and except for any loss or interruption of Hosting Services due to causes beyond the control of Provider.

   3.2. Subject to Section 3.1, Provider agrees to provide the Hosting Services in accordance with the Service Level Agreement set forth in <u>Schedule C</u>. In the event of any loss or interruption of Hosting Services other than as permitted in Section 3.1 of this Agreement, Customer's sole and exclusive remedy and Provider's sole liability will be as stated in the Service Level Agreement.

4. **Domain Name Registration**

   As part of the initial Hosting Services, Customer will provide Provider with a registered domain name. Upon Customer's written request, Provider will register a domain name selected by Customer provided that such domain name is available for registration and does not violate any policies of the registrars used by Provider or any law or regulation. Customer agrees to promptly reimburse to Provider the fees paid by Provider for registration and maintenance of such domain name.

5. [**Third Party Services**

   In the event that any of the Hosting Services and any Additional Services provided Customer (including, if applicable, credit card services or any third party content or data feeds) are supplied to Provider by third party ("Third Party Services"), such Third Party Services will be listed in <u>Schedule A</u> (as it may be amended from time to time) or an Additional Services Addendum. Payments that apply to Third Party Services, if applicable, are to be set forth in <u>Schedule B</u> (as it may be amended from time to time) or the applicable Additional Services Addendum.]

6. **Additional Hardware and Software**

   In the event that the Web Site requires additional hardware and software not included in the Hosting Services, Customer may request in writing that Provider (a) upgrade the level of Hosting Services, or (b) acquire additional hardware or software to be included in the Hosting Services. Provider will promptly review such request and submit to Customer, for its written acceptance, a proposal for additional hardware, software and/or any Additional Services Addendum required to fulfill Customer's request, including applicable pricing. If Customer accepts Provider's proposal in writing, Provider will proceed to use reasonable efforts to implement such proposal, and Customer will pay Provider as provided in such proposal.

7. **Web Site Updating**

   7.1. *Updating by Customer.* As part of the Hosting Services, on reasonable notice, Provider will provide Customer with reasonable access to one or more test servers to allow Customer to supply, transmit and apply revisions, updates, deletions, enhancements or modifications of the Web Site (the "Updates") and to test and review the Web Site as so modified.

   7.2. *Customer Consultants.* Customer may engage a third party ("Customer Consultant") to update and make other modifications to the Web Site, and Provider will cooperate with such Customer Consultant. Provider will provide each Customer Consultant with the same access to make Updates to the Web Site as Provider provides to Customer. Customer will require each Customer Consultant to sign a confidentiality agreement consistent with Customer's confidentiality obligation under this Agreement. Customer will be responsible for the acts and omissions of its Customer Consultant as if they were its own.

   7.3. *Additional Services.* If Customer's Updates require additional services or technology that are not within the scope of the Hosting Services as stated in this Agreement, Customer and Provider may negotiate and enter into an Additional Services Addendum setting forth the terms and conditions for Provider's support of such Updates.

8. **License and Proprietary Rights**

   8.1. *Proprietary Rights of Customer.* As between Customer and Provider, unless otherwise agreed in writing by the Parties, Customer Content will remain the property of Customer, including, without limitation, all copyrights, patents, trademarks, trade secrets and any other proprietary rights.

8.2.   *License to Provider.* Customer hereby grants to Provider a non-exclusive, worldwide, royalty-free license for the term of this Agreement to use, copy, install, archive, adapt, test, display, distribute and transmit through the Internet or other networks, modify and otherwise use Customer Content solely as is reasonably necessary to render the Hosting Services or any Additional Services to Customer under this Agreement.

8.3.   *Proprietary Rights of Provider.* The materials and technology, including but not limited to software, data, content, or information developed, supplied or provided by Provider or its suppliers, the means used by Provider to provide the Hosting Services and any Additional Services to Customer, and the copyrights, patents, trademarks, trade secrets, and other proprietary rights of Provider or its suppliers (collectively "Provider Technologies") will remain the property of Provider or its suppliers.

9.   **Customer Data Ownership and Use**

9.1.   "Customer Data" means (a) Customer's data, (b) data submitted by Web Site end users, and (c) data resulting from or used in transactions on the Web Site, including, without limitation, transaction and sales data from Web Site activity, end user contact information, and all other individually or personally identifiable information.

9.2.   As between Customer and Provider, Customer Data will be Customer's property. Provider will use such Customer Data only in the manner and for the purposes set forth in this Agreement or as otherwise authorized by Customer. Upon termination of this Agreement or Provider's Services for any reason, all such Customer Data will be made available to Customer, and Provider will thereafter make no copies, use or disclosure of Customer Data. Provider reserves the right to erase all copies of Customer Data ____ days after the termination of this Agreement.

9.3.   [Provider agrees to provide the measures for data security for Customer Data as stated in the Hosting Services stated in <u>Schedule A</u>.]

10.   **Confidentiality**

10.1.   *Definition of Confidential Information.* Each Party agrees that during the course of this Agreement, information that is confidential may be disclosed to the other Party, including, but not limited to, software, technical processes and formulas, source code, product designs, sales, cost and other unpublished financial information, product and business plans, advertising revenues, usage rates, advertising relationships, projections and marketing data ("Confidential Information").

10.2.   *Exclusions from Confidentiality.* Confidential Information, however, will not include information that the receiving Party can demonstrate (a) is, as of the time of its disclosure, or thereafter becomes publicly available without fault of the receiving Party, (b) was known to the receiving Party as of the time of its disclosure, (c) is independently developed by the receiving Party, or (d) is subsequently learned from a third party not under a confidentiality obligation to the providing Party. Except as provided for in this Agreement, each Party will not make any disclosure of the Confidential Information to anyone other than its employees and/or contractors who have a need to know in connection with this Agreement. Each Party will ensure that its employees and/or contractors are under confidentiality obligations with respect to the Confidential Information that are consistent with this Agreement. Each Party is responsible for the acts and omissions of its employees and/or contractors with regard to these obligations. The confidentiality obligations regarding Customer Data (including credit cardholder data) survive expiration or termination of this Agreement indefinitely; all other confidentiality obligations of the Parties and their employees and/or contractors will survive the expiration or termination of this Agreement for a period of two (2) years.

10.3. *Compelled Disclosure.* In the event that the receiving Party becomes legally compelled to disclose any of the Confidential Information of the disclosing Party, the receiving Party will provide the disclosing Party with prompt notice so that the disclosing Party may seek a protective order or other appropriate remedy.

10.4. *Remedy.* Each Party acknowledges that the other Party will not have an adequate remedy in the event that it breaches the provisions of this Agreement regarding Confidential Information and that such Party may suffer irreparable damage and injury in such event. The breaching Party agrees that the non-breaching Party, in addition to seeking any other available rights and remedies as may apply, will be entitled to seek an injunction restraining the breaching Party from committing or continuing such violation.

11. **Customer Content Matters**

11.1. *Responsibility for Customer Content.* Customer assumes sole responsibility for (a) obtaining authorizations and permissions for Customer Content (including without limitations any permissions for links to or interaction with third-party web sites), (b) ensuring the accuracy of Customer Content, (c) ensuring that the Customer Content does not infringe or violate any right of any third party and is not defamatory, and (d) complying with privacy law and other applicable legal requirements.

11.2. *Interactive Functionality.* Subject to Provider's written consent, not to be unreasonably refused, Customer may facilitate user forums, blogs, chat rooms, user content uploads, and other interactive features ("Interactive Functionality") using the Web Site and the Hosting Services. Depending on the nature of such functions and services, Provider reserves the right to require Customer to purchase Additional Services in order for Provider to support such functions and services. If Customer implements Interactive Functionality, it agrees to implement reasonable procedures to process complaints about resulting user-generated content and, if appropriate, remove infringing, illegal or offensive materials. [Customer agrees to include in the terms of use of the Web Site provisions binding on each user of the Web Site or the Hosting Services that the user will indemnify, defend, and hold harmless Provider from any such liability to the extent caused or contributed to by the end user.]

11.3. *Other Harmful Content or Conduct.* Customer will exclude and will not provide or permit Customer Content that is infringing, illegal or harmful to Provider or

Provider's computer infrastructure, including, without limitation: copyrighted material used without permission, threatening, disparaging, or hate-related content, pornographic or indecent materials or advertising for adult content, pirated software, or links to any of the above. Use of the Service for transmission of bulk unsolicited email (spam) is forbidden. Provider may suspend the Service or terminate this Agreement for Customer's breach of the provisions of this Section.

11.4.   *Excluding Customer Content.* Provider reserves the right, in its sole discretion, to exclude, disable, or remove from the Web Site any Customer Content on the Web Site that in Provider's good faith judgment materially impairs or degrades the operation of the Provider's systems, poses a risk of violating any law or violating or infringing third-party rights or which otherwise exposes or potentially exposes Provider to civil or criminal liability or public ridicule, provided that such right will not place an obligation on Provider to monitor or exert editorial control over the Web Site. Provider agrees to notify Customer promptly by email of any such removal of Customer Content.

12.   **Fees and Taxes**

12.1.   *Hosting Services Fees.* Customer will pay Provider all fees for the Hosting Services in accordance with the applicable fee and payment schedule set forth in <u>Schedule A</u> hereto. Provider expressly reserves the right to change its rates charged hereunder for the Hosting Services during any Renewal Term (as defined below). [Provider reserves the right to pass through to Customer any increase in rates charged for any Third Party Services.] Customer will pay to Provider all fees for Additional Services on a time and materials basis as set forth in <u>Schedule B</u> hereto, on an applicable Additional Services Addendum, or as otherwise agreed in writing.

12.2.   *Out-of-Pocket Expenses.* Customer will pay, or promptly reimburse Provider for, any reasonable [pre-approved] out-of-pocket expenses, including, without limitation, travel and travel-related expenses, incurred by Provider in connection with the performance of the Hosting Services and any Additional Services.

12.3.   *Late Payment.* Unless otherwise agreed in writing, Customer will pay to Provider all fees. expenses and any other amounts due under this Agreement within thirty (30) days of receipt of the applicable Provider invoice. Late charges will apply to late payments at the annual rate of ____ percent, compounded daily, or if less, the maximum rate allowable under applicable law.

12.4.   *Default for Non-Payment.* The failure of Customer to pay fees due[, unless disputed in good faith,] within ____ days after receiving written notice from Provider specifying that such fees are overdue is a material breach of this Agreement. For such breach, Provider may, at its option, suspend performance of the Hosting Services and/or any Additional Services or terminate this Agreement. Suspension will not relieve Customer from paying past due fees plus interest. Provider will be entitled to recover attorneys' fees and costs of collection in case of payment delinquency.

12.5. *Taxes.* Customer will pay or reimburse Provider for all sales, use, VAT, and all other taxes and all duties that are levied or imposed by reason of the performance by Provider under this Agreement; excluding, however, income taxes on net income which may be levied against Provider.

13. **Warranties**

13.1. *Provider Warranties.* Provider represents and warrants that Provider has the power and authority to enter into and perform its obligations under this Agreement.

13.2. *Customer Warranties.* Customer represents and warrants that Customer has the power and authority to enter into and perform its obligations under this Agreement.

13.3. *Disclaimer of Warranty.* EXCEPT FOR THE LIMITED WARRANTY SET FORTH IN THIS AGREEMENT, PROVIDER EXPRESSLY DISCLAIMS ALL WARRANTIES, EXPRESS OR IMPLIED, INCLUDING, WITHOUT LIMITATION, WARRANTIES OF MERCHANTABILITY, NON-INFRINGEMENT, AND FITNESS FOR A PARTICULAR PURPOSE.

14. **Indemnification**

14.1. *By Provider.* Provider agrees to defend, indemnify, and hold harmless Customer, its officers, directors, employees and agents from any and all costs, liabilities, damages and reasonable attorneys' fees incurred in or resulting from any third party claim or lawsuit alleging that any of the Provider Technologies infringes or violates any rights of third parties, including without limitation, rights of publicity, rights of privacy, patents, copyrights, trademarks, trade secrets, and/or other proprietary rights.

14.2. *By Customer.* Customer agrees to defend, indemnify, and hold harmless Provider, its officers, directors, employees and agents from any and all costs, liabilities, damages and reasonable attorneys' fees incurred in or resulting from any third party claim or lawsuit arising or alleged to arise from Customer Content, Customer Data, and use of the Web Site by Customer or any user, or any Interactive Functionality, including, without limitation, any end user material or content posted, communicated, published, or distributed by means of the Web Site and any claim that such use or such content or material infringes or violates any rights of third parties, including without limitation, rights of publicity, rights of privacy, patents, copyrights, trademarks, trade secrets, and/or other proprietary rights or constitutes defamation or any illegality or criminal offense.

15. **Procedure for Indemnification**

As a condition of obtaining indemnification and a defense under any applicable provision of this Agreement, the indemnified Party will promptly provide the indemnifying Party with written notice of any claim which the indemnified Party believes falls within the scope of the foregoing paragraphs and will cooperate in the defense of the claim. The indemnifying Party will control such defense and all negotiations for the settlement of any such claim. Any settlement intended to bind the indemnified Party will not be final without the indemnified Party's written consent, which will not be unreasonably withheld, provided that consent is not required if the disposition has no adverse impact on the indemnified Party and provides the indemnified Party with an unconditional release of all asserted claims.

16. **Limitation of Liability**

    16.1. Provider shall have no liability for consequential, exemplary, special, incidental or punitive damages even if Provider has been advised of the possibility of such damages.

    16.2. Provider shall have no liability for unauthorized access to, or alteration, theft or destruction of, the Web Site, Customer Data, Customer Content, or Customer's data files, programs or information through accident, fraudulent means, loss, devices or any other cause.

    16.3. The aggregate liability of Provider to Customer shall be limited to the amount actually paid to Provider by Customer under this Agreement during the _____ months immediately preceding the date on which such claim(s) accrued. This limitation applies to all claims and liabilities in the aggregate, including, without limitation, breach of contract, breach of warranty, negligence, strict liability, or misrepresentations.

17. **Termination and Renewal**

    17.1. *Term.* This Agreement will be effective on the Effective Date and thereafter will remain in effect for _____ (__) years from the initial date of public availability of the Web Site, unless earlier terminated as otherwise provided in this Agreement (the "Initial Term"). This Agreement will automatically be renewed beyond the Initial Term for successive one (1) year terms (each, a "Renewal Term") unless a Party provides the other Party with a written notice of termination at least sixty (60) days prior to the expiration of the Initial Term or the then-current Renewal Term.

    17.2. *Termination*

        17.2.1. Either Party may terminate this Agreement if a bankruptcy or insolvency proceeding is instituted against the other Party which is acquiesced in and not dismissed within sixty (60) days or if the other party ceases business operations.

        17.2.2. Either Party may terminate this Agreement if the other Party materially breaches any of its representations, warranties or obligations under this Agreement, and such breach is not cured within thirty (30) days of receipt of notice specifying the breach[, except that the cure period for failures of payment obligations will be ___ (__) days].

    17.3. *Termination and payment.* Upon any termination or expiration of this Agreement, Customer will pay all unpaid and outstanding fees through the effective date of termination or expiration of this Agreement.

17.4. [Termination of Third Party Services. Should any Third Party Services no longer be available for any reason outside the control of the Provider, Provider may terminate such Third Party Services by providing Customer with thirty (30) days' notice. Provider will use commercially reasonable efforts to assist Customer in obtaining the same or similar services as those terminated from an alternate third-party provider.]

17.5. *Survival.* The following Sections, together with accrued obligations, will survive termination: 8.1 (Proprietary Rights of Customer), 8.3 (Proprietary Rights of Provider), 9 (Customer Data Ownership), 10 (Confidentiality), 12 (Fees and Taxes), 13.3 (Warranty Disclaimers), 14 (Indemnification), 15 (Procedure for Indemnification), 16 (Limitation of Liability), 17.5 (Survival) and 18 (Miscellaneous).

18. **Miscellaneous**

18.1. *Independent Contractors.* Provider and Customer are independent contractors and not employees or agents of one another.

18.2. *Amendments.* No amendment, change, waiver, or discharge hereof will be valid unless in writing and signed by the Party against which such amendment, change, waiver, or discharge is sought to be enforced.

18.3. *Customer List.* Provider may use the name of and identify Customer as a Provider client, in advertising, publicity, or similar materials distributed or displayed to prospective clients, subject to Customer's written consent, which is not to be unreasonably refused.

18.4. *Force Majeure.* [Except for the payment of fees by Customer,] If the performance of any part of this Agreement by either Party is prevented, hindered, delayed or otherwise made impracticable by reason of any flood, riot, fire, judicial or governmental action, labor disputes, act of God or any other causes beyond the control of either Party, that Party will be excused from such to the extent that it is prevented, hindered or delayed by such causes.

18.5. *Governing Law.* This Agreement will be governed in all respects by the laws of the State of _____ without regard to its conflict of laws provisions. Customer and Provider agree that the sole venue and jurisdiction for disputes arising from this Agreement or its subject matter will be the appropriate state or federal courts located in the city of _____, and Customer and Provider hereby submit to the exclusive jurisdiction of such courts.

18.6. *Assignment.* This Agreement will be binding upon and inure to the benefit of the successors and permitted assigns of the Parties hereto. Neither Party may assign any of its rights or delegate any of its obligations under this Agreement to any third party without the express prior written consent of the other Party, except in the instance of a merger, company sale, sale of business operations, line of business sale, or acquisition of the assigning Party.

18.7.   *Notice.* All notices and other communications provided hereunder may be made or given by either Party by facsimile, by first-class mail, postage prepaid, or by courier to the mailing address or facsimile numbers set out below or such other address or facsimile numbers as such Party will have furnished in writing to the other Party in writing:

If to Customer, to: _____

If to Provider, to: _____

Notice is effective upon receipt.

18.8.   *Waiver.* The waiver or failure of either Party to exercise any right in any respect provided for herein will not be deemed a waiver of any further right hereunder or any later exercise of such right.

18.9.   *Severability.* If any provision of this Agreement is determined to be invalid under any applicable statute or rule of law, it is to that extent to be deemed omitted, and the balance of the Agreement will remain enforceable.

18.10.   *Counterparts.* This Agreement may be executed in several counterparts, all of which taken together will constitute the entire agreement between the Parties hereto.

18.11.   *Headings.* The Section headings used herein are for reference and convenience only and will not enter into the interpretation hereof.

18.12.   *Entire Agreement.* This Agreement and attached Schedules constitute the entire agreement between Customer and Provider with respect to the subject matter hereof and there are no representations, understandings or agreements which are not fully expressed in this Agreement.

IN WITNESS WHEREOF, the Parties have caused this Agreement to be executed by their duly authorized representatives as of the date first written above.

Customer   Provider

By: _____   By: _____
(Signature)   (Signature)

Name: _____   Name: _____

Title: _____   Title: _____

Date: _____   Date: _____

Schedule A
Hosting Services and Fees

Hosting Services and Fees:

[This Schedule can itemize application management and support services provided, such as installation and update support, web server and database software management, data and software backup, disaster recovery, security system operations, third party services, and help desk. It may also include a list of hardware and software that Provider will supply.]

[This Schedule should also include a list of fees for Hosting Services and any applicable Additional Services. Such fees might include amounts for lease, use or purchase of hardware or software, monthly fees for the Provider's Web Site management and oversight, and extra fees for excess use of data storage or bandwidth.]

Schedule B
Fees for Additional Services

[This Schedule would include labor charges, by the hour or the day, for professionals that provide Additional Services.]

Schedule C
Service Level Agreement

For the purposes of this Service Level Agreement (or "SLA"), "System" means the hardware, software, and other items provided by Provider (as detailed in <u>Schedule A)</u> and Provider's network infrastructure and Internet connectivity.

The remedies provided herein are the sole and exclusive remedies with respect to Provider's performance guarantee as stated in this SLA.

Provider's Uptime Guarantee

Based on the equipment and service configuration selected by the Customer, Provider offers performance guarantee that the System will be operational and available to interact with the Internet ("the Uptime Guarantee") of _____ percent. This guarantee and the applicable remedies are subject to the terms and conditions below.

Credits for Customer

Periods of unavailability in excess of those specified in the Uptime Guarantee will entitle Customer to a credit applicable to future monthly charges which Customer is obligated to pay Provider. The amount of the credit will be the greater of (a) 10% of the monthly fees outlined in **Schedule A** or (b) an amount calculated based upon the number of hours during a particular month (see example below) and the duration of any and all periods of unavailability in excess of Uptime Guarantee during such month. The formula for any such credit or refund is as follows:

$$\text{Credit} = \frac{\text{Hours in Excess of Uptime Guarantee in Month}}{\text{Hours in Month}} \times \text{Monthly Fee (in Schedule A)}$$

For the purposes of this formula, a period of unavailability will be deemed to occur entirely in the month in which such period of unavailability begins.

Procedure

When a period of unavailability is detected by the Customer, the Customer should contact the Provider by email or phone and advise Provider's staff of the problem. If the staff of Provider are able to confirm the Customer's report, the period of unavailability will be recorded. Such period of unavailability will be deemed to have begun at the earlier of the time such unavailability was reported to the Provider by Customer or the time such unavailability was detected by the Provider's monitoring tools.

[Customer Termination Option

In addition to the foregoing credit, Customer may terminate the Agreement at any time by providing Provider with ____ (__) days written notice of termination in the event that (i) the Web Site is unavailable for a total of ____ hours within any ____ day period or (ii) the Uptime Guarantee is not met for ____ or more weeks in a ____ consecutive week period.]

Limitations

Provider will not be responsible for periods of unavailability resulting from failure by Customer to approve reasonable modifications to the System reasonably recommended by Provider to prevent periods of unavailability if Provider has provided Customer with documentation to show the reason for such modification(s) and the manner in which such modification(s) will affect the System.

In addition, Provider will not be responsible for periods of unavailability to the extent Provider is able to prove that such periods of unavailability resulted from the following:

■ Failure of networks, hardware or software which are not part of the System.

■ Customer modifications to the System which are not approved by Provider, resulting from Customer's use of customizable software provided by a third party (i.e., a software provider other than Provider).

■ Any modifications made to operating systems without the consent of Provider.

■ Modifications to the System implemented by Provider, at the request of Customer, but not recommended or approved by Provider.

■ Unavailability occurring during periods of System testing, development, or problem diagnosis which are scheduled in advance with Customer's approval (and in such case, only during the period of scheduled downtime).

■ Planned facility and equipment maintenance upgrades and migration, which are scheduled in advance.

■ Normal maintenance periods which are scheduled every Wednesday between 4:00 am and 6:00 am [*(Indicate applicable time zone)*].

■ Content or applications, developed by third parties and installed or run on the System by the Customer or others authorized by Customer to have access to the System without Provider's approval or recommendation.

■ Incidents of force majeure.

■ Interruption of Hosting Services due to a denial of service or other hostile attack on the System or due to unexpected and unusually peak demands for access to the Web Site.

■ Co-located hardware not managed by Provider.

[System Monitoring

Provider will actively monitor the System for unavailability and proper operation 24 hours per day, 7 days per week, every day of the year. Provider does not guarantee that remote monitoring will be able to detect all problems or interruptions at the time they occur.]

[Schedule D
Terms and Conditions Regarding PCI Compliance

1. **Data Protection Compliance**

   1.1. *Compliance.* Provider will use commercially reasonable efforts to remain in compliance with the Payment Card Industry ("PCI") Data Security Standards for a Level 1 Service Provider.

   1.2. *Additional Services.* If due to changes in PCI-related requirements, additional hardware, software, or procedures are required, Provider may require Customer to purchase mutually agreed Additional Services as a condition of providing further PCI compliance.

   1.3. *Compliance Audit.* Customer may audit the compliance with such standards at Provider's site. These audits may take place no more than once per calendar year. PCI representatives or third party PCI-approved representatives may audit Provider on Customer's behalf, at Customer's sole cost. Customer agrees to provide to Provider reasonable notice of such audit.

2. **Nature of Obligations; Remedies**

   2.1. Compliance by Provider with the requirements of PCI is an agreement between Provider and Customer and there are no third party beneficiaries of such obligation. For the avoidance of doubt, no third party customer, bank, card issuer, network member, association or any other third party will have any right to assert any claim or cause of action against Provider. Provider disclaims any liability to any third party arising out of or relating to such standards.]

U.S. Department of Justice Checklist for Reporting a Theft of Trade Secrets Offense

United States Department of Justice

Checklist for Reporting a Theft of Trade Secrets Offense

If you or your company has become the victim of a theft of trade secrets offense, the U.S. Department of Justice asks that you please fill out the information indicated below and contact a federal law enforcement official to report the offense.

NOTE ON CONFIDENTIALITY: Federal law provides that courts "shall enter such orders and take such action as may be necessary and appropriate to preserve the confidentiality of trade secrets, consistent with the requirements of the Federal Rules of Criminal and Civil Procedure, the Federal Rules of Evidence, and all other applicable laws" 18 U.S.C. § 1835.

Prosecutors utilizing any of the information set forth below will generally request the court to enter an order to preserve the status of the information as a trade secret and prevent its unnecessary and harmful disclosure.

Background and Contact Information

1. Victim's Name:
2. Primary Location and Address:
3. Nature of Primary Business:
4. Law Enforcement Contact:

    Phone: Fax:

    Email: Pager/Mobile:

Description of the Trade Secret:

5. Generally describe the trade secret (e.g., source code, formula):

    Provide an estimated value of the trade secret identifying ONE of the methods and indicating ONE of the ranges listed below:

    Method

    ___Cost to develop the Trade Secret;

    ___Acquisition Cost (identify date and source of acquisition); or

    ___Fair Market Value if sold.

    Estimated Value:

    ___Under $50,000;

    ___Between $50,000 and $100,000;

    ___Between $100,000 and $1 million;

___Between $1 million and $5 million; or

___Over $5 million.

Identify a person knowledgeable about valuation, including that person's contact information:

General Physical Measures Taken to Protect the Trade Secret

6. Describe the general physical security precautions taken by the company, such as fencing the perimeter of the premises, visitor control systems, using alarming or self-locking doors, or hiring security personnel.

7. Has the company established physical barriers to prevent unauthorized viewing or access to the trade secret, such as "Authorized Personnel Only" signs at access points? (See below if computer-stored trade secret.) ___YES ___NO

8. Does the company require sign in/out procedures for access to and return of trade secret materials? ___YES ___NO

9. Are employees required to wear identification badges? ___YES ___ NO

10. Does the company have a written security policy? ___YES ___NO

    ■ How are employees advised of the security policy?

    ■ Are employees required to sign a written acknowledgment of the security policy? ___YES ___NO

    ■ Identify the person most knowledgeable about matters relating to the security policy, including title and contact information.

11. How many employees have access to the trade secret?

12. Was access to the trade secret limited to a "need to know" basis? ___YES ___NO

Confidentiality and Non-Disclosure Agreements

13. Does the company enter into confidentiality and non-disclosure agreements with employees and third-parties concerning the trade secret? ___YES ___NO

14. Has the company established and distributed written confidentiality policies to all employees? ___YES ___NO

15. Does the company have a policy for advising company employees regarding the company's trade secrets? ___YES ___NO

Computer-Stored Trade Secrets

16. If the trade secret is computer source code or other computer-stored information, how is access regulated (e.g., are employees given unique user names and passwords)?

17. If the company stores the trade secret on a computer network, is the network protected by a firewall? ___YES ___NO

18. Is remote access permitted into the computer network? ___YES ___NO

19. Is the trade secret maintained on a separate computer server? ___YES ___NO

20. Does the company prohibit employees from bringing outside computer programs or storage media to the premises? ___YES ___NO

21. Does the company maintain electronic access records such as computer logs? ___YES ___NO

Document Control

22. If the trade secret consisted of documents, were they clearly marked "CONFIDENTIAL" or "PROPRIETARY"? ___YES ___NO

23. Describe the document control procedures employed by the company, such as limiting access and sign in/out policies.

24. Was there a written policy concerning document control procedures and, if so, how were employees advised of it? ___YES ___NO

25. Identify the person most knowledgeable about the document control procedures, including title and contact information.

Employee Controls

26. Are new employees subject to a background investigation? ___YES ___NO

27. Does the company hold "exit interviews" to remind departing employees of their obligation not to disclose trade secrets? ___YES ___NO

Description of the Theft of Trade Secret

28. Identify the name(s) or location(s) of possible suspects, including the following information:

    - Name (Suspect #1):
    - Phone number:
    - Email address:
    - Physical address:
    - Employer:
    - Reason for suspicion:
    - Name (Suspect #2):
    - Phone number:
    - Email address:
    - Physical address:
    - Employer:
    - Reason for suspicion

29.   Was the trade secret stolen to benefit a third party, such as a competitor or another business?
___YES ___NO

If so, identify that business and its location:

30.   Do you have any information that the theft of the trade secret was committed to benefit a foreign government or instrumentality of a foreign government? ___YES ___NO

If so, identify the foreign government and describe that information.

31.   If the suspect is a current or former employee, describe all confidentiality and non-disclosure agreements in effect.

32.   Identify any physical locations tied to the theft of the trade secret, such as where it may be currently stored or used.

33.   If you have conducted an internal investigation into the theft or counterfeiting activities, please describe any evidence acquired.

Civil Enforcement Proceedings

34.   Has a civil enforcement action been filed against the suspects identified above?
___YES ___NO

- If so, identify the following:

    i.   Name of court and case number:

    ii.   Date of filing:

    iii. Names of attorneys:

    iv.   Status of case:

- If not, is a civil action contemplated?

    What type and when?

35.   Please provide any information concerning the suspected crime not described above that you believe might assist law enforcement.

Index